PENGUIN POETS

GERARD MANLEY HOPKINS

Gerard Manley Hopkins (1844–89) was born in Essex, the eldest son of a prosperous middle-class family. He was educated at Highgate School and Balliol College, Oxford, where he read Classics and began his lifelong friendship with Robert Bridges. In 1866 he entered the Roman Catholic Church and two years later he became a member of the Society of Jesus. In 1877 he was ordained and was priest in a number of parishes including a slum district in Liverpool. From 1882 to 1884 he taught at Stonyhurst College and in 1884 he became Classics Professor at University College, Dublin. In his lifetime Hopkins was hardly known as a poet, except to one or two friends; his poems were not published until 1918, in a volume edited by Robert Bridges.

POEMS AND PROSE OF
GERARD MANLEY HOPKINS

SELECTED WITH AN INTRODUCTION
AND NOTES
BY
W. H. GARDNER

PENGUIN BOOKS

Penguin Books Ltd, Harmondsworth, Middlesex, England
Viking Penguin Inc., 40 West 23rd Street, New York, New York 10010, U.S.A.
Penguin Books Australia Ltd, Ringwood, Victoria, Australia
Penguin Books Canada Ltd, 2801 John Street, Markham, Ontario, Canada L3R 1B4
Penguin Books (N.Z.) Ltd, 182–190 Wairau Road, Auckland 10, New Zealand

—

This selection first published 1953
Reprinted 1954, 1958, 1960, 1961, 1962, 1963, 1964, 1966, 1967, 1968,
1970, 1971, 1972, 1974, 1975 (twice), 1976, 1978 (twice),
1979, 1981, 1982, 1983, 1984 (twice)

—

Set, printed and bound in Great Britain by
Cox & Wyman Ltd, Reading
Set in Monotype Bembo

ACKNOWLEDGEMENTS

THE poems in this selection, taken originally from my Third Edition of *Poems of Gerard Manley Hopkins* (Oxford University Press, 1948), have since the ninth impression been gradually collated and brought into line in a number of instances with the text of the more authoritative Fourth Edition (O.U.P., 1967) by kind permission of the publishers, and of my co-editor in the Fourth Edition, Professor N. H. MacKenzie, from whom most of the emendations originated. The prose selections from the published works follow the texts of the O.U.P. editions of 1935–1959 (see below, p. 221), to the editors of which, Professor Claude Colleer Abbott and the late Humphry House, I am in many ways deeply indebted. I must also acknowledge the valuable contributions to the understanding of Hopkins made by the Rev. C. Devlin, S.J., and the writers whose works are listed on p. 255.

Moreover this selection would not have been possible without the generous cooperation of the Rev. Philip Caraman, S.J., who, acting for the copyright holders, the Society of Jesus, gave me permission to draw freely from Hopkins's writings. I am also grateful to the Rev. D. Anthony Bischoff, S.J., for allowing me to print passages from the Journal of 1866–1868, which he discovered in 1947 and which has now appeared in *The Journals and Papers of Gerard Manley Hopkins* (2nd edn.), 1959.

My thanks are also due to the following: the Oxford University Press, as literary executors of Robert Bridges, for permission to quote from R. B.'s notes to the First Edition of Hopkins's *Poems*; Mr L. Handley-Derry and the Librarian of the Bodleian for permission to reproduce facsimile poems from MS. book 'B'; the late Gerard Hopkins for valuable advice and facilities at all times; Mr E. L. Hillman for helping me with the proof-reading; and lastly my wife – for more assistance both manual and critical than I could ever specify.

W.H.G.

CONTENTS

SECTION B–PROSE

FROM NOTE-BOOKS, JOURNAL, ETC.

SELECTED LETTERS

SECTION C–EDITOR'S NOTES

ILLUSTRATIONS

INTRODUCTION[1]

WITH that boyish gusto which is sometimes found in Hopkins's letters to his relations and friends, he once remarked to Robert Bridges: 'What fun if you were a classic!' At that time Hopkins himself was an unpublished poet with very little prospect of even getting into print, to say nothing of being honoured by posterity. Now, however, the slow dialectic of time has brought in its compensations. Chiefly through the care and foresight of Bridges, the small but precious collection of Hopkins's poems has been saved from oblivion. Not only has this 'eccentric' and 'obscure' Victorian poet-priest attained the once undreamt of distinction of being widely read, discussed, and lectured on, but we can now reasonably assume that he himself has been raised to what might be called, in his own idiom, that 'higher cleave' of posthumous being – the status of a classic.

The permanent worth of Hopkins as a writer is threefold. Firstly, he is one of the most powerful and profound of our religious poets and is also one of the most satisfying of the so-called 'nature poets' in English; secondly, to isolate a merit which is really an essential part of his total quality, he is one of the acknowledged masters of original style – one of the few strikingly successful innovators in poetic language and rhythm; thirdly, the publication of much of his prose – notebooks, journals, letters, sermons – has given us a body of autobiographical and critical writing which, apart from its broader human interest, throws much light on the development of a unique artistic personality. It is no disparagement of Hopkins's prose to say that its value depends to a large extent, though not entirely, upon what it tells us about the poet himself, and especially about his intense practical concern with those interests which inform and shape his poetry, namely his religion, his personal reading of nature, his love of people, and his critical approach to art – and to

[1] In the following pages, bracketed Roman numbers refer to Hopkins's letters in this selection, while ordinary figures refer to the numbered poems. For the abbreviations *B*, *D*, *N*, and *F* see p. 221.

poetic technique in particular. Of Hopkins the poet much needs to
be said; but we may introduce him by observing that he succeeded
in breaking up, by a kind of creative violence, an outworn conven-
tion. He led poetry forward by taking it back – to its primal linguistic
origins: he showed how poetry could gain in resourcefulness and
power by incorporating in its own artistic processes those natural
principles of growth and adaptation which govern our everyday
speech – which give to a living, developing language its peculiar
tang, colour, range, and expressiveness. At the same time he was a
learned poet, who knew how to make full use of all that seemed to
him good in the whole European poetic tradition. He achieved one
important kind of perfection, which both invites and defies imita-
tion. He invites imitation because he uses a large number of highly
effective poetic and rhetorical devices, any one or more of which
can be imitated; he defies imitation because the Hopkins manner is
so essentially a part of the man himself, and is so sharply distinctive,
that anything resembling it seems at once to wear the look of
pastiche.

No one can read Hopkins for the first time without being struck
by two things: the strangeness of his style and the obvious genuine-
ness of his poetic gift. Looking for an author, we discover also a
man – a man of unusual integrity, both intellectual and moral. This
is not to say that Hopkins, as man and writer, had no faults. With
his shortcomings as a man and a priest he himself was always deeply
concerned – to the point of scrupulosity. As a prose writer he can
justly claim a certain indulgence, for, with the possible exception of
the Commentary on the *Spiritual Exercises*, none of his prose was
ever intended for publication. The natural subtlety of his intellect
and his love of detailed explanation sometimes make his style a
little crabbed or involved; but his spontaneous, earnest writing is
always the utterance of a vigorous and sensitive mind – often
humorous or witty, usually searching and stimulating, never
commonplace or pedestrian. On Hopkins's 'bad faults' as a poet his
friend and literary sponsor, Robert Bridges, wrote at some length in
his Preface to the First Edition of 1918. He pointed out the obscurity
– due to an extreme condensation of thought and language; the
grammatical licences, such as the occasional absence of an indispens-
able nominative relative pronoun (as in 'O Hero savest' for 'O Hero
that savest'); the ambiguous use of homophones, and the forced
ingenuity of a few (very few) of the rhymes. Bridges admitted that

most of these stylistic 'tricks' were seriously used and were integral
to the personal manner which produced so many 'rare masterly
beauties'. He was right in warning the common reader of the initial
difficulties he would encounter; but forgetting his Shakespeare,
Donne, and Browning, he made the extraordinary mistake of
declaring that any poetry which demanded 'a conscious effort of
interpretation' was necessarily bad poetry. Since 1918, the publica-
tion of Hopkins's letters and note-books has enabled us to see more
clearly what he was trying to do; and though many who are now
reading Hopkins for the first time may still be repelled by real or
supposed 'errors of taste', by 'occasional affectation', 'obscurity',
and 'oddity', they will surely find that after a reasonable effort of
interpretation most of the obscurities will (as Hopkins said) 'explode'
into meaning, and that the unusual features of grammar and diction
do, with few exceptions, subserve a very precise and genuine artistic
purpose. In 1878 Hopkins wrote to Bridges:

> 'Obscurity I do and will try to avoid so far as is consistent with
> excellences higher than clearness at a first reading ... As for
> affectation I do not believe I am guilty of it: you should point out
> instances, but as long as mere novelty and boldness strikes you as
> affectation your criticism strikes me as – as water of the Lower
> Isis.'

This poet's impressive quality, like his occasional faults, arose out
of his basic belief about the poetic nature:

> 'Every poet, I thought, must be original and originality a condi-
> tion of poetic genius; so that each poet is like a species in nature
> (not an *individuum genericum* or *specificum*) and can never recur.
> That nothing should be old or borrowed however cannot be.'

Hopkins's ideal was a poem, a work of art, which was 'beautiful to
individuation', by which he probably meant 'beautiful to the point
of bringing out all the complex individuality of the subject, which
includes, in effect, the individuality of the artist'. And this aim,
though justified in the total result, did at times lead to a striving after
'individuation' which produced the strange word or queer con-
struction without the necessary counterbalancing sense of fitness or
beauty. Hopkins assured Patmore that his 'thoughts involuntary

moved' in the language and rhythm that we know – that he did not write his poems from preconceived theories. That is undoubtedly true in the sense that no genuine poet in the act of poetic creation is consciously trying to make his poem justify a number of pre-conceived rules; but it must not conceal the fact that Hopkins had thought long and deeply about the principles of poetry. The best way to understand the technical and ethical foundations of his work as a whole is to trace briefly the development of his mind in relation to the main events of his life, and to that we shall now proceed.

II

Born at Stratford, Essex, in 1844, Gerard Manley Hopkins was the eldest of eight children and was brought up in a prosperous middle-class home. In 1843 his father, Manley Hopkins, had published a volume of verse dedicated to Thomas Hood. The mother was devout, and the father, besides writing books, had a passion for curious psychological problems and out-of-the-way knowledge – a quality which was handed on to the eldest son. In his family, music and drawing were sedulously cultivated, and two of Gerard's brothers became professional artists. He himself was an excellent draughtsman, and his later skill, as a poet, in communicating through words the essence and individuality of visual forms in nature was partly fostered by his early training with the pencil. Indeed, his first ambition was to be a painter, and throughout his impressionable schooldays and the first two years at Oxford the influence of Ruskin and the Pre-Raphaelites was as marked as that of the pious, contem-plative mother and the busy, intellectually-curious father.

At Highgate School he won the Poetry Prize in 1860, made many friends, championed the rights of the mere schoolboy against the tyranny of the headmaster, and coloured his reputation as a pre-cocious scholar by a streak of eccentricity and honourable notoriety: to prove his own strength of will and the fact that most people drank too much, he won a wager by abstaining from liquids for a whole week. Here at school the child was father to the man: lashed by the headmaster's tongue and riding-whip (I), Hopkins was con-firmed in those two tendencies, self-denial and independence of spirit, which later determined the character of his bare twenty-four years of adult life. At the same time, the sensuous side of the boy's nature is shown in the following typical passages from the Keatsian *A Vision of the Mermaids*, written in 1862:

> 'Plum-purple was the west; but spikes of light
> Spear'd open lustrous gashes, crimson-white;
> (Where the eye fix'd, fled the encrimsoning spot,
> And, gathering, floated where the gaze was not;)
> And through their parting lids there came and went
> Keen glimpses of the inner firmament:
> Fair beds they seem'd of water-lily flakes
> Clustering entrancingly in beryl lakes:
> Anon, across their swimming splendour strook,
> An intense line of throbbing blood-light shook
> A quivering pennon; then, for eye too keen,
> Ebb'd back beneath its snowy lids, unseen.' (ll. 7–18).

. . . . . .

> 'Soon – as when Summer of his sister Spring
> Crushes and tears the rare enjewelling,
> And boasting "I have fairer things than these"
> Plashes amidst the billowy apple-trees
> His lusty hands, in gusts of scented wind
> Swirling out bloom till all the air is blind
> With rosy foam and pelting blossom and mists
> Of driving vermeil-rain; and, as he lists,
> The dainty onyx-coronals deflowers,
> A glorious wanton; – all the wrecks in showers
> Crowd down upon a stream, and, jostling thick
> With bubbles bugle-eyed, struggle and stick
> On tangled shoals that bar the brook – a crowd
> Of filmy globes and rosy-floating cloud:
> So those Mermaidens crowded to my rock . . .' (ll. 84–98).

In 1863 Hopkins went up to Balliol College, Oxford, with an exhibition, and while reading Classics began his lifelong friendship with Robert Bridges. Hopkins's earliest diaries are full of sensitive observations on nature and poetic imagery. Our first extract (p. 89) shows with what zest he studied words and the 'onomatopoetic theory' of the origin of language. Thus early he evinced a feeling for combined meaning, sound, and suggestion which was later turned to good account in his mature poetry. Another interesting product of this formative period is that long letter to Baillie (II) in which he makes a shrewd critical distinction between the language of true poetry and what he calls 'Parnassian' – the personal dialect of a true poet when he is writing (as the great Victorians so often did) without inspiration. Most of the poems and verse-plays which Hopkins himself attempted between 1862 and 1868 were either derivative or abortive, though in the best of them, from the *Vision* quoted above to *The Habit of Perfection* (No. 4), we see with what technical skill and genuine poetic passion he could handle the conventional forms and metres.

Oxford in the 1860s was still resonant with echoes of the Tractarians. The Oxford Movement, begun in 1833, was a great effort to establish the Authority and Catholicity of the English Church and to infuse into it something of the medieval spirit of intellectual and practical piety. In 1845, John Henry Newman had gone over to the Church of Rome; but counter to the Romanizing tendency was the growing influence of the 'liberals' or Broad Church rationalists within the Protestant fold. Hence the leading High Churchmen (Anglo-Catholics) decided to rally round Dr E. B. Pusey in defence of the Anglican 'middle way'. Together with William Addis and other undergraduates, Hopkins became an ardent Puseyite and Ritualist; but, as Pusey realized, his disciples were being tugged hard by the Papacy on one side and by liberalism on the other. Foremost among the Broad Church rationalizers was Benjamin Jowett, Master of Balliol and Regius Professor of Greek, whose lectures Hopkins attended and the 'purity' of whose character he admired. Two other important influences directly brought to bear upon Hopkins were the humanism of Matthew Arnold (then Professor of Poetry) and the new Aestheticism as it was then just beginning to be formulated in the teaching and criticism of Walter Pater, who was one of Hopkins's tutors.

Among the many Oxford men with whom Hopkins kept up a correspondence, A. W. M. Baillie remained an agnostic to the end of his life; E. H. Coleridge adhered (in spite of Letter III) to the Anglican persuasion; Robert Bridges developed, through his poetry, a private cult of Beauty, while Addis and several more went over to the Catholics. With Hopkins the desire to find 'the one visible Church' was very strong, yet there were plenty of forces to pull him away from the magnetic example of Newman.

In 1865, while he was arguing about Authority and also mastering the classics, Hopkins was under the spell of two Anglican poets, George Herbert and Christina Rossetti. In the same year we detect, in his own poems, the first note of frustration and despair: 'My prayers all meet a brazen heaven/And fail or scatter all away.' At twenty-one he feels 'the long success of sin', and the backslidings recorded for confessional purposes in his diaries show the extent of his moral earnestness. Anticipating some of the great sonnets which were wrung from a far deeper level of experience in 1885, this second-year student says that prayer is now 'A warfare of my lips in truth/Battling with God . . .' Yet only a month later he could write:

'I have found the dominant of my range and state –
Love, O my God, to call Thee Love and Love.' (No. 2.)

Like other Anglo-Catholics, he practised the milder forms of asceticism. Like Milton, he strove to attain a perfect chastity of mind and body, not merely in the interests of Art, but in what he considered to be the higher interests of character, sanctity - 'immortal beauty' as he called it.[1] But in 1866, only a few months before he resolved to become a Catholic, he wrote a poem called *Nondum*, in one stanza of which he expressed a mood almost as sombre as that of James Thomson's *City of Dreadful Night:*

'We see the glories of the earth
But not the hand that wrought them all:
Night to a myriad worlds gives birth,
Yet like a lighted empty hall
Where stands no host at door or hearth
Vacant creation's lamps appal.'

Nevertheless, the glories of the earth were always important for Hopkins. Although his hopes of becoming a painter or poet were receding, he was still possessed by a zeal for noting anything that delighted his eye and stimulated his sense of form. And here it is necessary to consider his Journal, which runs, with only one break,[2] from May 1866 to February 1875. The entries range from bald weather reports to critical notes on Royal Academy paintings; but

[1] See below, pp. 140–1 and 198–9. [2] From July 24, 1866, to July 10, 1867.

the best part of the work consists of carefully written observations on natural phenomena – on colour, organic form, movement, in fact the intrinsic quality of any object which was capable of striking through the senses and into the mind with a feeling of novelty and discovery. Indeed, many vivid images and descriptions recorded in the Journal were 'stalled' by the poet's mind and used later, with a functional precision, in the mature poems. With a searching vision, which often has to coin or re-mint words to express itself, Hopkins describes trees, breaking waves, the ribbed glacier, and the distant hill whose contour is like a 'slow tune'; he eagerly observes the growth and disintegration of anything from a cloud to a bluebell. But he is mainly interested in all those aspects of a thing which make it distinctive and individual. He is always intent on examining that unified complex of characteristics which constitute 'the outward reflection of the inner nature of a thing'[1] – its individual essence. He was always looking for the law or principle which gave to any object or grouping of objects its delicate and surprising uniqueness. Very often this is, for Hopkins, the fundamental beauty which is the active principle of all true being, the source of all true knowledge and delight – even of religious ecstasy; for speaking of a bluebell he says: 'I know the beauty of our Lord by it.'

Now this feeling for intrinsic quality, for the unified pattern of essential characteristics, is the special mark of the artist, whose business is to select these characteristics and organize them into what Clive Bell has called 'significant form'. So too Hopkins must have felt that he had discovered a new aesthetic or metaphysical principle. As a name for that 'individually-distinctive' form (made up of various sense-data) which constitutes the rich and revealing 'oneness' of the natural object, he coined the word *inscape*; and for that energy of being by which all things are upheld, for that natural (but ultimately supernatural) stress which determines an *inscape* and keeps it in being – for that he coined the name *instress*. In our Journal extracts from May 3, 1866, onwards (especially May 6th and July 11th) we see him feeling his way towards a satisfying formulation of what he had discovered.

It was not until 1868 that the terms *inscape* and *instress* began to appear frequently, and in a distracting variety of contexts. Early in that year Pater had introduced Hopkins to Swinburne and the

---

[1] W. A. M. Peters, S.J., op. cit. below, p. 255.

painter Simeon Solomon, so it is possible that Hopkins's preoccupation with 'pattern', 'design', was in part due to his conversation with those aesthetes. But the trend of his thought is not hard to discern. *Instress* is akin to what Shelley (following Plato) called 'the One Spirit's plastic stress', which sweeps through the 'dull dense world' of matter and imposes on it the predestined forms and reflections of the Prime Good.[1] But *instress* is not only the unifying force *in* the object; it connotes also that impulse *from* the 'inscape' which acts on the senses and, through them, actualizes the inscape in the mind of the beholder (or rather 'perceiver', for inscape may be perceived through all the senses at once). Instress, then, is often the *sensation* of inscape – a quasi-mystical illumination, a sudden perception of that deeper pattern, order, and unity which gives meaning to external forms, e.g.:

> 'I saw the inscape though freshly, as if my eye were still growing, though with a companion the eye and the ear are for the most part shut and instress cannot come.' (p. 127).

'There lives the dearest freshness deep down things', Hopkins says in *God's Grandeur*, and in the Journal he writes:

> 'I thought how sadly beauty of inscape was unknown and buried away from simple people and yet how near at hand it was if they had eyes to see it and it could be called out everywhere again.'

Although, as he says, living people are commonly dead to the world of inscape, this something called inscape can still preserve in the dead thing the distinctive quality of the living:

> '... there is one notable dead tree, ... the inscape markedly holding its most simple and beautiful oneness up from the ground through a graceful swerve below (I think) the spring of the branches up to the tops of the timber.'

All the above has a direct bearing upon Hopkins the poet. In 1880, his friend Dixon, who had not yet heard of inscape, praised

---

[1] Cf. Hopkins in a letter to Patmore: 'Fineness, proportion of feature comes from a moulding force which succeeds in asserting itself over the resistance of cumbersome or restraining matter; ...' (*F*, 306).

him for his power of 'forcibly and delicately giving the essence of things in nature', and it is true to say that Hopkins's individual poetic style was directly influenced by the inscape of natural organic forms.[1] In 1879 he replied to a criticism by Bridges:

> 'No doubt my poetry errs on the side of oddness . . . But as air, melody, is what strikes me most of all in music and design in painting, so design, pattern or what I am in the habit of calling *inscape* is what I above all aim at in poetry. Now it is the virtue of design, pattern, or inscape to be distinctive and it is the vice of distinctiveness to become queer. This vice I cannot have escaped.'

Inscape in poetry is further explained by Hopkins himself: it is 'the essential and only lasting thing . . . species or individually-distinctive beauty of style'. He never quite believed in his own admission of literary 'vice', and his best defence is that he is never odd or queer without a purpose. The main reason for the initial strangeness of his style is the serious artistic purpose of 'inscaping' into a perfect unity (i) the inward fusion of thought and feeling,[2] and (ii) the corresponding outward harmony of rhythm and sound-texture. For Hopkins, inscape was 'the very soul of art'.

The theory of inscape probably owed something to Walter Pater. The Platonic dialogue *On the Origin of Beauty*, one third of which is given in this selection, might well have been written for that tutor, and Pater's influence can also be felt in some lecture notes on 'Poetry and Verse' (1874):

> 'Some matter or meaning is essential to [poetry] but only as an element necessary to support and employ the shape which is contemplated for its own sake. (Poetry is in fact speech employed to carry the inscape of speech for the inscape's sake – and therefore the inscape must be dwelt on.)'

There we have a suggestive theory of poetry coming very near to the aesthetic doctrine of 'art for art's sake'. Yet even before he left Oxford, Hopkins had realized that pure aestheticism, to the exclusion of every other purpose in art, was a dangerous single path to

---

[1] Cf. the 'hangers' in Sprung Rhythm and the 'hangers' of elm trees (below pp. 10 and 120).

[2] 'Feeling', in Hopkins, is no vague romantic emotion, but a sense of *value* – of nearness to, or remoteness from, God.

follow, as the case of Oscar Wilde subsequently proved.[1] Much of the power of Hopkins's mature poetry came from the tension between the inborn creative *personality* of the artist and the acquired religious *character* of the Jesuit priest. This tension sometimes resulted in what Bridges called 'the naked encounter of sensualism and asceticism'; but Bridges did not do justice to the fine and significant balance which Hopkins maintained between these two opposite but necessary forces.

To return to the life-story, the undergraduate Hopkins's main problem was solved when, in October 1866, he was received by Dr Newman into the Catholic Church. In the following year he took a First Class in 'Greats' and was proclaimed 'the star of Balliol'. For a few months after leaving the university he taught at Newman's Oratory School at Edgbaston; then, in 1868, after the holiday in Switzerland which is recorded in the Journal, he entered the Novitiate of the Society of Jesus. On becoming a Jesuit he burnt (as he thought) all the verses he had written, and 'resolved to write no more, as not belonging to my profession, unless by the wish of my superiors'. But, as he noted down in 1873, 'all the world is full of inscape, and chance left free to act falls into an order as well as purpose'. Thus in 1872, while studying medieval philosophy as part of his nine years' training for the priesthood, he came across the writings of Duns Scotus, and in that subtle thinker's 'principle of Individuation' and 'theory of knowledge' he discovered what seemed to be a philosophical corroboration of his own private theory of inscape and instress. 'From this time', he writes, 'I was flush with a new enthusiasm. It may come to nothing or it may be a mercy from God.' So much did in fact come of it that a few words about Scotus seem to be necessary.

Unlike St. Thomas Aquinas, official theologian of the Jesuit order, Scotus attached great importance to individuality and personality. The difference, he said, between the concept 'a man' and the concept 'Socrates' is due to the addition to the specific nature (*humanitas*) of an individualizing difference, or final perfection, which makes 'this man *this*' and not 'that'. To this final individualizing 'form' (which is, of course, inherent in the object as a whole) Scotus gave the name Thisness (*haecceitas*). Again, whereas Aquinas had said that the 'individual' is really unknowable (only the 'universal' being known), Scotus declared that the 'individual', on the

---

[1] Cf. Wilde's 'All art is quite useless'.

contrary, is immediately knowable by the intellect in union with the senses. By a 'first act of knowledge' the mind has a direct but vague intuition of the individual concrete object as a 'most special image' – a 'particular glimpse', so to speak, of the *haecceitas*. Further, it is through this knowledge of the singular that the mind, by abstracting and comparing in a 'second act', arrives eventually at its knowledge of the universal.

That is an over-simplified summary, but we can imagine how so much emphasis on the value of the concrete thing, the object of sense, must have appealed to the poet in Hopkins. 'Just then', he wrote, 'when I took in any inscape of the sky or sea I thought of Scotus'; and we may add that he was influenced by Scotus in the writing of at least a dozen of his best poems.[1] Nine years later, in *Duns Scotus's Oxford*, he described the Subtle Doctor as the one 'who of all men most sways my spirits to peace; / Of realty the rarest-veinèd unraveller.' This theologian seemed to give him a sanction for doing as a Christian poet what, as a Jesuit priest, he could not possibly do, that is, *assert* his individuality. For Hopkins, poetic creation occurred when the poet's own nature (his own 'inscape') had been instressed by some complementary inscape discovered in external Nature. The resulting poem is therefore a *new* inscape, and like all poetry must have, 'down to the least separable part, an individualizing touch'. Hence he could write to Bridges, as late as 1888:

'The effect of studying masterpieces is to make me admire and do otherwise. So it must be on every original artist to some degree, on me to a marked degree.'

But Scotism was not the only important formative influence in those seven fallow years between 1868 and 1875. The almost military discipline of the Society of Jesus is based on *The Spiritual Exercises*, written by its founder, St. Ignatius Loyola, and the religious character of Hopkins was so effectually moulded by this discipline that many of his poems are (or contain) poetic interpretations or embodiments of the Ignatian teaching. Sworn to chastity, poverty, and obedience, the Jesuit devotes his intellect and will to the service of Christ, and this deliberate sacrifice of personal ambition merits a supernatural liberation of the spirit for the higher service of

[1] E.g., Nos. 5, 8, 9, 11, 13, 15, 20, 21, 22, 34, 38, 48.

mankind. 'This life', Hopkins wrote to Baillie, 'though it is hard is God's will for me as I most intimately know, which is more than violets knee-deep.' In Hopkins's writings therefore we discern the 'poisĕd powers' of a saintly self-abnegation and an intense self-consciousness. As we see by the opening passage of his Commentary on the *Spiritual Exercises* (p. 145), he valued the human personality as the direct link between man and his Creator, a relationship which is part of that vast hierarchy of being which is made up of all creatures, animate and inanimate, with Christ as their summit. The value of haecceity, selfhood, inscape as a key to the universal is stressed in *Henry Purcell* (No. 22), and again in that markedly 'Scotist' sonnet 'As kingfishers catch fire' (No. 34). Each mortal thing expresses its own being ('Selves – goes itself; *myself* it speaks and spells'); but on the moral plane man, and especially the Jesuit, must orientate his life towards his highest spiritual good:

> 'There's none but truth can stead you. Christ is truth.'
> (No. 64.)

The full force of the impact upon Hopkins of the Ignatian discipline, with its supreme ideal of Sacrifice, is brought out in *The Windhover*, *The Soldier*, and *In Honour of St. Alphonsus Rodriguez*.

III

In 1874, while Hopkins was reading his theology in North Wales, he showed signs of those physical and nervous disabilities which weighed on him to the end of his life. The Journal entry for September 6th (p. 132) strongly suggests, moreover, that his artistic energies craved an outlet in literary and musical interests and activities. Then and later he was kindly treated by his superiors, being given frequent rest periods and many changes of occupation. In spite of moral scruples (p. 133), he did manage to learn Welsh, and he turned his knowledge of classical Welsh poetry to good account when, in December 1875, and at the wish of his Rector, he broke a seven years' silence and wrote his first great poem, *The Wreck of the Deutschland*. In this *tour de force* he incorporated almost all the elements of his 'new rhythm', his new 'inscaped' diction, and his deeply meditated Christian philosophy of life. Owing to the reasons set out in Letter XVI, the editor of the Jesuit magazine, *The Month*, could not print the work, and so began Hopkins's career as an almost unrecognized poet. Even Bridges refused to grapple and board *The Deutschland* a second time – a rebuff which drew from the disappointed author the wry humour of Letter XIII. Two years later *The Loss of the Eurydice* was itself, seemingly, a total loss, foundering on the same editorial rocks.

In 1877, the year of his ordination, Hopkins produced his most joyous sonnets on the instress of God in nature and the instressing of both God and nature in man. At the same time he showed, in *God's Grandeur* and *The Sea and the Skylark*, a critical reaction to the ruthless industrialism of the age. His concern about social conditions is partly explained by the 'Communist' letter of 1871 (IX) and is echoed later in the pregnant obscurities of *Tom's Garland* (No. 47). In 1874 Hopkins had renewed his intellectual contact with Bridges, and the letters which passed between them, full of mutual esteem, appraisal and encouragement, form a chapter in our literary history which is marred only by R. B.'s decision to destroy his own side of the correspondence and by his strange refusal, in 1909, to allow the Rev. Joseph Keating, S.J. to bring out a complete edition of Hopkins's poems.[1]

Between 1877 and 1881 Hopkins served as select preacher, missioner, or parish priest in London, Oxford, Liverpool, Glasgow, and Chesterfield. As a priest he was devout, conscientious, and everywhere liked, but he was not altogether suited either to preaching or to the more exacting kinds of parochial work. The poverty and squalor of the great industrial centres oppressed his spirit, and physical debility often reduced him to despair: 'all I want', he wrote, 'is a working strength.' Many of the poems of this period were inspired by his personal experiences as a priest, and most of them, like *The Handsome Heart* and the superb *Felix Randal*, show a deep anxiety for the spiritual welfare of the young and for the ultimate fate of 'dear and dogged man'.

In 1878 he reintroduced himself to his old schoolmaster, R. W. Dixon (XIV), and thenceforward wrote to him, as to Bridges, many long letters packed with criticism, theory, and self-revelation. On first reading some poems by Hopkins, the gentle Dixon immediately expressed his 'excited delight', his 'deep and intense admiration'.

[1] See *The Manuscripts of Gerard Manley Hopkins*, by D. Anthony Bischoff, S.J. [*Thought* (U.S.A.), Vol. xxvi, No. 103, pp. 556–7.]

Hopkins acknowledged the Canon's plaudits with 'great joy' and 'I thank you for your comforting praises'; but the latter could not rest until such work was published, and his well-meaning attempt to get *The Loss of the Eurydice* into a Carlisle newspaper provoked the pathetic and alarmed protest of Letters XVII and XVIII. Dixon, however, was not satisfied; and when in 1881 Hopkins entered his 'Third Year' Probation, which included a thirty-day silent 'retreat' for the renewal of his spiritual aims and ideals, the older and freer man remarked: 'I suppose you are determined to go on with it!' The reply was characteristic:

> 'I should be black with perjury if I drew back now. And beyond that I can say with St Peter: "To whom shall I go! *Tu verba vitae aeternae habes*." Besides all which, my mind is here more at peace than it has ever been and I would gladly live all my life, if it were to be so, in as great or greater seclusion from the world and be busied only with God.'

He admits that in his normal working life 'worldly interests freshen, and worldly ambitions revive'; but there can be no doubt that his will (both 'affective' and 'active') was now and always firmly set towards the ideal of renunciation and sanctity.

From 1882 to 1884 Hopkins taught Latin and Greek at Stonyhurst College, Blackburn, and the final appointment of his life was to the Chair of Classics at University College, Dublin, which was then managed and partly staffed by the Society of Jesus. In Ireland he felt that he was 'at a third remove' (No. 43), being separated from his Irish colleagues by national and political allegiances as he was now severed from his family and English friends by distance and religion. In spite of frequent holidays, his old physical weakness troubled him more and more; he complained that he always felt 'jaded'. By the time he had carried out his normal academic and social duties, he had no surplus energy with which to write the books that he believed he could and should write, such as a treatise on Sacrifice and a study of Greek metres. 'I am a eunuch', he wrote to Bridges, 'but it is for the kingdom of heaven's sake.' He could still, at times, turn to poetry; but, as he said, 'I have made writing so difficult' – and inspiration seldom came.[1] The number of fragments and promising

---

[1] See the note to Nos. 43–6, below, pp. 239–40.

unfinished poems which he left is due partly to the necessary limita-
tion of his experience and partly to the flagging of his physical and
imaginative powers. Nowhere has the frustration of the creative
spirit been more poignantly expressed than in Nos. 51 and 53. Yet
intellectually, Hopkins was far from idle. His letters to Bridges and
Dixon often contained long, detailed critiques of their manuscript
verse. In 1883 he cheerfully undertook the task of helping Patmore
to revise all his poems for a new edition. He also gave much time to
the study of musical composition, for which he had a small but
interesting gift and a great enthusiasm (XXII).

The desolations recorded in the sonnets of 1885 were in some
perceptible measure due to an entanglement of personal and pro-
fessional problems. In one set of retreat notes he is worried about
the part played by some of the Irish clergy in support of Irish
nationalism, and these qualms of an English patriot are immediately
followed by doubts about his own fitness for the position he held
and his personal responsibility for the right use of his talents. In his
letters, he sharply denounced the Home Rule policy of the 'traitor'
Gladstone, yet he was fully aware of the wrongs that Ireland had
suffered and was sternly critical, from a Catholic point of view, of
the secularist tendencies of England and the whole British Empire
(XXIV).

And what of the view, often asserted, that the last sonnets are,
for all their art, unmistakable symptoms of acute neurosis due to
thwarted impulses, both sexual and artistic? The first issue cannot be
discussed here, but even if an unwarrantably large concession were
made to the psychoanalytic diagnosis, the deeper spiritual signifi-
cances of the sonnets numbered 41 to 46 would remain untouched.
As an artist, Hopkins must have felt the lack of that success which
he often declared to be right and proper for his own poet-friends:
'I say deliberately and before God, I would have you and Canon
Dixon and all true poets remember that fame, the being known,
though one of the most dangerous things to man, is nevertheless the
true and appointed air, element, and setting of genius and its works.'
Yet for Hopkins himself the Jesuit standard, as we can see from Letter
XX, was quite different. In reading the last poems we must take
into account those Christian values and supernatural stresses which
he himself regarded as the prime realities. 'The life I lead', he dryly
told Dixon, 'is liable to many mortifications, but the want of fame
as a poet is not one of them.' Some critics have taken the signs

of inner conflict in these poems to be indications of fundamental doubt, a mood of rebellion, a submerged and rather unseemly scuffle between a Jesuit-Jekyll and a hedonist-Hyde. (He confessed that his own 'Hyde' was worse than R. L. Stevenson's; but then St. Augustine would have confessed the same.) Hopkins also said: 'I have never wavered in my vocation, but I have not lived up to it.' As for his poems, 'I could wish', he admitted, 'that my pieces could at some time become known but in some spontaneous way ... and without my forcing.' Nevertheless, we still have to account for the tense and tragic note of inhibition in No. 43:

>   'Only what word
> Wisest my heart breeds dark heaven's baffling ban
> Bars, or hell's spell thwarts. This to hoard unheard,
> Heard unheeded, leaves me a lonely began.'

Dixon found in Hopkins's poetry 'a *terrible pathos* – something of what you call temper in poetry: a right temper which goes to the point of the terrible; the terrible crystal.' The words 'temper' and 'crystal' express admirably the fusion of poetic passion and poetic form, especially as it is found in the poems numbered 39 to 46. As regards their content, such moods of 'desolation' conform to those periods of spiritual dryness which are carefully described, and prescribed for, by St Ignatius in the *Spiritual Exercises*. Desolation is the human shuddering recoil from the strain of a rigorous discipline – a sourness, loss of hope, of joy, almost a suspension of faith itself, which makes the victim feel that he is totally separated from his God. Nos. 44, 46, and 51 indicate not so much a conflict as a deep sense of privation; as Dr John Pick has said, they are, in a sense, love-letters:

>   'cries like dead letters sent
> To dearest him that lives alas! away.'

But Hopkins speaks also of a 'woe, world-sorrow' (No. 42), which suggests that he was inwardly grieved at the 'schism in the soul' of nineteenth-century man, at the common lack of a spiritual centre, at the inroads into the Christian ethos which were daily being made by scientific rationalism and materialism – that 'wilder beast from West' which was about to devour his Andromeda (No. 26). Such a precise and unromantic *Weltschmerz* would account for the pained comment, at the end of Letter XXVII, on the Rev. W. Addis's secession from the Roman Catholic Church. At the same time there is much to be said for the view that the spiritual dereliction of these last sonnets is akin to that 'dark night of the soul' which is described by mystics as an advanced phase in the progress of the soul towards the ineffable peace of union with God; for to be 'busied only with God' was Hopkins's fervent wish in 1881. Dixon's *'terrible pathos'* does not quite hit the centre of Hopkins's poetry. There is, from the *Deutschland* to the last sonnet, more of heroic acceptance than self-pity: underneath the despair and complaint the note of willing self-surrender to the higher necessity is always implicit.

That Hopkins, during the last four years of his life, was not continuously unhappy is proved by oral tradition, by the varied and frequent zest of his letters,[1] and above all by the bold experimentation and sensuous nature-poetry of such later pieces as *Harry Ploughman*, *Epithalamion*, and *That Nature is a Heraclitean Fire*, with its bright imagery and apocalyptic 'comfort':

> 'In a flash, at a trumpet crash,
> I am all at once what Christ is, ' since he was what I am, and
> This Jack, joke, poor potsherd, ' patch, matchwood, immortal diamond,
>   Is immortal diamond.'

Hopkins's deep underlying faith, from which he drew his powers of spiritual recovery, is also seen in *Carrion Comfort*, 'Patience, hard thing', and 'My own heart let me more have pity on'. In the bitter experiences of the later 'terrible' sonnets we may miss 'the roll, the rise, the carol, the creation' of some of the earlier poems; but in their austere concentration, their clear, incisive intensity, the sonnets of 1885–1889 are in many ways Hopkins's crowning achievement. They are the work of a man who, while putting the whole of his 'sad self' into a poem, could still preserve the sensitivity and control of the artist, and who must have found in the making (though unfortunately too seldom) a deep sense of relief and fulfilment.

[1] His last letter to Bridges (April 29, 1889) begins, 'I am ill to-day, but no matter for that as my spirits are good. And I want you too to "buck up", as we used to say at school, about those jokes over which you write in so dudgeonous a spirit.'

In the early part of 1889 Hopkins's health began to fail rapidly, and he contracted typhoid fever. Eventually peritonitis set in, and his parents were summoned from England. The last rites were administered, and on June 8th he died, his last words being, 'I am so happy, so happy'.

IV

Something more positive still remains to be said about Hopkins's prosody and style, and it is best to begin with the former. In *The Wreck of the Deutschland* he tried out and almost perfected what he called his 'new rhythm'. By this he meant primarily Sprung Rhythm, which is fully explained in the Author's Preface and Letter XVI. Many of the subsequent poems were written in Counterpoint Rhythm, and these two rhythmical modes, together with other refinements such as 'outrides' or 'outriding feet', were often elucidated in the MSS. by various stress- and expression-marks.[1] Most of these for a number of reasons, chiefly typographical, have always been omitted from the printed text, and in justification of this omission it should be stated that Hopkins, while feeling strongly the need for such guides to the correct speech-movement, felt also that they were 'objectionable', 'offensive'. Bridges wisely retained a few essential stress-marks, and to these a few more have been added; but most of the marks, even when they are consistent, are not indispensable. Many of them are illustrated in the Notes and there too will be found all the really essential 'outrides'. In the reading aloud of such poems as *The Windhover*, *Hurrahing in Harvest*, and *Felix Randal* (and Hopkins always insisted that his poems should be read with the *ear* and not with the eye)[2] it is often the 'outride' which tells us the poet's precise rhythmical intention. Moreover the author's own description of the metrical scheme of a poem has always, wherever it exists, been transcribed in the Notes.

Next to be considered is what may be called the sound-texture of the poetry, for this is really an integral part of the rhythm. Partly to give richness to his language, partly to bring out subtle relationships between ideas and images, and partly as a guide to the rhythmical stresses, Hopkins made greater use than any other English poet of alliteration, assonance, internal full- and half-rhyme,

[1] See the facsimile reproductions on pp. 233, 236, and 243.
[2] See notes to Nos. 39 and 48, pp. 238 and 242.

and those subtle vocalic scales which he called 'vowelling on' and 'vowelling off'. All these devices are generally employed with taste and control; they give intensity, variety in unity, and, strange to say, inevitability to the poetic thought; they contribute, in short, to that inscape of speech, that 'starriness', pattern, and melody without which poetry, for Hopkins, could hardly exist. The influence of the Welsh *cynghanedd* on this aspect of Hopkins's style is briefly illustrated in Notes B and C (p. 249). To sum up, before we can read one of these poems as Hopkins intended it to be read, we must first ascertain the number of stressed syllables in each line – unless, as in Nos. 36 and 65, the rhythm is 'free' – and also carefully study the 'outrides', when these occur;[1] we then allow the sense and feeling of the words (as these are 'fetched out' by alliteration, assonance, etc.) to determine the correct beat and movement of the verse. In the following there are no 'outrides':[2]

> Ínto the snóws she swéeps,
> Húrling the háven behínd,
> The Déutschland, on Súnday; and só the ský kéeps,
> For the ínfinite áir is unkínd,
>
> And the séa flínt-fláke, bláck-bácked in the régular blów,
> Sittíng Eástnortheást, in cúrsed quárter, the wínd;
>
> Wiry and whíte-fíery and whírlwind-swivellèd snów
> Spíns to the wídow-máking unchílding unfáthering déeps.
>
> (No. 5, st. 13.)

It should be noted that stressed syllables are usually *long*, either by nature or by position. Uncertainty in the stressing is often caused by the juxtaposition of two strong syllables which seem to be equally important; but this difficulty may be solved by the use of a half-stress (ˇ) for one of them, as in the scansion of the above stanza. Another solution would be the quick, equal stressing indicated by the mark ⌐——¬ in Hopkins's own note to No. 38 (below, p. 238), which would give us:

'And the séa flint-flake, black-backed in the régular blów . . .

[1] i.e. in Nos. 13, 15, 16, 20, 21, 22, 24, 30, 41, 48. For an explanation of 'outrides' see below, p. 10 and pp. 228-9.
[2] 'There are no outriding feet in the *Deutschland*' (G. M. H. in B, p. 45).

A good example of the way internal rhyme and alliteration bring out both the meaning and the rhythm in this 'Sprung' verse is to be found in No. 5, st. 12, lines 5–6:

> O Fáther, not under thý féathers nor éver as guéssing
> The *góal* was a *shóal*, of a fóurth the *dóom* to be *drówned* . . .'

Fate had ordained that the 'goal' of the Deutschland should be not New York but a sandbank; for a quarter of the emigrants, 'doom' and 'drowning' were indeed identical. Equally apt is the alliterative link between the italicized words in the following (*ibid.*, st. 11):

> 'But wé *dréam* we are róoted in éarth – *Dúst*!'

After 'rhythm', the main cause of initial difficulty is Hopkins's bold creative handling of language – both in the choice of words and in the position of words in the sentence. Hopkins said that poetical language 'should be the current language heightened, to any degree heightened and unlike itself, but not (I mean normally: passing freaks and graces are another thing) an obsolete one. This is Shakespeare's and Milton's practice . . .' As special 'graces' he admits a fair sprinkling of archaic and dialect words; but the chief characteristic of his rich and surprising vocabulary is the use he makes of all types of word, both 'shaggy' and 'combed', though he shows a marked preference for the pure Anglo-Saxon. Equally striking is his genius for compounding words to make new and distinctive wholes, whether by close fusion, on the analogy of familiar compounds ('quickgold', 'daredeaths', 'moonmarks'),[1] or by means of a hyphen ('*dapple-dawn-drawn* falcon'), or in an unhyphened adjectival group ('*Thóu mastering mé* God!', '*the rólling level únderneáth him steady* air').[2]

The purpose of this compounding is to weld together, in one concentrated image, all the essential characteristics of the object, to *inscape* them in words, to communicate to the reader that same 'instress of feeling' which first moved the poet himself. When he speaks, in *Harry Ploughman*, of the masculine beauty and power of the labourer as

> 'Chúrlsgrace too, chíld of Amánsstrength . . .'[2]

[1] Cf. 'quick*silver*', 'dare*devils*', '*birth*marks'.
[2] The two 'outrides', marked by loops, should be noted.

he does not mean 'a man's stréngth', which reminds us of an advertisement for Phosferine or Guinness; he means precisely *one* thing, 'Amansstrength' (with a great stress on –*man*–) – that union of health and braced muscular forces which characterizes this particular ploughman in action and is typical of all workmen of the same kind. This is one of the inscapes of the world which 'simple people' (most of us) normally miss. Hopkins's use of original compounds often enables him to fuse into one complex image a whole series of actions or states, as in his vivid inscape of the Incarnation:

> 'The heaven-flung, heart-fleshed, maiden-furled
>> Miracle-in-Mary-of-flame,
> Mid-numbered He in three of the thunder-throne!'
>
> (No. 5, st. 34.)

The second line contains a tmesis: 'Miracle-of-flame *in Mary*' is rearranged so that the position of 'in-Mary' suggests the furling of the child in the mother and also suggests that Mary herself is an intrinsic part of the miracle. It will be noticed too that all the words before and after 'He' constitute one long individualizing description of the Christ, Second Person of the Holy Trinity. Similarly in the delightful *Epithalamion* the poet gives us a dynamic and precise picture of bathers in a rock pool: he tells

>   'how the boys
> With dare and with downdolphinry and bellbright bodies
>> huddling out,
> Are earthworld, airworld, waterworld thorough hurled, all
>> by turn and turn about.'

In both the above examples Hopkins catches the inscape of a complex action, and a certain dramatic quality gives us the instress of the experience. The use of *dare* as a noun is typical of his Shakespearian feeling for the sharp immediacy of the mood and plunge, just as the Elizabethan *thorough* for 'through' shows his affection for an old word which still has an echo in current usage ('thoroughfare').

Of all poets who have revered Shakespeare, Hopkins has learnt most from the master's skill in utilizing the full resources of the English language. His own manner is in many ways a development of Shakespeare's latest condensed and elliptical style; but he goes much further than Shakespeare in manipulating and poethandling (so to speak) the stiff English sentence so as to make it a vehicle for his impassioned thought, casting out the dull colourless particles whenever he can and so placing his words that the most important get the greatest emphasis. Sometimes his violent transposition, omission, or clotting of words gives the impression of a man trying to utter all his thoughts at once; and then, as Bridges said, 'emphasis seems to oust euphony'. Most of the obscurities occasioned by this 'artistic wantonness' are touched on in the Notes; but it must be admitted that now and again his individualizing twists are too un-English to be pleasant, as when in *Tom's Garland* a navvy who need not go hungry becomes

> '(feel
> That ne'er need hunger, Tom . . .'

or when, in *The Lantern out of Doors*, he makes a weird clause out of an eye following a person receding through a crowd:

> '*wind*
> *What most I may eye after*, be in at the end
> I cannot, and out of sight is out of mind.'

But these palpable faults are comparatively few; usually, an image or turn of phrase which at first seems queer or obscure will not only 'explode' but will also justify itself as a strong or delicate harmony of thought, feeling, and sound. Consider, for instance, the magical concentration of

> 'I cast for comfort I can no more get
> By groping round my comfortless, than blind
> Eyes in their dark can day or thirst can find
> Thirst's all-in-all in all a world of wet.' (No. 46.)

Moreover in this poetry the flexibility of style which allows a passage of simple, almost colloquial language to rise naturally into sonorous incantation, as in *Felix Randal*, is matched by the poet's happy audacity in so placing an adjective that it modifies with relevant force two or even three words in the same sentence:

> 'Only what word
> *Wisest* my heart breeds dark heaven's baffling ban
> Bars . . .' (No. 43.)
> 'And *frightful* a nightfall folded *rueful* a day' (No. 5, st. 15.)

– which to me conveys as much as: 'And terribly, yet pitifully too, a menacing night closed down upon a hope-shattering day.' But examples of Hopkins's verve, variety, and subtlety could be multiplied, and most readers will find inexhaustible pleasure in winding their way, though somewhat gingerly at first, into this poet's meaning.

Lastly we must commend the range of Hopkins's imagery, from the simple childlike up to the complex metaphysical; the significant symbolism in such poems as Nos. 5 and 13; the objective value of his Christian vision of things earthly and divine; and no less the amazing architectonic of verse which buckles so many liberties of rhythm, diction, and syntax within the discipline of an elaborate stanza or the nicely proportioned parts of the Italian or Miltonic sonnet. The sonnet-form he moulds admirably to his purpose, now lengthening and now shortening it, in one poem extending and in the next contracting the line-length according to the nature (astringent or expansive) of the theme in hand.

If we consider quality before quantity, as in these days of overproduction we probably should, it is perhaps truer to say that Hopkins is one of our lesser *great* poets than to say, with the late Desmond MacCarthy, that he is one of our great *lesser* poets. It is not the 'Parnassian' redundancies and repetitions that count, but the essence; and Hopkins is nearly all essence. In him, as in the world's greater poets, the fusion of thought and form, the combination of rare insight and an even rarer power and music in the presentation, lifts the poetry from the personal to the universal plane. Though he is inimitable, Hopkins (as Mr Stephen Spender has said) 'ferments in other poets'. No one can really know him without acquiring a higher standard of poetic beauty, a sharper vision of the world, and a deeper sense of the underlying spiritual reality.

W. H. GARDNER

University of Natal,
   Pietermaritzburg.
   August 1952.

This new reprint incorporates, as did (prematurely) the 1966 reprint, some thirty improved readings which are among the many established mainly by my fellow editor, Professor N. H. MacKenzie, for the new Fourth Edition of *Poems of Gerard Manley Hopkins* (O.U.P., 1967). In acknowledging this debt I must warn readers that whenever new emendations in this Penguin reprint coincide with readings in the Oxford Fourth Edition, the text of the Fourth Edition is the *earlier* – the authoritative source.

The comma after 'plume' in line 9 of *The Windhover* (omitted in some previous impressions of this book) has now been restored, the change being authenticated in the new note on No. 13, l. 9 (p. 227). At the same time, a few other defective readings, inherited from earlier editions of the poems, have been carefully corrected. These emendations have full and unquestionable MS. authority, and the most important are as follows: Poem No. 1, st. 7, l. 4 (*tower*); No. 5, st. 12, l. 8 (*million*); No. 15, l. 1 (*rise*); No. 25, st. 1, l. 2 (*the wimpled lip*); No. 26, l. 4 (*dragon food*); No. 43, l. 4 (*my peace/my parting*); No. 56, l. 4 (*fineflour*). Furthermore, a number of minor misprints, which crept in when the book was reset, have now been removed.

1967   W.H.G.

SECTION A

POETRY

FOUR EARLY POEMS
(1865–1866)

*

I

THE ALCHEMIST IN THE CITY

M Y window shows the travelling clouds,
Leaves spent, new seasons, alter'd sky,
The making and the melting crowds:
The whole world passes; I stand by.

They do not waste their meted hours,
But men and masters plan and build:
I see the crowning of their towers,
And happy promises fulfill'd.

And I – perhaps if my intent
Could count on prediluvian age,
The labours I should then have spent
Might so attain their heritage,

But now before the pot can glow
With not to be discover'd gold,
At length the bellows shall not blow,
The furnace shall at last be cold.

Yet it is now too late to heal
The incapable and cumbrous shame
Which makes me when with men I deal
More powerless than the blind or lame.

No, I should love the city less
Even than this my thankless lore;
But I desire the wilderness
Or weeded landslips of the shore.

I walk my breezy belvedere
To watch the low or levant sun,
I see the city pigeons veer,
I mark the tower swallows run

Between the tower-top and the ground
Below me in the bearing air;
Then find in the horizon-round
One spot and hunger to be there.

And then I hate the most that lore
That holds no promise of success;
Then sweetest seems the houseless shore,
Then free and kind the wilderness.

Or ancient mounds that cover bones,
Or rocks where rockdoves do repair
And trees of terebinth and stones
And silence and a gulf of air.

There on a long and squarèd height
After the sunset I would lie,
And pierce the yellow waxen light
With free long looking, ere I die.

2

LET me be to Thee as the circling bird,
Or bat with tender and air-crisping wings
That shapes in half-light his departing rings,
From both of whom a changeless note is heard.

I have found my music in a common word,
Trying each pleasurable throat that sings
And every praisèd sequence of sweet strings,
And know infallibly which I preferred.

The authentic cadence was discovered late
Which ends those only strains that I approve,
And other science all gone out of date
And minor sweetness scarce made mention of:
I have found the dominant of my range and state –
Love, O my God, to call Thee Love and Love.

3

HEAVEN-HAVEN

A nun takes the veil

I HAVE desired to go
        Where springs not fail,
To fields where flies no sharp and sided hail
        And a few lilies blow.

And I have asked to be   *illusion*
        Where no storms come,
Where the green swell is in the havens dumb,
        And out of the swing of the sea.

4

THE HABIT OF PERFECTION

ELECTED Silence, sing to me
And beat upon my whorlèd ear,
Pipe me to pastures still and be
The music that I care to hear.

Shape nothing, lips; be lovely-dumb:
It is the shut, the curfew sent
From there where all surrenders come
Which only makes you eloquent.

Be shellèd, eyes, with double dark
And find the uncreated light:
This ruck and reel which you remark
Coils, keeps, and teases simple sight.

Palate, the hutch of tasty lust,
Desire not to be rinsed with wine:
The can must be so sweet, the crust
So fresh that come in fasts divine!

Nostrils, your careless breath that spend
Upon the stir and keep of pride,
What relish shall the censers send
Along the sanctuary side!

O feel-of-primrose hands, O feet
That want the yield of plushy sward,
But you shall walk the golden street
And you unhouse and house the Lord.

And, Poverty, be thou the bride
And now the marriage feast begun,
And lily-coloured clothes provide
Your spouse not laboured-at nor spun.

POEMS
(1876–1889)

*

AUTHOR'S PREFACE

THE poems in this book[1] are written some in Running Rhythm, the common rhythm in English use, some in Sprung Rhythm, and some in a mixture of the two. And those in the common rhythm are some counterpointed, some not.

Common English rhythm, called Running Rhythm[2] above, is measured by feet of either two or three syllables and (putting aside the imperfect feet at the beginning and end of lines and also some unusual measures, in which feet seem to be paired together and double or composite feet arise) never more nor less.

Every foot has one principal stress or accent, and this or the syllable it falls on may be called the Stress of the foot and the other part, the one or two unaccented syllables, the Slack.[3] Feet (and the rhythms made out of them) in which the Stress comes first are called Falling Feet and Falling Rhythms, feet and rhythm in which the Slack comes first are called Rising Feet and Rhythms, and if the Stress is between two Slacks there will be Rocking Feet and Rhythms. These distinctions are real and true to nature; but for purposes of scanning it is a great convenience to follow the example of music and take the stress always first, as the accent or the chief accent always comes first in a musical bar. If this is done there will be in common English verse only two possible feet – the

[1] That is, the MS. book retained by Robert Bridges and known as 'B' (not to be confused with *B* – below, p. 221). Bridges tells us that this Preface, which does not apply to the Early Poems, 'must have been written in 1883 or not much later'. (Ed.)

[2] G. M. H. used also the term 'Standard Rhythm': see notes to Nos. 8–12. (Ed.)

[3] In the following footnotes (and Notes to the poems) the Stress = (/) and the Slack = (×) or (× × etc.). (Ed.)

so-called accentual Trochee and Dactyl, and correspondingly only two possible uniform rhythms, the so-called Trochaic and Dactylic. But they may be mixed and then what the Greeks called a Logaoedic Rhythm arises.[1] These are the facts and according to these the scanning of ordinary regularly-written English verse is very simple indeed and to bring in other principles is here unnecessary.

But because verse written strictly in these feet and by these principles will become same and tame the poets have brought in licences and departures from rule to give variety, and especially when the natural rhythm is rising, as in the common ten-syllable or five-foot verse, rhymed or blank. These irregularities are chiefly Reversed Feet and Reversed or Counterpoint Rhythm, which two things are two steps or degrees of licence in the same kind. By a reversed foot I mean the putting the stress where, to judge by the rest of the measure, the slack should be and the slack where the stress, and this is done freely at the beginning of a line and, in the course of a line, after a pause; only scarcely ever in the second foot or place and never in the last, unless when the poet designs some extraordinary effect; for these places are characteristic and sensitive and cannot well be touched. But the reversal of the first foot and of some middle foot after a strong pause is a thing so natural that our poets have generally done it, from Chaucer down, without remark and it commonly passes unnoticed and cannot be said to amount to a formal change of rhythm, but rather is that irregularity which all natural growth and motion shews. If however the reversal is repeated in two feet running, especially so as to include the sensitive second foot, it must be due either to great want of ear or else is a calculated effect, the superinducing or *mounting* of a new rhythm upon the old; and since the new or mounted rhythm is actually heard and at the same time the mind naturally supplies the natural or standard foregoing rhythm, for we do not forget

[1] E.g. in G. M. H.'s imitation of Swinburne's metre in *Ad Mariam* (3rd Edn., No. 26).

     × × | ′ ×   × | ′ × | ′ × × | ′ ×
'We have suffered the sons of Winter in sorrow' (II.1) (Ed.).

what the rhythm is that by rights we should be hearing, two
rhythms are in some manner running at once and we have some-
thing answerable to counterpoint in music, which is two or more
strains of tune going on together, and this is Counterpoint
Rhythm.[1] Of this kind of verse Milton is the great master and the
choruses of *Samson Agonistes* are written throughout in it – but
with the disadvantage that he does not let the reader clearly know
what the ground-rhythm is meant to be and so they have struck
most readers as merely irregular. And in fact if you counterpoint
throughout, since one only of the counter rhythms is actually
heard, the other is really destroyed or cannot come to exist, and
what is written is one rhythm only and probably Sprung Rhythm,
of which I now speak.

Sprung Rhythm, as used in this book, is measured by feet of
from one to four syllables, regularly, and for particular effects any
number of weak or slack syllables may be used. It has one stress,
which falls on the only syllable, if there is only one, or, if there
are more, then scanning as above, on the first, and so gives rise to
four sorts of feet, a monosyllable and the so-called accentual
Trochee, Dactyl, and the First Paeon.[2] And there will be four
corresponding natural rhythms; but nominally the feet are mixed
and any one may follow any other. And hence Sprung Rhythm

---

[1] First heard in *God's Grandeur*:

/×|/× | × / | × / | × /

'Generations have trod, have trod, have trod,' (l. 5). The twirl ⌣ was
used in the MSS. to mark reversed feet. (Ed.). See also Letter XVI, p. 186.

[2] E.g. in *The Wreck of the Deutschland*:

(a) Monosyllabic feet:

× | / | / | /

'The sour scythe cringe, . . .' (xi. 8.)

/ × | / | / |

'Jesu, heart's light,' (xxx. 1.)

(b) Paeons:

/ × × × | / × × × | / × × × |

'Startle the poor sheep back! is the shipwrack then a . . .'

(xxxi. 8.)

For extended paeons see Notes to *ibid.*, xxxi. 6 and xxxv. 3. (Ed.)

differs from Running Rhythm in having or being only one nominal rhythm, a mixed or 'logaoedic' one, instead of three, but on the other hand in having twice the flexibility of foot, so that any two stresses may either follow one another running or be divided by one, two, or three slack syllables. But strict Sprung Rhythm cannot be counterpointed. In Sprung Rhythm, as in logaoedic rhythm generally, the feet are assumed to be equally long or strong and their seeming inequality is made up by pause or stressing.

Remark also that it is natural in Sprung Rhythm for the lines to be *rove over*,[1] that is for the scanning of each line immediately to take up that of the one before, so that if the first has one or more syllables at its end the other must have so many the less at its beginning; and in fact the scanning runs on without break from the beginning, say, of a stanza to the end and all the stanza is one long strain, though written in lines asunder.

Two licences are natural to Sprung Rhythm. The one is rests, as in music; but of this an example is scarcely to be found in this book, unless in the *Echos*, second line.[2] The other is *hangers* or *outrides*, that is one, two, or three slack syllables added to a foot and not counting in the nominal scanning. They are so called because they seem to hang below the line or ride forward or backward from it in another dimension than the line itself, according to a principle needless to explain here.[3] These outriding half feet or hangers are marked by a loop underneath them, and plenty of them will be found.

The other marks are easily understood, namely accents, where the reader might be in doubt which syllable should have the stress; slurs, that is loops *over* syllables, to tie them together into the time of one; little loops at the end of a line to shew that the rhyme goes on to the first letter of the next line; what in music are called

---

[1] 'Rove' is apparently the past participle of the nautical *reeve*, though G. M. H. speaks of 'the "over-reaving" of the verse at which I so much aim'. (*B*, p. 86.) (Ed.)

[2] No. 36; but see also the first line of No. 39 (Ed.)

[3] More clearly explained in G. M. H.'s note to No. 15 (below, p. 228). For examples of outrides see Notes *passim*, Nos. 13, 15, 21, &c. (Ed.)

pauses ⌒, to shew that the syllable should be dwelt on; and twirls ⌣,[1] to mark reversed or counterpointed rhythm.[2]

Note on the nature and history of Sprung Rhythm – Sprung Rhythm is the most natural of things. For (1) it is the rhythm of common speech and of written prose, when rhythm is perceived in them. (2) It is the rhythm of all but the most monotonously regular music, so that in the words of choruses and refrains and in songs written closely to music it arises. (3) It is found in nursery rhymes, weather saws, and so on; because, however these may have been once made in running rhythm, the terminations having dropped off by the change of language, the stresses come together and so the rhythm is sprung. (4) It arises in common verse when reversed or counterpointed, for the same reason.

But nevertheless in spite of all this and though Greek and Latin lyric verse, which is well known, and the old English verse seen in *Pierce Ploughman* are in sprung rhythm, it has in fact ceased to be used since the Elizabethan age, Greene being the last writer who can be said to have recognized it. For perhaps there was not, down to our days, a single, even short, poem in English in which sprung rhythm is employed – not for single effects or in fixed places – but as the governing principle of the scansion. I say this because the contrary has been asserted: if it is otherwise the poem should be cited.

Some of the sonnets of this book[3] are in five-foot, some in six-foot or Alexandrine lines.

Nos. 13 and 22[4] are Curtal-Sonnets, that is they are constructed in proportions resembling those of the sonnet proper, namely 6+4 instead of 8+6, with however a halfline tailpiece (so that the equation is rather $\frac{12}{2}+\frac{9}{2} = \frac{21}{2} = 10\frac{1}{2}$).

---

[1] MS. has ⌣, a mistake (see next footnote). (Ed.)

[2] These marks and others are illustrated in the notes to one or more of the poems numbered 36, 38, 42, 44, 47, 48, and 50. For the 'little loops' to indicate linked rhyme see note to No. 5, st. xiv. 3-4; for 'hurried feet' see notes to Nos. 42, 47, and 48; for the 'quiver or circumflexion (⌣) making one syllable nearly two' see notes to Nos. 44 and 48; for the 'slur' and the mark ∧ ('strong stress, which does not differ much from ⌒') see notes to No. 48. (Ed.)

[3] See above, p. 7, note 1.   [4] Nos. 14 and 23 in the present edition.

POEMS
(1876–1889)

*

5

THE WRECK
OF THE DEUTSCHLAND

*To the
happy memory of five Franciscan nuns
exiles by the Falck Laws
drowned between midnight and morning of
Dec. 7th, 1875*

PART THE FIRST

I

Thou mastering me
God! giver of breath and bread;
World's strand, sway of the sea;
Lord of living and dead;
Thou hast bound bones and veins in me, fastened me flesh,
And after it almost unmade, what with dread,
Thy doing: and dost thou touch me afresh?
Over again I feel thy finger and find thee.

2

I did say yes
O at lightning and lashed rod;
Thou heardst me truer than tongue confess
Thy terror, O Christ, O God;
Thou knowest the walls, altar and hour and night:
The swoon of a heart that the sweep and the hurl of thee trod
Hard down with a horror of height:
And the midriff astrain with leaning of, laced with fire of stress.

3

The frown of his face
Before me, the hurtle of hell
Behind, where, where was a, where was a place?
I whirled out wings that spell
And fled with a fling of the heart to the heart of the Host.
My heart, but you were dovewinged, I can tell,
Carrier-witted, I am bold to boast,
To flash from the flame to the flame then, tower from the grace
to the grace.

4

I am soft sift
In an hourglass – at the wall
Fast, but mined with a motion, a drift,
And it crowds and it combs to the fall;
I steady as a water in a well, to a poise, to a pane,
But roped with, always, all the way down from the tall
Fells or flanks of the voel, a vein
Of the gospel proffer, a pressure, a principle, Christ's gift.

5

I kiss my hand
To the stars, lovely-asunder
Starlight, wafting him out of it; and
Glow, glory in thunder;
Kiss my hand to the dappled-with-damson west;
Since, tho' he is under the world's splendour and wonder,
His mystery must be instressed, stressed;
For I greet him the days I meet him, and bless when I understand.

6

Not out of his bliss
Springs the stress felt
Nor first from heaven (and few know this)
Swings the stroke dealt —
Stroke and a stress that stars and storms deliver,
That guilt is hushed by, hearts are flushed by and melt —
But it rides time like riding a river
(And here the faithful waver, the faithless fable and miss).

7

It dates from day
Of his going in Galilee;
Warm-laid grave of a womb-life grey;
Manger, maiden's knee;
The dense and the driven Passion, and frightful sweat;
Thence the discharge of it, there its swellings to be,
Though felt before, though in high flood yet —
Where none would have known of it, only the heart, being hard
at bay,

8

Is out with it! Oh,
We lash with the best or worst
Word last! How a lush-kept plush-capped sloe
Will, mouthed to flesh-burst,
Gush! – flush the man, the being with it, sour or sweet,
Brim, in a flash, full! – Hither then, last or first,
To hero of Calvary, Christ's feet –
Never ask if meaning it, wanting it, warned of it – men go.

9

Be adored among men,
God, three-numberèd form;
Wring thy rebel, dogged in den,
Man's malice, with wrecking and storm.
Beyond saying sweet, past telling of tongue,
Thou art lightning and love, I found it, a winter and warm;
Father and fondler of heart thou hast wrung:
Hast thy dark descending and most art merciful then.

10

With an anvil-ding
And with fire in him forge thy will
Or rather, rather then, stealing as Spring
Through him, melt him but master him still:
Whether at once, as once at a crash Paul,
Or as Austin, a lingering-out swéet skill,
Make mercy in all of us, out of us all
Mastery, but be adored, but be adored King.

PART THE SECOND

11

'Some find me a sword; some
The flange and the rail; flame,
Fang, or flood' goes Death on drum,
And storms bugle his fame.
But wé dream we are rooted in earth – Dust!
Flesh falls within sight of us, we, though our flower the same,
Wave with the meadow, forget that there must
The sour scythe cringe, and the blear share come.

12

On Saturday sailed from Bremen,
American-outward-bound,
Take settler and seamen, tell men with women,
Two hundred souls in the round –
O Father, not under thy feathers nor ever as guessing
The goal was a shoal, of a fourth the doom to be drowned;
Yet did the dark side of the bay of thy blessing
Not vault them, the million of rounds of thy mercy not reeve
even them in?

13

Into the snows she sweeps,
Hurling the haven behind,
The Deutschland, on Sunday; and so the sky keeps,
For the infinite air is unkind,
And the sea flint-flake, black-backed in the regular blow,
Sitting Eastnortheast, in cursed quarter, the wind;
Wiry and white-fiery and whirlwind-swivellèd snow
Spins to the widow-making unchilding unfathering deeps.

14

She drove in the dark to leeward,
　　She struck – not a reef or a rock
But the combs of a smother of sand: night drew her
　　Dead to the Kentish Knock;
And she beat the bank down with her bows and the ride of
　　her keel:
The breakers rolled on her beam with ruinous shock;
　　And canvas and compass, the whorl and the wheel
Idle for ever to waft her or wind her with, these she endured.

15

Hope had grown grey hairs,
　　Hope had mourning on,
Trenched with tears, carved with cares,
　　Hope was twelve hours gone;
And frightful a nightfall folded rueful a day
Nor rescue, only rocket and lightship, shone,
　　And lives at last were washing away:
To the shrouds they took, – they shook in the hurling and horrible
　　airs.

16

One stirred from the rigging to save
　　The wild woman-kind below,
With a rope's end round the man, handy and brave –
　　He was pitched to his death at a blow,
For all his dreadnought breast and braids of thew:
They could tell him for hours, dandled the to and fro
　　Through the cobbled foam-fleece. What could he do
With the burl of the fountains of air, buck and the flood of the
　　wave?

17

They fought with God's cold –
And they could not and fell to the deck
(Crushed them) or water (and drowned them) or rolled
With the sea-romp over the wreck.
Night roared, with the heart-break hearing a heart-broke
rabble,
The woman's wailing, the crying of child without check –
Till a lioness arose breasting the babble,
A prophetess towered in the tumult, a virginal tongue told.

18

Ah, touched in your bower of bone,
Are you! turned for an exquisite smart,
Have you! make words break from me here all alone,
Do you! – mother of being in me, heart.
O unteachably after evil, but uttering truth,
Why tears! is it? tears; such a melting, a madrigal start!
Never-eldering revel and river of youth,
What can it be, this glee? the good you have there of your own?

19

Sister, a sister calling
A master, her master and mine! –
And the inboard seas run swirling and hawling;
The rash smart sloggering brine
Blinds her; but she that weather sees one thing, one;
Has one fetch in her: she rears herself to divine
Ears, and the call of the tall nun
To the men in the tops and the tackle rode over the storm's
brawling.

20

She was first of a five and came
Of a coifèd sisterhood.
(O Deutschland, double a desperate name!
O world wide of its good!
But Gertrude, lily, and Luther, are two of a town,
Christ's lily and beast of the waste wood:
From life's dawn it is drawn down,
Abel is Cain's brother and breasts they have sucked the same.)

21

Loathed for a love men knew in them,
Banned by the land of their birth,
Rhine refused them. Thames would ruin them;
Surf, snow, river and earth
Gnashed: but thou art above, thou Orion of light;
Thy unchancelling poising palms were weighing the worth,
Thou martyr-master: in thy sight
Storm flakes were scroll-leaved flowers, lily showers – sweet
heaven was astrew in them.

22

Five! the finding and sake
And cipher of suffering Christ.
Mark, the mark is of man's make
And the word of it Sacrificed.
But he scores it in scarlet himself on his own bespoken,
Before time-taken, dearest prizèd and priced –
Stigma, signal, cinquefoil token
For lettering of the lamb's fleece, ruddying of the rose-flake.

23

      Joy fall to thee, father Francis,
       Drawn to the Life that died;
  With the gnarls of the nails in thee, niche of the lance, his
      Lovescape crucified
And seal of his seraph-arrival! and these thy daughters
    And five-livèd and leavèd favour and pride,
     Are sisterly sealed in wild waters,
To bathe in his fall-gold mercies, to breathe in his all-fire glances.

24

      Away in the loveable west,
     On a pastoral forehead of Wales,
  I was under a roof here, I was at rest,
     And they the prey of the gales;
She to the black-about air, to the breaker, the thickly
Falling flakes, to the throng that catches and quails
    Was calling 'O Christ, Christ, come quickly':
The cross to her she calls Christ to her, christens her wild-worst Best.

25

     The majesty! what did she mean?
    Breathe, arch and original Breath.
  Is it love in her of the being as her lover had been?
    Breathe, body of lovely Death.
They were else-minded then, altogether, the men
Woke thee with a *we are perishing* in the weather of Gen-
     nesareth.
   Or is it that she cried for the crown then,
The keener to come at the comfort for feeling the combating keen?

26

For how to the heart's cheering
The down-dugged ground-hugged grey
Hovers off, the jay-blue heavens appearing
Of pied and peeled May!
Blue-beating and hoary-glow height; or night, still higher,
With belled fire and the moth-soft Milky Way,
What by your measure is the heaven of desire,
The treasure never eyesight got, nor was ever guessed what for
the hearing?

27

No, but it was not these.
The jading and jar of the cart,
Time's tasking, it is fathers that asking for ease
Of the sodden-with-its-sorrowing heart,
Not danger, electrical horror; then further it finds
The appealing of the Passion is tenderer in prayer apart:
Other, I gather, in measure her mind's
Burden, in wind's burly and beat of endragonèd seas.

28

But how shall I . . . make me room there:
Reach me a . . . Fancy, come faster –
Strike you the sight of it? look at it loom there,
Thing that she . . . there then! the Master,
Ipse, the only one, Christ, King, Head:
He was to cure the extremity where he had cast her;
Do, deal, lord it with living and dead;
Let him ride, her pride, in his triumph, despatch and have done
with his doom there.

29

Ah! there was a heart right!
There was single eye!
Read the unshapeable shock night
And knew the who and the why;
Wording it how but by him that present and past,
Heaven and earth are word of, worded by? –
The Simon Peter of a soul! to the blast
Tarpeian-fast, but a blown beacon of light.

30

Jesu, heart's light,
Jesu, maid's son,
What was the feast followed the night
Thou hadst glory of this nun? –
Feast of the one woman without stain.
For so conceived, so to conceive thee is done;
But here was heart-throe, birth of a brain,
Word, that heard and kept thee and uttered thee outright.

31

Well, she has thee for the pain, for the
Patience; but pity of the rest of them!
Heart, go and bleed at a bitterer vein for the
Comfortless unconfessed of them –
No not uncomforted: lovely-felicitous Providence
Finger of a tender of, O of a feathery delicacy, the breast of the
Maiden could obey so, be a bell to, ring of it, and
Startle the poor sheep back! is the shipwrack then a harvest,
does tempest carry the grain for thee?

32

I admire thee, master of the tides,
Of the Yore-flood, of the year's fall;
The recurb and the recovery of the gulf's sides,
The girth of it and the wharf of it and the wall;
Stanching, quenching ocean of a motionable mind;
Ground of being, and granite of it: past all
Grasp God, throned behind
Death with a sovereignty that heeds but hides, bodes but abides;

33

With a mercy that outrides
The all of water, an ark
For the listener; for the lingerer with a love glides
Lower than death and the dark;
A vein for the visiting of the past-prayer, pent in prison,
The-last-breath penitent spirits – the uttermost mark
Our passion-plungèd giant risen,
The Christ of the Father compassionate, fetched in the storm of
his strides.

34

Now burn, new born to the world,
Double-naturèd name,
The heaven-flung, heart-fleshed, maiden-furled
Miracle-in-Mary-of-flame,
Mid-numberèd He in three of the thunder-throne!
Not a dooms-day dazzle in his coming nor dark as he came;
Kind, but royally reclaiming his own;
A released shower, let flash to the shire, not a lightning of fire
hard-hurled.

35

Dame, at our door
Drowned, and among our shoals,
Remember us in the roads, the heaven-haven of the
Reward:
Our King back, oh, upon English souls!
Let him easter in us, be a dayspring to the dimness of us, be
a crimson-cresseted east,
More brightening her, rare-dear Britain, as his reign rolls,
Pride, rose, prince, hero of us, high-priest,
Our hearts' charity's hearth's fire, our thoughts' chivalry's throng's
Lord.

6

PENMAEN POOL

For the Visitors' Book at the Inn

Who long for rest, who look for pleasure
Away from counter, court, or school
O where live well your lease of leisure
But here at, here at Penmaen Pool?

You'll dare the Alp? you'll dart the skiff?
Each sport has here its tackle and tool:
Come, plant the staff by Cadair cliff;
Come, swing the sculls on Penmaen Pool.

What's yonder? – Grizzled Dyphwys dim:
The triple-hummocked Giant's Stool,
Hoar messmate, hobs and nobs with him
To halve the bowl of Penmaen Pool.

And all the landscape under survey,
At tranquil turns, by nature's rule,
Rides repeated topsyturvy
In frank, in fairy Penmaen Pool.

And Charles's Wain, the wondrous seven,
And sheep-flock clouds like worlds of wool,
For all they shine so, high in heaven,
Shew brighter shaken in Penmaen Pool.

The Mawddach, how she trips! though throttled
If floodtide teeming thrills her full,
And mazy sands all water-wattled
Waylay her at ebb, past Penmaen Pool.

But what's to see in stormy weather,
When grey showers gather and gusts are cool?
Why, raindrop-roundels looped together
That lace the face of Penmaen Pool.

Then even in weariest wintry hour
Of New Year's month or surly Yule
Furred snows, charged tuft above tuft, tower
From darksome darksome Penmaen Pool.

And ever, if bound here hardest home,
You've parlour-pastime left and (who'll
Not honour it?) ale like goldy foam
That frocks an oar in Penmaen Pool.

Then come who pine for peace or pleasure
Away from counter, court, or school,
Spend here your measure of time and treasure
And taste the treats of Penmaen Pool.

7

THE SILVER JUBILEE:

*to James First Bishop of Shrewsbury on the 25th Year
of his Episcopate July 28, 1876*

THOUGH no high-hung bells or din
Of braggart bugles cry it in –
   What is sound? Nature's round
Makes the Silver Jubilee.

Five and twenty years have run
Since sacred fountains to the sun
   Sprang, that but now were shut,
Showering Silver Jubilee.

Feasts, when we shall fall asleep,
Shrewsbury may see others keep;
   None but you this her true,
This her Silver Jubilee.

Not today we need lament
Your wealth of life is some way spent:
   Toil has shed round your head
Silver but for Jubilee.

Then for her whose velvet vales
Should have pealed with welcome, Wales,
   Let the chime of a rhyme
Utter Silver Jubilee.

8

GOD'S GRANDEUR

THE world is charged with the grandeur of God.
  It will flame out, like shining from shook foil;
  It gathers to a greatness, like the ooze of oil
Crushed. Why do men then now not reck his rod?
Generations have trod, have trod, have trod;
  And all is seared with trade; bleared, smeared with toil;
  And wears man's smudge and shares man's smell: the soil
Is bare now, nor can foot feel, being shod.

And for all this, nature is never spent;
  There lives the dearest freshness deep down things;
And though the last lights off the black West went
  Oh, morning, at the brown brink eastward, springs –
Because the Holy Ghost over the bent
  World broods with warm breast and with ah! bright wings.

9

THE STARLIGHT NIGHT

LOOK at the stars! look, look up at the skies!
  O look at all the fire-folk sitting in the air!
  The bright boroughs, the circle-citadels there!
Down in dim woods the diamond delves! the elves'-eyes!
The grey lawns cold where gold, where quickgold lies!
  Wind-beat whitebeam! airy abeles set on a flare!
  Flake-doves sent floating forth at a farmyard scare!
Ah well! it is all a purchase, all is a prize.

Buy then! bid then! – What? – Prayer, patience, alms, vows.
Look, look: a May-mess, like on orchard boughs!
  Look! March-bloom, like on mealed-with-yellow sallows!
These are indeed the barn; withindoors house
The shocks. This piece-bright paling shuts the spouse
  Christ home, Christ and his mother and all his hallows.

10

SPRING

NOTHING is so beautiful as Spring –
  When weeds, in wheels, shoot long and lovely and lush;
  Thrush's eggs look little low heavens, and thrush
Through the echoing timber does so rinse and wring
The ear, it strikes like lightnings to hear him sing;
  The glassy peartree leaves and blooms, they brush
  The descending blue; that blue is all in a rush
With richness; the racing lambs too have fair their fling.

What is all this juice and all this joy?
  A strain of the earth's sweet being in the beginning
In Eden garden. – Have, get, before it cloy,
  Before it cloud, Christ, lord, and sour with sinning,
Innocent mind and Mayday in girl and boy,
  Most, O maid's child, thy choice and worthy the winning.

11

THE LANTERN OUT OF DOORS

SOMETIMES a lantern moves along the night,
  That interests our eyes. And who goes there?
  I think; where from and bound, I wonder, where,
With, all down darkness wide, his wading light?

Men go by me whom either beauty bright
   In mould or mind or what not else makes rare:
   They rain against our much-thick and marsh air
Rich beams, till death or distance buys them quite.

Death or distance soon consumes them: wind
   What most I may eye after, be in at the end
I cannot, and out of sight is out of mind.

Christ minds: Christ's interest, what to avow or amend
   There, éyes them, heart wánts, care haúnts, foot fóllows kínd,
Their ránsom, théir rescue, ánd first, fást, last friénd.

12

THE SEA AND THE SKYLARK

On ear and ear two noises too old to end
   Trench – right, the tide that ramps against the shore;
   With a flood or a fall, low lull-off or all roar,
Frequenting there while moon shall wear and wend.

Left hand, off land, I hear the lark ascend,
   His rash-fresh re-winded new-skeinèd score
   In crisps of curl off wild winch whirl, and pour
And pelt music, till none's to spill nor spend.

How these two shame this shallow and frail town!
   How ring right out our sordid turbid time,
Being pure! We, life's pride and cared-for crown,

   Have lost that cheer and charm of earth's past prime:
Our make and making break, are breaking, down
   To man's last dust, drain fast towards man's first slime.

13

THE WINDHOVER

To Christ our Lord

I CAUGHT this morning morning's minion, king-
    dom of daylight's dauphin, dapple-dawn-drawn Falcon, in his
        riding
Of the rolling level underneath him steady air, and striding
High there, how he rung upon the rein of a wimpling wing
In his ecstasy! then off, off forth on swing,
    As a skate's heel sweeps smooth on a bow-bend: the hurl and
        gliding
    Rebuffed the big wind. My heart in hiding
Stirred for a bird, – the achieve of, the mastery of the thing!

Brute beauty and valour and act, oh, air, pride, plume, here
    Buckle! AND the fire that breaks from thee then, a billion
Times told lovelier, more dangerous. O my chevalier!

    No wonder of it: shéer plód makes plough down sillion
Shine, and blue-bleak embers, ah my dear,
    Fall, gall themselves, and gash gold-vermilion.

14

PIED BEAUTY

GLORY be to God for dappled things –
    For skies of couple-colour as a brinded cow;
        For rose-moles in all stipple upon trout that swim;
Fresh-firecoal chestnut-falls; finches' wings;
    Landscape plotted and pieced – fold, fallow, and plough;
        And áll trádes, their gear and tackle and trim.

All things counter, original, spare, strange;
    Whatever is fickle, freckled (who knows how?)
      With swift, slow; sweet, sour; adazzle, dim;
He fathers-forth whose beauty is past change:
          Praise him.

15

HURRAHING IN HARVEST   *Sept 1 1877*

SUMMER ends now; now, barbarous in beauty, the stooks rise
    Around; up above, what wind-walks! what lovely behaviour
    Of silk-sack clouds! has wilder, wilful-wavier
Meal-drift moulded ever and melted across skies?

I walk, I lift up, I lift up heart, eyes,
    Down all that glory in the heavens to glean our Saviour;
    And, éyes, heárt, what looks, what lips yet gave you a
Rapturous love's greeting of realer, of rounder replies?

And the azurous hung hills are his world-wielding shoulder
    Majestic – as a stallion stalwart, very-violet-sweet! –
These things, these things were here and but the beholder
    Wanting; which two when they once meet,
The heart réars wíngs bold and bolder
    And hurls for him, O half hurls earth for him off under his feet.

16

THE CAGED SKYLARK

As a dare-gale skylark scanted in a dull cage
    Man's mounting spirit in his bone-house, mean house, dwells –
    That bird beyond the remembering his free fells;
This in drudgery, day-labouring-out life's age.

Though aloft on turf or perch or poor low stage,
   Both sing sometímes the sweetest, sweetest spells,
   Yet both droop deadly sómetimes in their cells
Or wring their barriers in bursts of fear or rage.

Not that the sweet-fowl, song-fowl, needs no rest –
Why, hear him, hear him babble and drop down to
     his nest,
   But his own nest, wild nest, no prison.

Man's spirit will be flesh-bound when found at best,
But uncumberèd: meadow-down is not distressed
   For a rainbow footing it nor he for his bónes rísen.

17

IN THE VALLEY OF THE ELWY

I REMEMBER a house where all were good
   To me, God knows, deserving no such thing:
   Comforting smell breathed at very entering,
Fetched fresh, as I suppose, off some sweet wood.
That cordial air made those kind people a hood
   All over, as a bevy of eggs the mothering wing
   Will, or mild nights the new morsels of Spring:
Why, it seemed of course; seemed of right it should.

Lovely the woods, waters, meadows, combes, vales,
All the air things wear that build this world of Wales;
   Only the inmate does not correspond:
God, lover of souls, swaying considerate scales,
Complete thy creature dear O where it fails,
   Being mighty a master, being a father and fond.

18

THE LOSS OF THE EURYDICE

Foundered March 24, 1878

THE Eurydice – it concerned thee, O Lord:
Three hundred souls, O alas! on board,
    Some asleep unawakened, all un-
warned, eleven fathoms fallen   4

Where she foundered! One stroke
Felled and furled them, the hearts of oak!
    And flockbells off the aerial
Downs' forefalls beat to the burial.   8

For she did pride her, freighted fully, on
Bounden bales or a hoard of bullion? –
    Precious passing measure,
Lads and men her lade and treasure.   12

She had come from a cruise, training seamen –
Men, boldboys soon to be men:
    Must it, worst weather,
Blast bole and bloom together?   16

No Atlantic squall overwrought her
Or rearing billow of the Biscay water:
    Home was hard at hand
And the blow bore from land.   20

And you were a liar, O blue March day.
Bright sun lanced fire in the heavenly bay;
    But what black Boreas wrecked her? he
Came equipped, deadly-electric,   24

A beetling baldbright cloud thorough England
Riding: there did storms not mingle? and
    Hailropes hustle and grind their
Heavengravel? wolfsnow, worlds of it, wind there?   28

Now Carisbrook keep goes under in gloom:
Now it overvaults Appledurcombe;
    Now near by Ventnor town
It hurls, hurls off Boniface Down.   32

Too proud, too proud, what a press she bore!
Royal, and all her royals wore.
    Sharp with her, shorten sail!
Too late; lost; gone with the gale.   36

This was that fell capsize.
As half she had righted and hoped to rise
    Death teeming in by her portholes
Raced down decks, round messes of mortals.   40

Then a lurch forward, frigate and men;
'All hands for themselves' the cry ran then;
    But she who had housed them thither
Was around them, bound them or wound them with her.   44

Marcus Hare, high her captain,
Kept to her – care-drowned and wrapped in
    Cheer's death, would follow
His charge through the champ-white water-in-a-wallow,   48

All under Channel to bury in a beach her
Cheeks: Right, rude of feature,
    He thought he heard say
'Her commander! and thou too, and thou this way.'   52

It is even seen, time's something server,
In mankind's medley a duty-swerver,
    At downright 'No or yes?'
Doffs all, drives full for righteousness.   56

Sydney Fletcher, Bristol-bred,
(Low lie his mates now on watery bed)
    Takes to the seas and snows
As sheer down the ship goes.   60

Now her afterdraught gullies him too down;
Now he wrings for breath with the deathgush brown;
    Till a lifebelt and God's will
Lend him a lift from the sea-swill.   64

Now he shoots short up to the round air;
Now he gasps, now he gazes everywhere;
    But his eye no cliff, no coast or
Mark makes in the rivelling snowstorm.   68

Him, after an hour of wintry waves,
A schooner sights, with another, and saves,
    And he boards her in Oh! such joy
He has lost count what came next, poor boy, –   72

They say who saw one sea-corpse cold
He was all of lovely manly mould,
    Every inch a tar,
Of the best we boast our sailors are.   76

Look, foot to forelock, how all things suit! he
Is strung by duty, is strained to beauty,
    And brown-as-dawning-skinned
With brine and shine and whirling wind.   80

O his nimble finger, his gnarled grip!
Leagues, leagues of seamanship
   Slumber in these forsaken
Bones, this sinew, and will not waken.   84

He was but one like thousands more,
Day and night I deplore
   My people and born own nation,
Fast foundering own generation.   88

I might let bygones be – our curse
Of ruinous shrine no hand or, worse,
   Robbery's hand is busy to
Dress, hoar-hallowèd shrines unvisited;   92

Only the breathing temple and fleet
Life, this wildworth blown so sweet,
   These daredeaths, ay this crew, in
Unchrist, all rolled in ruin –   96

Deeply surely I need to deplore it,
Wondering why my master bore it,
   The riving off that race
So at home, time was, to his truth and grace   100

That a starlight-wender of ours would say
The marvellous Milk was Walsingham Way
   And one – but let be, let be:
More, more than was will yet be. –   104

O well wept, mother·have lost son;
Wept, wife; wept, sweetheart would be one:
   Though grief yield them no good
Yet shed what tears sad truelove should.   108

But to Christ lord of thunder
Crouch; lay knee by earth low under:
    'Holiest, loveliest, bravest,
Save my hero, O Hero savest.   112

And the prayer thou hearst me making
Have, at the awful overtaking,
    Heard; have heard and granted
Grace that day grace was wanted.'   116

Not that hell knows redeeming,
But for souls sunk in seeming
    Fresh, till doomfire burn all,
Prayer shall fetch pity eternal.   120

19

THE MAY MAGNIFICAT

MAY is Mary's month, and I
Muse at that and wonder why:
    Her feasts follow reason,
    Dated due to season –

Candlemas, Lady Day;
But the Lady Month, May,
    Why fasten that upon her,
    With a feasting in her honour?

Is it only its being brighter
Than the most are must delight her?
    Is it opportunest
    And flowers finds soonest?

Ask of her, the mighty mother:
Her reply puts this other
    Question: What is Spring? –
    Growth in every thing –

Flesh and fleece, fur and feather,
Grass and greenworld all together;
    Star-eyed strawberry-breasted
    Throstle above her nested

Cluster of bugle blue eggs thin
Forms and warms the life within;
    And bird and blossom swell
    In sod or sheath or shell.

All things rising, all things sizing
Mary sees, sympathising
    With that world of good,
    Nature's motherhood.

Their magnifying of each its kind
With delight calls to mind
    How she did in her stored
    Magnify the Lord.

Well but there was more than this:
Spring's universal bliss
    Much, had much to say
    To offering Mary May.

When drop-of-blood-and-foam-dapple
Bloom lights the orchard-apple
    And thicket and thorp are merry
    With silver-surfèd cherry.

And azuring-over greyball makes
Wood banks and brakes wash wet like lakes
    And magic cuckoocall
    Caps, clears, and clinches all –

This ecstasy all through mothering earth
Tells Mary her mirth till Christ's birth
    To remember and exultation
    In God who was her salvation.

20

BINSEY POPLARS

felled 1879

M Y aspens dear, whose airy cages quelled,
Quelled or quenched in leaves the leaping sun,
All felled, felled, are all felled;
    Of a fresh and following folded rank
        Not spared, not one
        That dandled a sandalled
    Shadow that swam or sank
On meadow and river and wind-wandering weed-
    winding bank.

O if we but knew what we do
    When we delve or hew –
    Hack and rack the growing green!
        Since country is so tender
    To touch, her being só slender,
    That, like this sleek and seeing ball
    But a prick will make no eye at all,
    Where we, even where we mean

To mend her we end her,
When we hew or delve:
After-comers cannot guess the beauty been.
Ten or twelve, only ten or twelve
Strokes of havoc únselve
The sweet especial scene,
Rural scene, a rural scene,
Sweet especial rural scene.

21

DUNS SCOTUS'S OXFORD

TOWERY city and branchy between towers;
Cuckoo-echoing, bell-swarmèd, lark-charmèd, rook-racked,
river-rounded;
The dapple-eared lily below thee; that country and town did
Once encounter in, here coped and poisèd powers;

Thou hast a base and brickish skirt there, sours
That neighbour-nature thy grey beauty is grounded
Best in; graceless growth, thou hast confounded
Rural rural keeping – folk, flocks, and flowers.

Yet ah! this air I gather and I release
He lived on; these weeds and waters, these walls are what
He haunted who of all men most sways my spirits to peace;

Of realty the rarest-veinèd unraveller; a not
Rivalled insight, be rival Italy or Greece;
Who fired France for Mary without spot.

22

HENRY PURCELL

The poet wishes well to the divine genius of Purcell and praises him that, whereas other musicians have given utterance to the moods of man's mind, he has, beyond that, uttered in notes the very make and species of man as created both in him and in all men generally.

HAVE fair fallen, O fair, fair have fallen, so dear
To me, so arch especial a spirit as heaves in Henry Purcell,
An age is now since passed, since parted; with the reversal
Of the outward sentence low lays him, listed to a heresy, here.

Not mood in him nor meaning, proud fire or sacred fear,
Or love, or pity, or all that sweet notes not his might nursle:
It is the forgèd feature finds me; it is the rehearsal
Of own, of abrúpt sélf there so thrusts on, so throngs the ear.

Let him oh! with his air of angels then lift me, lay me! only I'll
Have an eye to the sakes of him, quaint moonmarks, to his pelted
    plumage under
Wings: so some great stormfowl, whenever he has walked his
    while

The thunder purple seabeach, plumèd purple-of-thunder,
If a wuthering of his palmy snow pinions scatter a colossal smile
Off him, but meaning motion fans fresh our wits with wonder.

23

PEACE

WHEN will you ever, Peace, wild wooddove, shy wings shut,
Your round me roaming end, and under be my boughs?
When, when, Peace, will you, Peace? I'll not play hypocrite
To own my heart: I yield you do come sometimes; but
That piecemeal peace is poor peace. What pure peace allows
Alarms of wars, the daunting wars, the death of it?

O surely, reaving Peace, my Lord should leave in lieu
Some good! And so he does leave Patience exquisite,
That plumes to Peace thereafter. And when Peace here does house
He comes with work to do, he does not come to coo,
        He comes to brood and sit.

24

THE BUGLER'S FIRST COMMUNION

A BUGLER boy from barrack (it is over the hill
There) – boy bugler, born, he tells me, of Irish
      Mother to an English sire (he
Shares their best gifts surely, fall how things will),

This very very day came down to us after a boon he on
My late being there begged of me, overflowing
      Boon in my bestowing,
Came, I say, this day to it – to a First Communion.

Here he knelt then ín regimental red.
Forth Christ from cupboard fetched, how fain I of feet
      To his youngster take his treat!
Low latched in leaf light housel his too huge godhead.

There! and your sweetest sendings, ah divine,
By it, heavens, befall him! as a heart Christ's darling, dauntless;
      Tongue true, vaunt- and tauntless;
Breathing bloom of a chastity in mansex fine.

Frowning and forefending angel-warder
Squander the hell-rook ranks sally to molest him;
      March, kind comrade, abreast him;
Dress his days to a dexterous and starlight order.

How it dóes my heart good, visiting at that bleak hill,
When limber liquid youth, that to all I teach
      Yields tender as a pushed peach,
Hies headstrong to its wellbeing of a self-wise self-will!

Then though I should tread tufts of consolation
Dáys áfter, só I in a sort deserve to
      And do serve God to serve to
Just such slips of soldiery Christ's royal ration.

Nothing élse is like it, no, not all so strains
Us: fresh youth fretted in a bloomfall all portending
      That sweet's sweeter ending;
Realm both Christ is heir to and thére réigns.

O now well work that sealing sacred ointment!
O for now charms, arms, what bans off bad
      And locks love ever in a lad!
Let mé though see no more of him, and not disappointment

Those sweet hopes quell whose least me quickenings lift,
In scarlet or somewhere of some day seeing
That brow and bead of being,
An our day's God's own Galahad. Though this child's drift

Seems by a divíne doom chánnelled, nor do I cry
Disaster there; but may he not rankle and roam
In backwheels though bound home? –
That left to the Lord of the Eucharist, I here lie by;

Recorded only, I have put my lips on pleas
Would brandle adamantine heaven with ride and jar, did
Prayer go disregarded:
Forward-like, but however, and like favourable heaven heard
these.

25

MORNING, MIDDAY, AND EVENING SACRIFICE

THE dappled die-away
Cheek and the wimpled lip,
The gold-wisp, the airy-grey
Eye, all in fellowship –
This, all this beauty blooming,
This, all this freshness fuming,
Give God while worth consuming.

Both thought and thew now bolder
And told by Nature: Tower;
Head, heart, hand, heel, and shoulder
That beat and breathe in power –

This pride of prime's enjoyment
Take as for tool, not toy meant
And hold at Christ's employment.

The vault and scope and schooling
And mastery in the mind,
In silk-ash kept from cooling,
And ripest under rind –
What life half lifts the latch of,
What hell stalks towards the snatch of,
Your offering, with despatch, of!

26

ANDROMEDA

Now Time's Andromeda on this rock rude,
With not her either beauty's equal or
Her injury's, looks off by both horns of shore,
Her flower, her piece of being, doomed dragon food.
  Time past she has been attempted and pursued
By many blows and banes; but now hears roar
A wilder beast from West than all were, more
Rife in her wrongs, more lawless, and more lewd.

  Her Perseus linger and leave her tó her extremes? –
Pillowy air he treads a time and hangs
His thoughts on her, forsaken that she seems,
  All while her patience, morselled into pangs,
Mounts; then to alight disarming, no one dreams,
With Gorgon's gear and barebill / thongs and fangs.

27

THE CANDLE INDOORS

SOME candle clear burns somewhere I come by.
I muse at how its being puts blissful back
With yellowy moisture mild night's blear-all black,
Or to-fro tender trambeams truckle at the eye.
By that window what task what fingers ply,
I plod wondering, a-wanting, just for lack
Of answer the eagerer a-wanting Jessy or Jack
There / God to aggrándise, God to glorify. –

Come you indoors, come home; your fading fire
Mend first and vital candle in close heart's vault:
You there are master, do your own desire;
What hinders? Are you beam-blind, yet to a fault
In a neighbour deft-handed? are you that liar
And, cast by conscience out, spendsavour salt?

28

THE HANDSOME HEART:

at a Gracious Answer

'BUT tell me, child, your choice; what shall I buy
You?' – 'Father, what you buy me I like best.'
With the sweetest air that said, still plied and pressed,
He swung to his first poised purport of reply.

What the heart is! which, like carriers let fly –
Doff darkness, homing nature knows the rest –
To its own fine function, wild and self-instressed,
Falls light as ten years long taught how to and why.

Mannerly-hearted! more than handsome face –
Beauty's bearing or muse of mounting vein,
All, in this case, bathed in high hallowing grace ...

Of heaven what boon to buy you, boy, or gain
Not granted! – Only ... O on that path you pace
Run all your race, O brace sterner that strain!

29

AT THE WEDDING MARCH

GOD with honour hang your head,
Groom, and grace you, bride, your bed
With lissome scions, sweet scions,
Out of hallowed bodies bred.

Each be other's comfort kind:
Déep, déeper than divined,
Divine charity, dear charity,
Fast you ever, fast bind.

Then let the March tread our ears:
I to him turn with tears
Who to wedlock, his wonder wedlock,
Déals tríumph and immortal years.

30

FELIX RANDAL

FELIX RANDAL the farrier, O is he dead then? my duty all ended,
Who have watched his mould of man, big-boned and hardy-
    handsome
Pining, pining, till time when reason rambled in it and some
Fatal four disorders, fleshed there, all contended?

Sickness broke him. Impatient, he cursed at first, but mended
Being anointed and all; though a heavenlier heart began some
Months earlier, since I had our sweet reprieve and ransom
Tendered to him. Ah well, God rest him all road ever he
offended!

This seeing the sick endears them to us, us too it endears.
My tongue had taught thee comfort, touch had quenched thy
        tears,
Thy tears that touched my heart, child, Felix, poor Felix Randal;

How far from then forethought of, all thy more boisterous
        years,
When thou at the random grim forge, powerful amidst peers,
Didst fettle for the great grey drayhorse his bright and battering
        sandal!

31

BROTHERS

How lovely the elder brother's
Life all laced in the other's,
Lóve-laced! – what once I well
Witnessed; so fortune fell.
When Shrovetide, two years gone,   5
Our boys' plays brought on
Part was picked for John,
Young Jóhn; then fear, then joy
Ran revel in the elder boy.
Their night was come now; all   10
Our company thronged the hall;
Henry, by the wall,
Beckoned me beside him;
I came where called, and eyed him
By meanwhiles; making mý play   15

Turn most on tender byplay.
For, wrung all on love's rack,
My lad, and lost in Jack,
Smiled, blushed, and bit his lip;
Or drove, with a diver's dip,   20
Clutched hands down through clasped knees –
Truth's tokens tricks like these,
Old tell tales, with what stress
He hung on the imp's success.
Now the other was bráss-bóld: 25
Hé had no work to hold
His heart up at the strain;
Nay, roguish ran the vein.
Two tedious acts were past;
Jack's call and cue at last;   30
When Henry, heart-forsook,
Dropped eyes and dared not look.
Eh, how áll rúng!
Young dog, he did give tongue!
But Harry – in his hands he has flung   35
His tear-tricked cheeks of flame
For fond love and for shame.
    Ah Nature, framed in fault,
There's comfort then, there's salt;
Nature, bad, base, and blind,   40
Dearly thou canst be kind;
There dearly thén, deárly,
I'll cry thou canst be kind.

32

SPRING AND FALL

to a young child

MÁRGARÉT, áre you gríeving
Over Goldengrove unleaving?
Leáves líke the things of man, you
With your fresh thoughts care for, can you?
Ah! ás the heart grows older
It will come to such sights colder
By and by, nor spare a sigh
Though worlds of wanwood leafmeal lie;
And yet you will weep and know why.
Now no matter, child, the name:
Sórrow's spríngs áre the same.
Nor mouth had, no nor mind, expressed
What heart heard of, ghost guessed:
It ís the blight man was born for,
It is Margaret you mourn for.

33

INVERSNAID

THIS darksome burn, horseback brown,
His rollrock highroad roaring down,
In coop and in comb the fleece of his foam
Flutes and low to the lake falls home.

A windpuff-bonnet of fáwn-fróth
Turns and twindles over the broth
Of a pool so pitchblack, féll-frówning,
It rounds and rounds Despair to drowning.

Degged with dew, dappled with dew
Are the groins of the braes that the brook treads through,
Wiry heathpacks, flitches of fern,
And the beadbonny ash that sits over the burn.

What would the world be, once bereft
Of wet and of wilderness? Let them be left,
O let them be left, wildness and wet;
Long live the weeds and the wilderness yet.

34

As kingfishers catch fire, dragonflies draw flame;
As tumbled over rim in roundy wells
Stones ring; like each tucked string tells, each hung bell's
Bow swung finds tongue to fling out broad its name;
Each mortal thing does one thing and the same:
Deals out that being indoors each one dwells;
Selves — goes itself; *myself* it speaks and spells,
Crying *Whát I dó is me: for that I came.*

I say móre: the just man justices;
Keeps gráce: thát keeps all his goings graces;
Acts in God's eye what in God's eye he is —
Chríst — for Christ plays in ten thousand places,
Lovely in limbs, and lovely in eyes not his
To the Father through the features of men's faces.

35

RIBBLESDALE

EARTH, sweet Earth, sweet landscape, with leavès throng
And louchèd low grass, heaven that dost appeal
To, with no tongue to plead, no heart to feel;
That canst but only be, but dost that long —

Thou canst but bé, but that thou well dost; strong
Thy plea with him who dealt, nay does now deal,
Thy lovely dale down thus and thus bids reel
Thy river, and o'er gives all to rack or wrong.

And what is Earth's eye, tongue, or heart else, where
Else, but in dear and dogged man? – Ah, the heir
To his own selfbent so bound, so tied to his turn,
To thriftless reave both our rich round world bare
And none reck of world after, this bids wear
Earth brows of such care, care and dear concern.

36

THE LEADEN ECHO AND THE GOLDEN ECHO

(Maiden's song from St. Winefred's Well)

THE LEADEN ECHO

How to kéep – is there ány any, is there none such, nowhere
    known some, bow or brooch or braid or brace, láce, latch or
    catch or key to keep
Back beauty, keep it, beauty, beauty, beauty, . . . from vanishing
    away?
Ó is there no frowning of these wrinkles, rankèd wrinkles deep,
Dówn? no waving off of these most mournful messengers, still
    messengers, sad and stealing messengers of grey?
No there's none, there's none, O no there's none,
Nor can you long be, what you now are, called fair,
Do what you may do, what, do what you may,
And wisdom is early to despair:
Be beginning; since, no, nothing can be done
To keep at bay   10
Age and age's evils, hoar hair,

Ruck and wrinkle, drooping, dying, death's worst, winding sheets,
    tombs and worms and tumbling to decay;
So be beginning, be beginning to despair.
O there's none; no no no there's none:
Be beginning to despair, to despair,
Despair, despair, despair, despair.

THE GOLDEN ECHO

    Spare!
There ís one, yes I have one (Hush there!);
Only not within seeing of the sun,
Not within the singeing of the strong sun,
Tall sun's tingeing, or treacherous the tainting of the earth's air,
Somewhere elsewhere there is ah well where! one,
Oñe. Yes I cán tell such a key, I dó know such a place,
Where whatever's prized and passes of us, everything that's fresh
    and fast flying of us, seems to us sweet of us and swiftly away
    with, done away with, undone,
Úndone, done with, soon done with, and yet dearly and danger-
    ously sweet
Of us, the wimpled-water-dimpled, not-by-morning-matchèd
    face,   10
The flower of beauty, fleece of beauty, too too apt to, ah! to fleet,
Never fleets móre, fastened with the tenderest truth
To its own best being and its loveliness of youth: it is an ever-
    lastingness of, O it is an all youth!
Come then, your ways and airs and looks, locks, maiden gear,
    gallantry and gaiety and grace,
Winning ways, airs innocent, maiden manners, sweet looks, loose
    locks, long locks, lovelocks, gaygear, going gallant, girlgrace –
Resign them, sign them, seal them, send them, motion them with
    breath,
And with sighs soaring, soaring síghs deliver
Them; beauty-in-the-ghost, deliver it, early now, long before
    death

Give beauty back, beauty, beauty, beauty, back to God, beauty's
    self and beauty's giver.
See; not a hair is, not an eyelash, not the least lash lost; every hair
Is, hair of the head, numbered.   21
Nay, what we had lighthanded left in surly the mere mould
Will have waked and have waxed and have walked with the wind
    what while we slept,
This side, that side hurling a heavyheaded hundredfold
What while we, while we slumbered.
O then, weary then whý should we tread? O why are we so
    haggard at the heart, so care-coiled, care-killed, so fagged,
    so fashed, so cogged, so cumbered,
When the thing we freely fórfeit is kept with fonder a care,
Fonder a care kept than we could have kept it, kept
Far with fonder a care (and we, we should have lost it) finer,
    fonder
A care kept. – Where kept? Do but tell us where kept, where. –
Yonder. – What high as that! We follow, now we follow. –
    Yonder, yes yonder, yonder,
Yonder.   31

37

THE BLESSED VIRGIN COMPARED
TO THE AIR WE BREATHE

           WILD air, world-mothering air,
           Nestling me everywhere,
           That each eyelash or hair
           Girdles; goes home betwixt
           The fleeciest, frailest-flixed
           Snowflake; that's fairly mixed
           With, riddles, and is rife
           In every least thing's life;
           This needful, never spent,
           And nursing element;   10

My more than meat and drink,
My meal at every wink;
This air, which, by life's law,
My lung must draw and draw
Now but to breathe its praise,
Minds me in many ways
Of her who not only
Gave God's infinity
Dwindled to infancy
Welcome in womb and breast,   20
Birth, milk, and all the rest
But mothers each new grace
That does now reach our race –
Mary Immaculate,
Merely a woman, yet
Whose presence, power is
Great as no goddess's
Was deemèd, dreamèd; who
This one work has to do –
Let all God's glory through,   30
God's glory which would go
Through her and from her flow
Off, and no way but so.

I say that we are wound
With mercy round and round
As if with air: the same
Is Mary, more by name.
She, wild web, wondrous robe,
Mantles the guilty globe,
Since God has let dispense   40
Her prayers his providence:
Nay, more than almoner,
The sweet alms' self is her
And men are meant to share
Her life as life does air.

If I have understood,
She holds high motherhood
Towards all our ghostly good
And plays in grace her part
About man's beating heart,   50
Laying, like air's fine flood,
The deathdance in his blood;
Yet no part but what will
Be Christ our Saviour still.
Of her flesh he took flesh:
He does take fresh and fresh,
Though much the mystery how,
Not flesh but spirit now
And makes, O marvellous!
New Nazareths in us,   60
Where she shall yet conceive
Him, morning, noon, and eve;
New Bethlems, and he born
There, evening, noon, and morn –
Bethlem or Nazareth,
Men here may draw like breath
More Christ and baffle death;
Who, born so, comes to be
New self and nobler me
In each one and each one   70
More makes, when all is done,
Both God's and Mary's Son.
    Again, look overhead
How air is azurèd;
O how! nay do but stand
Where you can lift your hand
Skywards: rich, rich it laps
Round the four fingergaps.
Yet such a sapphire-shot,
Charged, steepèd sky will not   80

Stain light. Yea, mark you this:
It does no prejudice.
The glass-blue days are those
When every colour glows,
Each shape and shadow shows.
Blue be it: this blue heaven
The seven or seven times seven
Hued sunbeam will transmit
Perfect, not alter it.
Or if there does some soft, 90
On things aloof, aloft,
Bloom breathe, that one breath more
Earth is the fairer for.
Whereas did air not make
This bath of blue and slake
His fire, the sun would shake,
A blear and blinding ball
With blackness bound, and all
The thick stars round him roll
Flashing like flecks or coal, 100
Quartz-fret, or sparks of salt,
In grimy vasty vault.
  So God was god of old:
A mother came to mould
Those limbs like ours which are
What must make our daystar
Much dearer to mankind;
Whose glory bare would blind
Or less would win man's mind.
Through her we may see him 110
Made sweeter, not made dim,
And her hand leaves his light
Sifted to suit our sight.
  Be thou then, O thou dear
Mother, my atmosphere;

My happier world, wherein
To wend and meet no sin;
Above me, round me lie
Fronting my forward eye
With sweet and scarless sky;   120
Stir in my ears, speak there
Of God's love, O live air,
Of patience, penance, prayer:
World-mothering air, air wild,
Wound with thee, in thee isled,
Fold home, fast fold thy child.

38

TO WHAT SERVES MORTAL BEAUTY?

To what serves mortal beauty [|] – dangerous; does set danc-
ing blood – the O-seal-that-so [|] feature, flung prouder form
Than Purcell tune lets tread to? [|] See: it does this: keeps warm
Men's wits to the things that are; [|] what good means – where a
    glance
Master more may than gaze, [|] gaze out of countenance.
Those lovely lads once, wet-fresh [|] windfalls of war's storm,
How then should Gregory, a father, [|] have gleanèd else from
    swarm-
ed Rome? But God to a nation [|] dealt that day's dear chance.
  To man, that needs would worship [|] block or barren stone,
Our law says: Love what are [|] love's worthiest, were all known;
World's loveliest – men's selves. Self [|] flashes off frame and face.
What do then? how meet beauty? [|] Merely meet it; own,
Home at heart, heaven's sweet gift; [|] then leave, let that alone.
Yea, wish that though, wish all, [|] God's better beauty, grace.

39

SPELT FROM SIBYL'S LEAVES

EARNEST, earthless, equal, attuneable, ⏐ vaulty, voluminous, . . .
    stupendous
Evening strains to be time's vást, ⏐ womb-of-all, home-of-all,
    hearse-of-all night.
Her fond yellow hornlight wound to the west, ⏐ her wild hollow
    hoarlight hung to the height
Waste; her earliest stars, earl-stars, ⏐ stárs principal, overbend us,
Fíre-féaturing heaven. For earth ⏐ her being has unbound, her
    dapple is at an end, as-
tray or aswarm, all throughther, in throngs; ⏐ self ín self steepèd
    and páshed – qúite
Disremembering, dísmémbering ⏐ áll now. Heart, you round me
    right
With: Óur évening is over us; óur night ⏐ whélms, whélms, ánd
    will end us.
Only the beak-leaved boughs dragonish ⏐ damask the tool-smooth
    bleak light; black,
Ever so black on it. Óur tale, O óur oracle! ⏐ Lét life, wáned,
    ah lét life wind
Off hér once skéined stained véined varíety ⏐ upon, áll on twó
    spools; párt, pen, páck
Now her áll in twó flocks, twó folds – black, white; ⏐ right,
    wrong; reckon but, reck but, mind
But thése two; wáre of a wórld where bút these ⏐ twó tell, each
    off the óther; of a rack
Where, selfwrung, selfstrung, sheathe- and shelterless, ⏐ thóughts
    agaínst thoughts ín groans grínd.

40

(THE SOLDIER)

YES. Whý do we áll, seeing of a soldier, bless him? bless
Our redcoats, our tars? Both these being, the greater part,
But frail clay, nay but foul clay. Here it is: the heart,
Since, proud, it calls the calling manly, gives a guess
That, hopes that, makesbelieve, the men must be no less;
It fancies, feigns, deems, dears the artist after his art;
And fain will find as sterling all as all is smart,
And scarlet wear the spirit of wár thére express.

Mark Christ our King. He knows war, served this soldiering
    through;
He of all can reeve a rope best. There he bides in bliss
Now, and séeing somewhére some mán do all that man can do,
For love he leans forth, needs his neck must fall on, kiss,
And cry 'O Christ-done deed! So God-made-flesh does too:
Were I come o'er again' cries Christ 'it should be this'.

41

(CARRION COMFORT)

NOT, I'll not, carrion comfort, Despair, not feast on thee;
Not untwist – slack they may be – these last strands of man
In me ór, most weary, cry *I can no more*. I can;
Can something, hope, wish day come, not choose not to be.
But ah, but O thou terrible, why wouldst thou rude on me
Thy wring-world right foot rock? lay a lionlimb against me?
    scan
With darksome devouring eyes my bruisèd bones? and fan,
O in turns of tempest, me heaped there; me frantic to avoid thee
    and flee?

Why? That my chaff might fly; my grain lie, sheer and clear.
Nay in all that toil, that coil, since (seems) I kissed the rod,
Hand rather, my heart lo! lapped strength, stole joy, would laugh,
    chéer.
Cheer whom though? the hero whose heaven-handling flung me,
    fóot tród
Me? or me that fought him? O which one? is it each one? That
    night, that year
Of now done darkness I wretch lay wrestling with (my God!)
    my God.

42

relentlessly
Despair

No worst, there is none. Pitched past pitch of grief,
More pangs will, schooled at forepangs, wilder wring.
Comforter, where, where is your comforting?
Mary, mother of us, where is your relief?
My cries heave, herds-long; huddle in a main, a chief
Woe, wórld-sorrow; on an áge-old anvil wince and sing –
Then lull, then leave off. Fury had shrieked 'No ling-
ering! Let me be fell: force I must be brief'.

O the mind, mind has mountains; cliffs of fall
Frightful, sheer, no-man-fathomed. Hold them cheap
May who ne'er hung there. Nor does long our small
Durance deal with that steep or deep. Here! creep,
Wretch, under a comfort serves in a whirlwind: all
Life death does end and each day dies with sleep.

43

To seem the stranger lies my lot, my life
Among strangers. Father and mother dear,
Brothers and sisters are in Christ not near
And he my peace/my parting, sword and strife.

England, whose honour O all my heart woos, wife
To my creating thought, would neither hear
Me, were I pleading, plead nor do I: I wear-
y of idle a being but by where wars are rife.

I am in Ireland now; now I am at a thírd
Remove. Not but in all removes I can
Kind love both give and get. Only what word
Wisest my heart breeds dark heaven's baffling ban
Bars or hell's spell thwarts. This to hoard unheard,
Heard unheeded, leaves me a lonely began.

44

I WAKE and feel the fell of dark, not day.
What hours, O what black hours we have spent
This night! what sights you, heart, saw; ways you went!
And more must, in yet longer light's delay.
    With witness I speak this. But where I say
Hours I mean years, mean life. And my lament
Is cries countless, cries like dead letters sent
To dearest him that lives alas! away.

I am gall, I am heartburn. God's most deep decree
Bitter would have me taste: my taste was me;
Bones built in me, flesh filled, blood brimmed the curse.
    Selfyeast of spirit a dull dough sours. I see
The lost are like this, and their scourge to be
As I am mine, their sweating selves; but worse.

45

PATIENCE, hard thing! the hard thing but to pray,
But bid for, Patience is! Patience who asks
Wants war, wants wounds; weary his times, his tasks;
To do without, take tosses, and obey.

Rare patience roots in these, and, these away,
Nowhere. Natural heart's ivy, Patience masks
Our ruins of wrecked past purpose. There she basks
Purple eyes and seas of liquid leaves all day.

We hear our hearts grate on themselves: it kills
To bruise them dearer. Yet the rebellious wills
Of us we do bid God bend to him even so.
    And where is he who more and more distils
Delicious kindness? – He is patient. Patience fills
His crisp combs, and that comes those ways we know.

Reply to 44   46   *HE HAS BEEN TOO
                                    DRAMATIC IN*

My own heart let me more have pity on; let   *PAST*
Me live to my sad self hereafter kind,
Charitable; not live this tormented mind   *+ there is no*
With this tormented mind tormenting yet.   *point in*
    I cast for comfort I can no more get   *tormenting*
By groping round my comfortless, than blind   *himself*
Eyes in their dark can day or thirst can find
Thirst's all-in-all in all a world of wet.

Soul, self; come, poor Jackself, I do advise
You, jaded, let be; call off thoughts awhile
Elsewhere; leave comfort root-room; let joy size
At God knows when to God knows what; whose smile
's not wrung, see you; unforeseen times rather – as skies
Betweenpie mountains – lights a lovely mile.

*Needs to calm a bit then he will
down   find comfort +
              solitude like
              catching a glimpse of
              the sky between the
              mountains*

47

TOM'S GARLAND:

upon the Unemployed

TOM – garlanded with squat and surly steel
Tom; then Tom's fallowbootfellow piles pick
By him and rips out rockfire homeforth – sturdy Dick;
Tom Heart-at-ease, Tom Navvy: he is all for his meal
Sure, 's bed now. Low be it: lustily he his low lot (feel
That ne'er need hunger, Tom; Tom seldom sick,
Seldomer heartsore; that treads through, prickproof, thick
Thousands of thorns, thoughts) swings though. Commonweal
Little Í reck ho! lacklevel in, if all had bread:
What! Country is honour enough in all us – lordly head,
With heaven's lights high hung round, or, mother-ground
That mammocks, mighty foot. But nó way sped,
Nor mind nor mainstrength; gold go garlanded
With, perilous, O nó; nor yet plod safe shod sound;
        Undenizened, beyond bound
Of earth's glory, earth's ease, all; no one, nowhere,
In wide the world's weal; rare gold, bold steel, bare
        In both; care, but share care –
This, by Despair, bred Hangdog dull; by Rage,
Manwolf, worse; and their packs infest the age.

48

HARRY PLOUGHMAN

HARD as hurdle arms, with a broth of goldish flue
Breathed round; the rack of ribs; the scooped flank; lank
Rope-over thigh; knee-nave; and barrelled shank –
        Head and foot, shoulder and shank –

By a grey eye's heed steered well, one crew, fall to;
Stand at stress. Each limb's barrowy brawn, his thew
That onewhere curded, onewhere sucked or sank –
               Soared or sank –,
Though as a beechbole firm, finds his, as at a roll-call, rank
And features, in flesh, what deed he each must do –
          His sinew-service where do.

He leans to it, Harry bends, look. Back, elbow, and liquid waist
In him, all quail to the wallowing o' the plough: 's cheek crim-
   sons; curls
Wag or crossbridle, in a wind lifted, windlaced –
         See his wind- lilylocks -laced;
Churlsgrace, too, child of Amansstrength, how it hangs or hurls
Them – broad in bluff hide his frowning feet lashed! raced
With, along them, cragiron under and cold furls –
        With-a-fountain's shining-shot furls.

49

THAT NATURE IS A HERACLITEAN FIRE
AND OF THE
COMFORT OF THE RESURRECTION

CLOUD-PUFFBALL, torn tufts, tossed pillows ▏flaunt forth, then
   chevy on an air-
built thoroughfare: heaven-roysterers, in gay-gangs ▏they throng;
   they glitter in marches.
Down roughcast, down dazzling whitewash, ▏wherever an elm
   arches,
Shivelights and shadowtackle in long ▏lashes lace, lance, and
   pair.

Delightfully the bright wind boisterous ˈ ropes, wrestles, beats
    earth bare
Of yestertempest's creases; ˈ in pool and rut peel parches
Squandering ooze to squeezed ˈ dough, crust, dust; stanches,
    starches
Squadroned masks and manmarks ˈ treadmire toil there
Footfretted in it. Million-fuelèd, ˈ nature's bonfire burns on.
But quench her bonniest, dearest ˈ to her, her clearest-selvèd
    spark
Man, how fast his firedint, ˈ his mark on mind, is gone!
Both are in an unfathomable, all is in an enormous dark
Drowned. O pity and indig ˈ nation! Manshape, that shone
Sheer off, disseveral, a star, ˈ death blots black out; nor mark
        Is any of him at all so stark
But vastness blurs and time ˈ beats level. Enough! the Resurrection,
A heart's-clarion! Away grief's gasping, ˈ joyless days, dejection.
        Across my foundering deck shone
A beacon, an eternal beam. ˈ Flesh fade, and mortal trash
Fall to the residuary worm; ˈ world's wildfire, leave but ash:
        In a flash, at a trumpet crash,
I am all at once what Christ is, ˈ since he was what I am, and
This Jack, joke, poor potsherd, ˈ patch, matchwood, immortal
    diamond,
        Is immortal diamond.

50

In honour of
ST. ALPHONSUS RODRIGUEZ
Laybrother of the Society of Jesus

HONOUR is flashed off exploit, so we say;
And those strokes once that gashed flesh or galled shield
Should tongue that time now, trumpet now that field,
And, on the fighter, forge his glorious day.

On Christ they do and on the martyr may;
But be the war within, the brand we wield
Unseen, the heróic breast not outward-steeled,
Earth hears no hurtle then from fiercest fray.

Yet God (that hews mountain and continent,
Earth, all, out; who, with trickling increment,
Veins violets and tall trees makes more and more)
Could crowd career with conquest while there went
Those years and years by of world without event
That in Majorca Alfonso watched the door.

51

Justus quidem tu es, Domine, si disputem tecum; verumtamen
justa loquar ad te: Quare via impiorum prosperatur? &c.

THOU art indeed just, Lord, if I contend
With thee; but, sir, so what I plead is just.
Why do sinners' ways prosper? and why must
Disappointment all I endeavour end?
    Wert thou my enemy, O thou my friend,
How wouldst thou worse, I wonder, than thou dost
Defeat, thwart me? Oh, the sots and thralls of lust
Do in spare hours more thrive than I that spend,
Sir, life upon thy cause. See, banks and brakes
Now, leavèd how thick! lacèd they are again
With fretty chervil, look, and fresh wind shakes
Them; birds build – but not I build; no, but strain,
Time's eunuch, and not breed one work that wakes.
Mine, O thou lord of life, send my roots rain.

52

THE shepherd's brow, fronting forked lightning, owns
The horror and the havoc and the glory
Of it. Angels fall, they are towers, from heaven – a story
Of just, majestical, and giant groans.
But man – we, scaffold of score brittle bones;
Who breathe, from groundlong babyhood to hoary
Age gasp; whose breath is our *memento mori* –
What bass is *our* viol for tragic tones?
He! Hand to mouth he lives, and voids with shame;
And, blazoned in however bold the name,
Man Jack the man is, just; his mate a hussy.
And I that die these deaths, that feed this flame,
That . . . in smooth spoons spy life's masque mirrored: tame
My tempests there, my fire and fever fussy.

53

TO R. B.

THE fine delight that fathers thought; the strong
Spur, live and lancing like the blowpipe flame,
Breathes once and, quenchèd faster than it came,
Leaves yet the mind a mother of immortal song.
Nine months she then, nay years, nine years she long
Within her wears, bears, cares and combs the same:
The widow of an insight lost she lives, with aim
Now known and hand at work now never wrong.

Sweet fire the sire of muse, my soul needs this;
I want the one rapture of an inspiration.
O then if in my lagging lines you miss
The roll, the rise, the carol, the creation,
My winter world, that scarcely breathes that bliss
Now, yields you, with some sighs, our explanation.

SOME UNFINISHED POEMS
AND FRAGMENTS
(1876–1889)

*

54

MOONRISE

I AWOKE in the Midsummer not-to-call night, ' in the white
    and the walk of the morning:
The moon, dwindled and thinned to the fringe ' of a fingernail
    held to the candle,
Or paring of paradisaïcal fruit, ' lovely in waning but lustreless,
Stepped from the stool, drew back from the barrow, ' of dark
    Maenefa the mountain;
A cusp still clasped him, a fluke yet fanged him, ' entangled him,
    not quit utterly.
This was the prized, the desirable sight, ' unsought, presented so
    easily,
Parted me leaf and leaf, divided me, ' eyelid and eyelid of slumber.

55

THE WOODLARK

Teevo cheevo cheevio chee:
O where, what can thát be?
Weedio-weedio: there again!
So tiny a trickle of sóng-strain;
And all round not to be found
For brier, bough, furrow, or gréen ground
Before or behind or far or at hand
Either left either right
Anywhere in the súnlight.

Well, after all! Ah but hark –
'I am the little wóodlark.
The skylark is my cousin and he
Is known to men more than me.
Round a ring, around a ring
And while I sail (must listen) I sing.

To-day the sky is two and two
With white strokes and strains of the blue.
The blue wheat-acre is underneath
And the braided ear breaks out of the sheath,
The ear in milk, lush the sash,
And crush-silk poppies aflash,
The blood-gush blade-gash
Flame-rash rudred
Bud shelling or broad-shed
Tatter-tassel-tangled and dingle-a-danglèd
Dandy-hung dainty head.

And down . . . the furrow dry
Sunspurge and oxeye
And lace-leaved lovely
Foam-tuft fumitory.

I ám so véry, O só very glád
That I dó thínk there is not to be had
[Anywhere any more joy to be in.
Cheevio:] when the cry within
Says Go on then I go on
Till the longing is less and the good gone,
But down drop, if it says Stop,
To the all-a-leaf of the tréetop.
And after that off the bough
[Hover-float to the hedge brow.]

Through the velvety wind V-winged
[Where shake shadow is sun's-eye-ringed]
To the nest's nook I balance and buoy
With a sweet joy of a sweet joy,
Sweet, of a sweet, of a sweet joy
Of a sweet – a sweet – sweet – joy.'

56

CHEERY BEGGAR

BEYOND Mágdalen and by the Bridge, on a place called there
  the Plain,
  In Summer, in a burst of summertime
  Following falls and falls of rain,
When the air was sweet-and-sour of the flown fineflour of
Those goldnails and their gaylinks that hang along a lime;

. . . .

  The motion of that man's heart is fine
  Whom want could not make píne, píne
That struggling should not sear him, a gift should cheer him
Like that poor pocket of pence, poor pence of mine.

. . . .

57

  THE furl of fresh-leaved dogrose down
  His cheeks the forth-and-flaunting sun
  Had swarthed about with lion-brown
    Before the Spring was done.

  His locks like all a ravel-rope's-end,
    With hempen strands in spray –
  Fallow, foam-fallow, hanks – fall'n off their ranks,
    Swung down at a disarray.

Or like a juicy and jostling shock
    Of bluebells sheaved in May
Or wind-long fleeces on the flock
    A day off shearing day.

Then over his turnèd temples – here –
    Was a rose, or, failing that,
Rough-Robin or five-lipped campion clear
    For a beauty-bow to his hat,
And the sunlight sidled, like dewdrops, like dandled
        diamonds
Through the sieve of the straw of the plait.

    .   .   .   .

58

ST. WINEFRED'S WELL

ACT I. SC. 1

Enter Teryth from riding, Winefred following.

T. WHAT is it, Gwen, my girl? ❘ why do you hover and haunt
    me?
W. You came by Caerwys, sir? ❘
T.   I came by Caerwys.
W.   There
    Some messenger there might have ❘ met you from my uncle.
T. Your uncle met the messenger – ❘ met me; and this the
    message:
    Lord Beuno comes to-night. ❘
W.   To-night, sir!
T.   Soon, now: therefore
    Have all things ready in his room. ❘
W.   There needs but little doing.
T. Let what there needs be done. ❘ Stay! with him one com-
    panion,

His deacon, Dirvan. Warm | twice over must the welcome be,

But both will share one cell. – | This was good news, Gwenvrewi.

W. Ah yes!

T.   Why, get thee gone then; | tell thy mother I want her.

Exit Winefred.

10

No man has such a daughter. | The fathers of the world

Call no such maiden 'mine'. | The deeper grows her dearness

And more and more times laces | round and round my heart,

The more some monstrous hand | gropes with clammy fingers there,

Tampering with those sweet bines, | draws them out, strains them, strains them;

Meantime some tongue cries 'What, Teryth! | what, thou poor fond father!

How when this bloom, this honeysuckle, | that rides the air so rich about thee,

Is all, all sheared away, | thus!' Then I sweat for fear.

Or else a funeral, | and yet 'tis not a funeral,

Some pageant which takes tears | and I must foot with feeling that   20

Alive or dead my girl | is carried in it, endlessly

Goes marching thro' my mind. | What sense is this? It has none.

This is too much the father; | nay the mother. Fanciful!

I here forbid my thoughts | to fool themselves with fears.

Enter Gwenlo.

. . . .

Act II. – *Scene, a wood ending in a steep bank over a dry dene.
Winefred having been murdered within, re-enter Caradoc with a
bloody sword.*

C.   My héart, where have we been? | What have we séen, my
         mind?
     What stroke has Carádoc's right arm dealt? | what done?
         Head of a rebel
     Struck óff it has; written | upon lovely limbs,
     In bloody lessons, lessons | of earnest, of revenge;
     Monuments of my earnest, | records of my revenge,
     On one that went against me | whéreas I had warned her –
     Warned her! well she knew. | I warned her of this work.
     What work? what harm's done? There is | no harm done,
         none yet;
     Perhaps we struck no blow, | Gwenvrewi lives perhaps;
     To makebelieve my mood was – | mock. O I might think so
     But here, here is a workman | from his day's task sweats.   11
     Wiped I am sure this was; | it seems not well; for still,
     Still the scarlet swings | and dances on the blade.
     So be it. Thou steel, thou butcher,
     I cán scour thee, fresh burnish thee, | sheathe thee in thy dark
         lair; these drops
     Never, never, never | in their blue banks again.
     The woeful, Cradock, O | the woeful word! Then what,
     What have we seen? Her head, | sheared from her shoulders,
         fall,
     And lapped in shining hair, | roll to the bank's edge; then
     Down the beetling banks, | like water in waterfalls,   20
     It stooped and flashed and fell | and ran like water away.
     Her eyes, oh and her eyes!
     In all her beauty, and sunlight | to it is a pit, den, darkness,
     Foam-falling is not fresh to it, | rainbow by it not beaming,
     In all her body, I say, | no place was like her eyes,
     No piece matched those eyes | kept most part much cast down
     But, being lifted, immortal, | of immortal brightness.

Several times I saw them, ˡ thrice or four times turning;
Round and round they came ˡ and flashed towards heaven:
    O there,
There they did appeal. ˡ Therefore airy vengeances   30
Are afoot; heaven-vault fast purpling ˡ portends, and what
    first lightning
Any instant falls means me. ˡ And I do not repent;
I do not and I will not ˡ repent, not repent.
The blame bear who aroused me. ˡ What I have done violent
I have líke a líon dóne, ˡ líonlíke dóne,
Honouring an uncontrolled ˡ royal wrathful nature,
Mantling passion in a grandeur, ˡ crimson grandeur.
Now be my pride then perfect, ˡ áll one piece. Henceforth
In a wide world of defiance ˡ Caradoc lives alone,   39
Loyal to his own soul, laying ˡ his ówn law down, no law nor
Lord now curb him for ever. ˡ O daring! O deep insight!
What is virtue? Valour; ˡ only the heart valiant.
And right? Only resolution; ˡ will, his will unwavering
Who, like me, knowing his nature ˡ to the heart home,
    nature's business,
Despatches with no flinching. ˡ But will flesh, O can flésh
Second this fiery strain? ˡ Not always; O no no!
We cannot live this life out; ˡ sometimes we must weary
And in this darksome world ˡ what comfort can I find?
Down this darksome world ˡ cómfort whére can I find
When 'ts light I quenched; its rose, ˡ time's one rich rose, my
    hand,   50
By her bloom, fast by ˡ her fresh, her fleecèd bloom,
Hideous dáshed dówn, leaving ˡ earth a winter withering
With no now, no Gwenvrewi. ˡ I must miss her most
That might have spared her were it ˡ but for passion-sake.
    Yes,
To hunger and not have, yét ˡ hope ón for, to storm and
    strive and
Be at every assault fresh foiled, ˡ worse flung, deeper dis-
    appointed,

The turmoil and the torment, ' it has, I swear, a sweetness,
Keeps a kind of joy in it, ' a zest, an edge, an ecstasy,
Next after sweet success. ' I am not left even this;   59
I all my being have hacked ' in half with her neck: one part,
Reason, selfdisposal, ' choice of better or worse way,
Is corpse now, cannot change; ' my other self, this soul,
Life's quick, this kínd, this kéen self-feeling,
With dreadful distillation ' of thoughts sour as blood,
Must all day long taste murder. ' What do nów then? Do?
   Nay,
Déed-bound I am; one deed tréads all dówn here ' cramps all
   doing. What do? Not yield,
Not hope, not pray; despair; ' ay, that: brazen despair out,
Brave all, and take what comes – ' as here this rabble is come,
Whose bloods I reck no more of, ' no more rank with hers
Than sewers with sacred oils. ' Mankind, that mob, comes.
Come!   70

Enter a crowd, among them Teryth, Gwenlo, Beuno.

 .   .   .   .

*After Winefred's raising from the dead and the breaking
                out of the fountain.*

BEUNO. O now while skies are blue, ' now while seas are salt,
   While rushy rains shall fall ' or brooks shall fleet from
      fountains,
   While sick men shall cast sighs, ' of sweet health all des-
      pairing,
   While blind men's eyes shall thírst after ' daylight, draughts
      of daylight,
   Or deaf ears shall desire that ' lípmusic that's lóst upon them,
   While cripples are, while lepers, ' dancers in dismal limb-
      dance,
   Fallers in dreadful frothpits, ' waterfearers wild,
   Stone, palsy, cancer, cough, ' lung-wasting, womb-not-
      bearing,

Rupture, running sores, ^ı what more? in brief, in burden,
As long as men are mortal ^ı and God merciful,   10
So long to this sweet spot, ^ı this leafy lean-over,
This Dry Dene, nów no longer dry ^ı nor dumb, but moist
  and musical
With the uproll and the downcarol ^ı of day and night
  delivering
Water, which keeps thy name, ^ı (for not in róck written,
But in pale water, fráil water, ^ı wild rash and reeling water,
That will not wear a print, ^ı that will not stain a pen,
Thy venerable record, ^ı virgin, is recorded).
Here to this holy well ^ı shall pilgrimages be,
And not from purple Wales only ^ı nor from elmy England,
But from beyond seas, Erin, ^ı France and Flanders, every-
  where,
Pilgrims, still pilgrims, móre ^ı pílgrims, still more poor
  pilgrims.

. . . .

What sights shall be when some ^ı that swung, wretches, on
  crutches
Their crutches shall cast from them, ^ı on heels of air de-
  parting,
Or they go rich as roseleaves ^ı hence that loathsome cáme
  hither!
Not now to náme even
Those dearer, more divine ^ı boons whose haven the heart is.

. . . .

As sure as what is most sure, ^ı sure as that spring primroses
Shall new-dapple next year, ^ı sure as to-morrow morning,
Amongst come-back-again things, ^ı thíngs with a revival,
  things with a recovery,
Thy name . . .   30

. . . .

59

(MARGARET CLITHEROE)

GOD'S counsel cólumnar-severe
But chaptered in the chief of bliss
Had always doomed her down to this –
Pressed to death. He plants the year;
The weighty weeks without hands grow,
Heaved drum on drum; but hands also
Must deal with Margaret Clitheroe.

The very victim would prepare.
Like water soon to be sucked in
Will crisp itself or settle and spin
So she: one sees that here and there
She mends the way she means to go.
The last thing Margaret's fingers sew
Is a shroud for Margaret Clitheroe.

The Christ-ed beauty of her mind
Her mould of features mated well.
She was admired. The spirit of hell
Being to her virtue clinching-blind
No wonder therefore was not slow
To the bargain of its hate to throw
The body of Margaret Clitheroe.

Great Thecla, the plumed passionflower,
Next Mary mother of maid and nun

.   .   .   .

And every saint of bloody hour
And breath immortal thronged that show;
Heaven turned its starlight eyes below
To the murder of Margaret Clitheroe.

She was a woman, upright, outright;
Her will was bent at God. For that
Word went she should be crushed out flat

.   .   .   .

Fawning fawning crocodiles
Days and days came round about
With tears to put her candle out;
They wound their winch of wicked smiles
To take her; while their tongues would go
God lighten your dark heart – but no,
Christ lived in Margaret Clitheroe.

She held her hands to, like in prayer;
They had them out and laid them wide
(Just like Jesus crucified);
They brought their hundredweights to bear.
Jews killed Jesus long ago
God's son; these (they did not know)
God's daughter Margaret Clitheroe.

When she felt the kill-weights crush
She told His name times-over three;
I suffer this she said *for Thee.*
After that in perfect hush
For a quarter of an hour or so
She was with the choke of woe. –
It is over, Margaret Clitheroe.

She caught the crying of those Three,
The Immortals of the eternal ring,
The Utterer, Utterèd, Uttering,
And witness in her place would she.
She not considered whether or no
She pleased the Queen and Council. So
To the death with Margaret Clitheroe!

Within her womb the child was quick.
Small matter of that then! Let him smother
And wreck in ruins of his mother.

. . . .

60

REPEAT that, repeat,
Cuckoo, bird, and open ear wells, heart-springs, delightfully
     sweet,
With a ballad, with a ballad, a rebound
Off trundled timber and scoops of the hillside ground, hollow
     hollow hollow ground:
The whole landscape flushes on a sudden at a sound.

61

ON A PIECE OF MUSIC

How all's to one thing wrought!
The members, how they sit!
O what a tune the thought
Must be that fancied it.

Nor angel insight can
Learn how the heart is hence:
Since all the make of man
Is law's indifference.

[Who shaped these walls has shewn
The music of his mind,
Made known, though thick through stone,
What beauty beat behind.]

Not free in this because
His powers seemed free to play:
He swept what scope he was
To sweep and must obey.

Though down his being's bent
Like air he changed in choice,
That was an instrument
Which overvaulted voice.

What makes the man and what
The man within that makes:
Ask whom he serves or not
Serves and what side he takes.

For good grows wild and wide,
Has shades, is nowhere none;
But right must seek a side
And choose for chieftain one.

Therefore this masterhood,
This piece of perfect song,
This fault-not-found-with good
Is neither right nor wrong,

No more than red and blue,
No more than Re and Mi,
Or sweet the golden glue
That's built for by the bee.

[Who built these walls made known
The music of his mind,
Yet here he has but shewn
His ruder-rounded rind,
His brightest blooms lie there unblown,
His sweetest nectar hides behind.]

62

(ASH-BOUGHS)
a.

Not of áll my eyes see, wandering on the world,
Is anything a milk to the mind so, so sighs deep
Poetry tó it, as a tree whose boughs break in the sky.
Say it is ásh-boughs: whether on a December day and furled
Fast ór they in clammyish lashtender combs creep
Apart wide and new-nestle at heaven most high.
They touch heaven, tabour on it; how their talons sweep
The smouldering enormous winter welkin! May
Mells blue and snow white through them, a fringe and fray
Of greenery: it is old earth's groping towards the steep
　　　Heaven whom she childs us by.

(Variant from line 7.)　　　*b.*

　They touch, they tabour on it, hover on it; here, there hurled,
　　　With talons sweep
　The smouldering enormous winter welkin. Eye,
　　　But more cheer is when May
　Mells blue with snowwhite through their fringe and fray
　Of greenery and old earth gropes for, grasps at steep
　　　Heaven with it whom she childs things by.

63

　　Thee, God, I come from, to thee go,
　　All day long I like fountain flow
　　From thy hand out, swayed about
　　Mote-like in thy mighty glow.

　　What I know of thee I bless,
　　As acknowledging thy stress
　　On my being and as seeing
　　Something of thy holiness.

Once I turned from thee and hid,
Bound on what thou hadst forbid;
Sow the wind I would; I sinned:
I repent of what I did.

Bad I am, but yet thy child.
Father, be thou reconciled,
Spare thou me, since I see
With thy might that thou art mild.

I have life before me still
And thy purpose to fulfil;
Yea a debt to pay thee yet:
Help me, sir, and so I will.

But thou bidst, and just thou art,
Me shew mercy from my heart
Towards my brother, every other
Man my mate and counterpart.

． ． ． ． ． ． ．

64

ON THE PORTRAIT OF TWO BEAUTIFUL
YOUNG PEOPLE

A Brother and Sister

O I admire and sorrow! The heart's eye grieves
Discovering you, dark tramplers, tyrant years.
A juice rides rich through bluebells, in vine leaves,
And beauty's dearest veriest vein is tears.

Happy the father, mother of these! Too fast:
Not that, but thus far, all with frailty, blest
In one fair fall; but, for time's aftercast,
Creatures all heft, hope, hazard, interest.

And are they thus? The fine, the fingering beams
Their young delightful hour do feature down
That fleeted else like day-dissolvèd dreams
Or ringlet-race on burling Barrow brown.

She leans on him with such contentment fond
As well the sister sits, would well the wife;
His looks, the soul's own letters, see beyond,
Gaze on, and fall directly forth on life.

But ah, bright forelock, cluster that you are
Of favoured make and mind and health and youth,
Where lies your landmark, seamark, or soul's star?
There's none but truth can stead you. Christ is truth.

There's none but good can bé good, both for you
And what sways with you, maybe this sweet maid;
None good but God – a warning wavèd to
One once that was found wanting when Good weighed.

Man lives that list, that leaning in the will
No wisdom can forecast by gauge or guess,
The selfless self of self, most strange, most still,
Fast furled and all foredrawn to No or Yes.

Your feast of; that most in you earnest eye
May but call on your banes to more carouse.
Worst will the best. What worm was here, we cry,
To have havoc-pocked so, see, the hung-heavenward
    boughs?

Enough: corruption was the world's first woe.
What need I strain my heart beyond my ken?
O but I bear my burning witness though
Against the wild and wanton work of men.

.   .   .   .

EPITHALAMION

HARK, hearer, hear what I do; lend a thought now, make
    believe
We are leafwhelmed somewhere with the hood
Of some branchy bunchy bushybowered wood,
Southern dene or Lancashire clough or Devon cleave,
That leans along the loins of hills, where a candycoloured, where
    a gluegold-brown
Marbled river, boisterously beautiful, between
Roots and rocks is danced and dandled, all in froth and water-
    blowballs, down.
We are there, when we hear a shout
That the hanging honeysuck, the dogeared hazels in the cover
Makes dither, makes hover
And the riot of a rout
Of, it must be, boys from the town
Bathing: it is summer's sovereign good.

By there comes a listless stranger: beckoned by the noise
He drops towards the river: unseen
Sees the bevy of them, how the boys
With dare and with downdolphinry and bellbright bodies
    huddling out,
Are earthworld, airworld, waterworld thorough hurled, all by
    turn and turn about.

This garland of their gambols flashes in his breast
Into such a sudden zest
Of summertime joys
That he hies to a pool neighbouring; sees it is the best
There; sweetest, freshest, shadowiest;
Fairyland; silk-beech, scrolled ash, packed sycamore, wild
    wychelm, hornbeam fretty overstood

By. Rafts and rafts of flake-leaves light, dealt so, painted on the air,
Hang as still as hawk or hawkmoth, as the stars or as the angles
    there,
Like the thing that never knew the earth, never off roots
Rose. Here he feasts: lovely all is! No more: off with – down
    he dings
His bleachèd both and woolwoven wear:
Careless these in coloured wisp
All lie tumbled-to; then with loop-locks
Forward falling, forehead frowning, lips crisp
Over finger-teasing task, his twiny boots
Fast he opens, last he offwrings
Till walk the world he can with bare his feet
And come where lies a coffer, burly all of blocks
Built of chancequarrièd, selfquainèd rocks
And the water warbles over into, filleted with glassy grassy
    quicksilvery shivès and shoots
And with heavenfallen freshness down from moorland still brims,
Dark or daylight on and on. Here he will then, here he will the
    fleet
Flinty kindcold element let break across his limbs
Long. Where we leave him, froliclavish, while he looks about
    him, laughs, swims.

Enough now; since the sacred matter that I mean
I should be wronging longer leaving it to float
Upon this only gambolling and echoing-of-earth note –
What is . . . the delightful dene?
Wedlock. What is water? Spousal love.

    .   .   .   .
    .   .   .   .

Father, mother, brothers, sisters, friends
Into fairy trees, wild flowers, wood ferns
Rankèd round the bower

    .   .   .   .

SECTION B

PROSE

AN EARLY DIARY

September 24, 1863

Horn.

The various lights under which a horn may be looked at have given rise to a vast number of words in language. It may be regarded as a projection, a climax, a badge of strength, power or vigour, a tapering body, a spiral, a wavy object, a bow, a vessel to hold withal or to drink from, a smooth hard material not brittle, stony, metallic or wooden, something sprouting up, something to thrust or push with, a sign of honour or pride, an instrument of music, etc. From the shape, *kernel* and *granum, grain, corn.* From the curve of a horn, *κορωνις, *corona, crown.* From the spiral *crinis,* meaning ringlets, locks. From its being the highest point comes our *crown* perhaps, in the sense of the top of the head, and the Greek κέρας, horn, and κάρα, head, were evidently identical; then for its sprouting up and growing, compare *keren, cornu,* κέρας, horn with grow, *cresco, grandis,* grass, great, *groot.* For its curving, *curvus* is probably from the root *horn* in one of its forms. κορώνη in Greek and *corvus, cornix* in Latin and *crow* (perhaps also *raven,* which may have been *craven* originally) in English bear a striking resemblance to *cornu, curvus.* So also γέρανος, *crane, heron, herne.* Why these birds should derive their names from *horn* I cannot presume to say. The tree *cornel,* Latin *cornus* is said to derive its name from the hard horn-like nature of its wood, and the *corns* of the foot perhaps for the same reason. *Corner* is so called from its shape, indeed the Latin is *cornu.* Possibly (though this is rather ingenious than likely, I think) *grin* may mean to curve up the ends of the mouth like horns. Mountains are called *horn* in Switzerland; now we know from Servius that *herna* meant *saxum* whence the Hernici, *Rock-men,* derive

---

* κορωνις is the name for the flourish at the end of a book, and also for the mark over a crasis, shaped thus '. (G. M. H.'s note.)

their name; *herna* is a horn-like crag. ἔρνος, a shoot, is so called from its horn-like growth. Curiously enough the expression κεράων ἔρνος[1] occurs in Oppian, and another word, ἔρνυξ, in the *Poetics* of Aristotle. Or it is possible that ἔρνος may be so called from its shooting up as, not in the shape of, a horn.

Expressions. He hath raised up a horn of salvation for us.

－－－－－

• • • • • • •

See *horn* above. On the other hand the derivation of *granum*, *grain* may be referred to the head.

Grind, gride, gird, grit, groat, grate, greet, κρούειν, *crush, crash,* κροτεῖν etc.

Original meaning to *strike, rub,* particularly *together*. That which is produced by such means is the *grit*, the *groats* or crumbs, like *fragmentum* from *frangere, bit* from *bite. Crumb, crumble* perhaps akin. To *greet*, to strike the hands together (?). *Greet*, grief, wearing, *tribulation. Grief* possibly connected. *Gruff*, with a sound as of two things rubbing together. I believe these words to be onomatopoetic. *Gr* common to them all representing a particular sound. In fact I think the onomatopoetic theory has not had a fair chance.[2] Cf. *Crack, creak, croak, crake, graculus, crackle*. These must be onomatopoetic.

－－－－－

• • • • • •

April (?), 1864

Moonlight hanging or dropping on treetops like blue cobweb.

－－－－－

Also the upper sides of little grotted waves turned to the sky have soft pale-coloured cobwebs on them, the under sides green.

－－－－－

[1] i.e. growth (= shooting) of horns.

[2] 'The onomatopoetic origin of many words and roots' was urged by Frederic Farrar in his *Essay on the Origin of Language* (1860). See the present editor's *Gerard Manley Hopkins*, Vol. II, pp. 397-9.

Note that the beaded oar, dripping, powders or sows the smooth with dry silver drops.

Poetry at Oxford.
It is a happy thing that there is no royal road to poetry. The world should know by this time that one cannot reach Parnassus except by flying thither. Yet from time to time more men go up and either perish in its gullies fluttering *excelsior* flags or else come down again with full folios and blank countenances. Yet the old fallacy keeps its ground. Every age has its false alarms.

. . . .

1866

For Lent. No puddings on Sundays. No tea except if to keep me awake and then without sugar. Meat only once a day. No verses in Passion week or on Fridays. No lunch or meat on Fridays. Not to sit in armchair except can work in no other way. Ash Wednesday and Good Friday bread and water.

Drops of rain hanging on rails etc. seen with only the lower rim lighted like nails (of fingers). Screws of brooks and twines. Soft chalky look with more shadowy middles of the globes of cloud on a night with a moon faint or concealed. Mealy clouds with a not brilliant moon. Blunt buds of the ash. Pencil buds of the beech. Lobes of the trees. Cups of the eyes. Gathering back the lightly hinged eyelids. Bows of the eyelids. Pencil of eyelashes. Juices of the eyeball. Eyelids like leaves, petals, caps, tufted hats, handkerchiefs, sleeves, gloves. Also of the bones sleeved in flesh. Juices of the sunrise. Joins and veins of the same. Vermilion look of the hand held against a candle with the darker parts as the middles of the fingers and especially the knuckles covered with ash.

. . . .

ON THE ORIGIN OF BEAUTY:
A PLATONIC DIALOGUE
(1865)

It was at the beginning of the Long Vacation, and Oxford was nearly empty. The Professor of the newly founded chair of Aesthetics, whose lectures had been unattended during the term, came one day in the evening to New College gardens and found John Hanbury a scholar of the college walking there. They knew each other, and had taken two or three turns under the chestnuts together, when a stranger came up to them and asked if these were Worcester Gardens.

'This is New College' said Hanbury: 'may I direct you to Worcester?' No, the stranger said, he had only wished to know the name; and, then shewing a sketching-block, he asked if there would be any objection to his sketching there. 'Not at all' said Hanbury: 'shall I bring a chair? My rooms are close by.' He always drew standing, he said, and Hanbury and the Professor moved away.

'What was that paradox I heard of yours?' asked the Professor: 'about criticism it was.'

'O it was nothing' said Hanbury drawing back.

'But let me hear it defended. Everybody likes a good paradox. The Frenchman said the marriage-tie was in every case a bad thing, for if the married tired of each other it bound them together against their will, and if they did not it was superfluous. I like that: do not you?'

'But mine is not a good paradox' said Hanbury; 'it is hardly one at all: at all events I do not see how to avoid the conclusion it brings me to. I was saying that in poetry purely common-sense criticism was not enough by itself: that is true, is it not?'

'Certainly.'

'And criticism is not advocacy: it is rather judicial, is it not?'

'Judicial, it should be.'

'And judgments depend on laws, on established laws. Now taste has few rules, and those not scientific and easily disputed, and I might add, often disputed. Am I right?'

'At least, go on' said the Professor.

'If a man disputes your judgment in taste, how can you prove he is wrong? If a man thinks beautiful what you think bad, you must believe he is sincere when he tells you so; and if he is educated how are you to say that his judgment is worse than yours? In fact *de gustibus non est disputandum.*[1] Criticism therefore in matters of taste cannot be judicial. And purely common-sense criticism is not enough, we agreed. So criticism in matters of taste has no weight at all. That was it: do not be severe on it.'

'I will respect it, my dear Hanbury, I will respect it, though I do not quite think you have proved your point. However I will not answer you directly, for do you know I am not so sure about *de gustibus,* which is going further back?'

'Indeed' said Hanbury. 'Well if you think there are ascertainable laws, I should be glad of it for one; for when one is morally sure that one is right, it is a pity not to be able to refer to a logical ground for one's belief.'

'I have my theory' said the Professor; 'but I am afraid –'

'Do let me hear it' said Hanbury: 'I shall be a disciple I am sure.'

'My first' said the Professor 'it will be then. But may I pursue the Socratic method? May I take up the dialectic battledore which you have just laid down?'

'The dialectic battledore do you call it? I shall be so glad to be the – what is that called now? I have been about thirteen years out of the nursery. The shuttlecock, of course – to be the shuttlecock to it.'

'Now where shall I begin?' said the Professor. 'I will begin here', and he pulled off one of the large lowest fans of the chestnuts. 'Do you think this beautiful?'

'That? The chestnut-fan? Certainly: I have always thought the chestnut one of the most finely foliaged of trees.'

[1] 'One mustn't argue about tastes.'

'You see it consists of seven leaves, the middle largest, diminishing towards the stalk, so that those nearest the stalk are smallest.'

'I see' said Hanbury 'I had never noticed there were seven before.'

'Now if we look about we shall find – yes there is one. There is a fan, do you see? with only six leaves. Nature is irregular in these things. Can you reach it? Now which do you think the more beautiful, the one with six, or the one with seven, leaves? Shut out, if you can, the remembrance that the six-leaved one is an anomaly or imperfection: consider it symmetrical.'

'Well I daresay the six-leaved one may improve the foliage by variety, but in themselves the seven-leaved one is the handsomer.'

'Just so' said the Professor; 'but could you give any reason?'

'I suppose, as they are like in all other respects, it is that seven is a prettier number than six, and that would agree with the mystical character attached to the number seven.'

'Yes, but let me understand' said the Professor. 'Now is 101 a prettier number than 100?'

'101? I do not know. No, I think 100 is. No: of course in fact it depends on 100 or 101 of what.'

'Suppose then I had two great chestnut-fans, one with 100, one with 101, leaves, which would be the handsomer? You will say you could not tell till you saw them. But now, following the arrangements of these six-leaved and seven-leaved fans, in the 100-leaved there would be 50 radiating leaves on either side and a gap in the middle, in the 101-leaved 50 on either side and one, the greatest, in the middle. Do you see?'

'Perfectly. And I think the 101-leaved, or in fact the odd-leaved one whatever its number of leaves, would be the handsomer; not, as you seem to shew, from the abstract excellence of an odd number, but because – well, I suppose because to have the greatest leaf in the middle is the handsomer way.'

'But which is the more symmetrical?' asked the Professor. 'Is not the six-leaved one?'

'Both have symmetry; yet, as you say, the six-leaved one seems the more so, supposing it of course to be really symmetrical, which this specimen is not.'

'Is not this' asked the Professor 'because it is naturally divided into two equal parts of three leaves each, while the seven-leaved is not, and cannot be symmetrical in the same way unless we physically cut the greatest leaf down the middle.'

'Yes that is it; I see' said Hanbury.

'And so you judge the less markedly symmetrical to be the handsomer. Still the seven-leaved one has much symmetry. But now look at the tree from which I pulled it. Do you like it better as it is, or would you have the boughs start from the trunk at the same height on opposite sides, symmetrically pair and pair?'

'As it is, certainly.'

'Or again look at the colouring of the sky.'

'But' put in Hanbury 'colouring is not a thing of symmetry.'

'No: but now what is symmetry? Is it not regularity?'

'I should say, the greatest regularity' said Hanbury.

'So it is. But is it not that sort of regularity which is measured by length and breadth and thickness? Music for instance might be regular, but not symmetrical ever; is it not so?'

'Quite so' said Hanbury.

'Let us say regularity then. The sky, you see, is blue above, then comes a pale indescribable hue, and then the red of the sundown. You admire it do you not?'

'Very much' said Hanbury.

'But the red is the richest colour, is it not?'

'Now it is: yes.'

'Should you then like the whole sky to be of one uniform rich red?'

'Certainly not.'

'Or the red and blue to end sharply with a straight line, without anything as a gobetween?'

'No: I like the gradation.'

'Again then you approve of variety over absolute uniformity. And variety is opposed to regularity, is it not? while uniformity is regularity. Is it not so?'

'Certainly. I am to conclude then that beauty is produced by irregularity' said Hanbury.

'Ah! you run on very fast' said the Professor. 'I never said that. Once more, if you please, I must send my shuttlecock up to the sky. You will no doubt with your feathers of vantage see better than I can, considering how my view is cut off by the buildings of the College, that rows of level cloud run along the west of the sky.'

'At all events' said he 'I can see them.'

'Do you think they would be better away?' asked the Professor.

'No: they add to the beauty of the sunset sky.'

'Notice however that they are pretty symmetrical. They are straight, and parallel with the sky-line and with each other, and of a uniform colour, and other things in them are symmetrical. Should you admire them more if they were shapeless?'

'I think not' said Hanbury.

'Again when we say anyone has regular features, do we mean praise or blame?'

'Praise.'

'We were speaking of the chestnut-trees, of their unsymmetrical growth. Now is the oak an unsymmetrical tree?'

'Very much so; O quite a rugged boldly-irregular tree: and this I should say was one of the things which make us invest it with certain qualities it has in poetry and in popular and national sentiment' said Hanbury.

'Very observant. You mean of course when it grows at liberty, rather than when influenced by confinement, cutting and so forth.'

'Yes: what I say will of course be truest of the tree when uninfluenced by man.'

'Very good. Now have you ever noticed that when the oak has grown to its full stature uninfluenced, the outline of its head is drawn by a long curve, I should think it would be that of a parabola, which, if you look at the tree from a little way off, is of almost mathematical correctness?'

'Dear me, is it indeed so? No, I had never noticed it, but now that you name it, I do seem to find something in me which verifies what you say.'

'Do you happen to remember' asked the Professor 'that fine

oak at the top of the hill above Elsfield where you have such a wide view?'

'Of course I do. Yes a very fine tree.'

'If you had analysed your admiration of it I think you would have had to lay a good deal of it to that strict parabolic outline. Or again if one of the three side-leaves of this seven-leaved chestnut-fan be torn off, it will be less beautiful, will it not? And this, I am sure you will now say, because the symmetry is destroyed.'

'Yes' said Hanbury. 'Then beauty, you would say perhaps, is a mixture of regularity and irregularity.'

'Complex beauty, yes. But let us inquire a little further. What is regularity? Is it not obedience to law? And what is law? Does it not mean that several things, or all the parts of one thing, are like each other?'

'Let me understand' said Hanbury.

'I fear I ply my battledore so fiercely that the best of shuttle-cocks has not time to right itself between the blows; but I will be steadier. Is not a straight line regular? and a circle?'

'Nothing can be more so' said Hanbury.

'And any part of a straight line or of a circle is exactly like another of the same size, is it not?'

'Exactly.'

'They are in fact consistent with themselves, and alike through-out.'

'Yes they are.'

'Regularity then is consistency or agreement or likeness, either of a thing to itself or of several things to each other.'

'I understand the first part of what you say, but – I am very sorry again to trouble you – not quite the second.'

'It is my fault' said the Professor. 'I mean that although a leaf might have an outline on one side so irregular that no law could be traced in it, yet if the other side exactly agreed with it, you would say there was law or regularity about the leaf to make one side like the other. Or if the leaf of a tree were altogether irregular, supposing such a thing were to be found in nature, yet all the leaves on the tree were exactly like it, having precisely that same irregularity, then you would recognise the presence of law about the tree.'

'Yes: I understand perfectly now.'

'Then regularity is likeness or agreement or consistency, and irregularity is the opposite, that is difference or disagreement or change or variety. Is it so?'

'Certainly.'

'Then the beauty of the oak and the chestnut-fan and the sky is a mixture of likeness and difference or agreement and disagreement or consistency and variety or symmetry and change.'

'It seems so, yes.'

'And if we did not feel the likeness we should not think them so beautiful, or if we did not feel the difference we should not think them so beautiful. The beauty we find is from the comparison we make of the things with themselves, seeing their likeness and difference, is it not?'

'Yes. But let me think a little. This may be the nature of the beauty in the things you have spoken of and of many others, but I do not at all yet see how it applies to all things, and I should like to ask you to account for some of them. Let me collect some instances.'

He stood looking out through a loophole in one of the towers of the old wall. Meanwhile the sketcher, who had long been drawing in a desultory way, moved from the stand he had taken up, as though meaning to walk about. He had become more interested in this philosophy of the Gardens than in his sketching, for in the clear air of the evening he had heard almost everything that was said, and the questioner and answerer had raised their voices: he was loath to lose the end of the debate. Hanbury hearing him move turned and asked if he would come in and have some tea. He thanked him and accepted the offer. It was then debated whether the party should go in at once or no, and it was agreed they should for the present at least continue to walk about. Hanbury in courtesy began to talk on indifferent subjects, but the stranger begged the discussion might be continued.

'I am afraid' he said 'I have heard more than I had any business to do, but I have become so interested that I – one's fondness for painting will be the best excuse for the interest a discussion on beauty has for one. Perhaps I might serve as alternative shuttlecock, while Mr. Hanbury' – he had heard the name from the Professor's mouth in the course of the talk – 'is collecting his instances. I hardly think I entirely understood the last of what was said.'

'If you will be so kind' said the Professor. 'But I fear that in the ardour of the game I thump the shuttlecock far too hard, in order to bring out the more resonant answers. I know quite well what sort of things Hanbury is going to bring forward, and in the meantime I would gladly fortify my first ground, which I took only with regard to things of abstract beauty. Of course everyone would allow as a truism that in making beautiful shapes (and the same will hold for the other kinds of abstract beauty) we must not have things too symmetrical; and most would allow we must not have them too unsymmetrical and rugged; but what this means and leads to they do not so much seem to consider. Now let me take an instance from those excellent frescoes which are being added to the new smoking-room at the Union –'

'Excuse me' said the painter: 'I have come up to paint those frescoes, so perhaps you would find me too much prejudiced for them to serve your purpose as examples.'

'Indeed' said the others 'then your name is Middleton, we are to presume.'

'Yes' said he, 'but pray do not let the discussion be interrupted on account of my frescoes. You will, I am sure, find another instance.'

'I will return then to the chestnut-fan' said the Professor. Hanbury went in to make tea, promising soon to be back, and the Professor continued. 'Each leaf is symmetrical is it not? Counting from the rib or spine which runs down the back of the middle leaf, each side of the fan answers to the other, does it not?'

'Quite so.'

'With the exception' went on the Professor, 'of such slight

inequalities or imperfections as are always to be found in nature. And these would not be expressed at all in an idealised chestnut-fan used in Art, would they? I mean of course not in a landscape picture, but in such a formalised and conventionalised shape as the chestnut-fan would have in decoration and architecture and so on.'

'Yes' said Middleton; 'It would then be quite symmetrical.'

'But yet it would not have lost its beauty, would it? – But I am really ashamed to ask these questions.'

'Not at all, not at all' said Middleton; 'I beg you will not be so. No, it would not have lost its beauty. It is in fact one of the most beautiful natural shapes at the disposal of Art.'

'And what was said of the whole fan is also true of each leaf of it, that it is symmetrical: but now let us see what this symmetry comes to. For first one side answers to the other, but yet there is a leaf, the middle one, which belongs to neither one side nor the other. Hanbury and I had agreed that this contrast of two opposite things, symmetry and the violation of it, was here preferable to pure symmetry. Next it radiates, but the radiation of leaves is not carried all the way round. Would it be improved by more regular radiation, do you think?'

'O no: whatever the beauties of regular radiation may be, the particular beauty of the chestnut-fan depends on its not being so radiated.'

'Here again then contrast is preferred to agreement. Then the leaves are pretty much alike but not of the same size. You would not have them of the same size, I am sure, thus again preferring contrast to agreement. And one sees that, although differing, they differ by a law, diminishing as they do towards the stalk; and this I presume is more beautiful than if they differed irregularly, so that the contrast of regularity with variety is once more preferred to agreement, the agreement it would be in this case of entire irregularity. Is it not so?'

'I think so, yes.'

'Although from their diminishing they do not form part of that most regular of figures the circle, yet in their diminishing they shape out another figure, do they not? partly regular, though containing variety; I mean that of a Greek Omega.'[1]

'Yes, I see how you mean.'

'Furthermore, although leaf answers to leaf on each side of the central one, you will see that the equal leaves are not diametrically opposite to each other – I use "diametrically" in its strict sense, opposite as the one half of a diameter is to the one on the other side of the centre –, with the exception of two of them.'

'No, I see' said Middleton: 'the greatest is opposite the stalk, which is the slimmest thing belonging to the fan; then the two next greatest, which are nearest to the middle one, are opposite to the two smallest, which are nearest to the stalk; only the two between these two last-mentioned pairs are both opposite and answering to each other. All this I see; and I understand that you would point out the contrast made by the regularity of the continuous diameter with the irregularity of the unequal opposite *radii*.'

'That is just what I would say' said the Professor. 'Then it is not the radiation which is the beauty of the fan, but the radiation heightened by its cessation near the stalk.'

'Yes.'

'Nor the agreement of side with side, but that agreement as reflected on by the one dominant leaf which belongs to neither side.'

'Yes.'

'Nor the likeness of the leaves, but their likeness as thrown up by their difference in size.'

'Yes.'

'Nor their inequality, but the inequality as tempered by their regular diminishing.'

'Yes.'

'Nor their each having a diametrical opposite, but that opposite being the least answering to themselves in the whole fan.'

'Yes.'

'I might say even more. It seems then that it is not the excellence

[1] i.e. the letter.

of any two things (or more) in themselves, but those two things as viewed by the light of each other, that makes beauty. Do you understand?'

'I think so, but might I ask you still further to explain?'

'I had reserved what I think will be my best proof for the last' said the Professor. 'The leaves of most trees may be roughly described as being formed by the intersection of two equal circles, in fact the figure called *vesica piscis*, but the leaves of this fan are not so. They are narrow near the stalk, they pass outwards with a long concave curve, then more than half-way up they turn, form a pair of rounded shoulders, so to speak, and then come round sharply to the point. Look here for instance,' and he pulled one off the tree.

'Yes, the curve is more complex than in most trees; but I am not sure I do not admire the commoner shape better in leaves.'

'Yes' said the Professor, 'but now would you have the fan made of that commoner sort? I have made a mock fan, see, with lime leaves.'

'Certainly not' said Middleton. 'The more complex curve is far more beautiful in the fan, for it leaves long narrow slits of light between the leaves, and in other respects the composition is finer and richer.'

'Ah! that is the pith of the matter – "its composition." But I am afraid to go on; I am talking to one who will laugh to see me fall into some snare as I trespass over his own grounds.'

'Pray go on' said Middleton.

'If I am to do so' said the Professor 'I shall put these next questions in fear and trembling. Do not painters speak of balancing mass by mass in the composition of their pictures?'

'They do.'

'If they balance mass by mass, the mass in one part of a picture must be unbalanced until that in another part is put in.'

'Of course.'

'If unbalanced then, the picture is unbeautiful.'

'Yes, in that respect.'

'Now suppose when the picture was finished with two masses

balanced, a copy were made from it, and one mass put in, not the one that was put in the first in the original picture but the other, and then the copying stopped; the picture would then be un-balanced as before, would it not?'

'Just as the first picture was, yes.'

'And it would be unbeautiful, would it not?'

'Yes.'

'But the finished picture was beautiful.'

'Yes.'

'The picture that had only one mass put in was unbeautiful: now as it was to be beautiful when both masses were put in, we might suppose the beauty must lie all in that mass which was yet to come: when however we in our second picture, anxious to have our beauty as soon as possible, put the second mass in first, pregnant as it was with graces, lo and behold! the result was as uninteresting as when we had the first mass alone put in. What are we to say then? The beauty does not lie in this mass or in that, but in what? In this mass as supported by that, and in that as supported by this. Is it so?'

'Exactly.'

'And artists call this composition. Does not then the beauty lie in the relation between the masses?'

'It seems it does.'

'Beauty then is a relation.'

'I suppose it is.'

'And things which have relation are near enough to have some-thing in common, but not near enough to be one and the same, are they not?'

'Yes.'

'And to perceive the likeness and difference of things, or their relation, we must compare them, must we not?'

'Yes.'

'Beauty therefore is a relation, and the apprehension of it a comparison. The sense of beauty in fact is a comparison, is it not?'

'So it would appear.'

'I have not yet said *what* the relation is' said the Professor, when he was interrupted by Hanbury who had returned some time since.

'Well' said he 'I must own, with all my wish for the logical ground I spoke of in discussions of taste, I feel it very unworthy to think that beauty resolves itself into a relation. However, it may be that the particular kind of beauty in a chestnut-fan, which seems after all a geometrical sort of thing, may be explained as you say, and you seem to have pulled it to pieces to exhibit that, so that I am either convinced or I really do not know what to say to the contrary; but I am sure there is in the higher forms of beauty – at least I seem to feel – something mystical, something I don't know how to call it. Is not there now something beyond what you have explained?'

'Oh! my dear friend, when one sets out with *a priori* notions – I am afraid I have lost the only chance of a disciple I ever had.'

'Not at all, I hope' said Middleton.

'No, no' said Hanbury; 'if you will explain on your theory what I am now going to put forward I will then believe it will apply to everything else. But now where is the relation you speak of, and the comparison, in this for instance?

> O blithe New-comer! I have heard,
> I hear thee and rejoice.
> O Cuckoo! Shall I call thee Bird
> Or but a wandering Voice?

Now is there not something mystical there, or is it all in plain broad daylight?'

'A mathematical thing, measured by compasses, that is what you think I should make it, do you not?'

'Well yes, if you put the words into my mouth.'

'But' went on the Professor 'if I am to undertake the analysis of so subtle a piece of beauty as you have tasked me with, might I do it by the aid of candlelight? for it is now dark, you see, and wet underfoot and one is almost cold, I think. I hope the tea is not.'

'Ah! the tea' said Hanbury; and they went in . . .

May 2, 1866. We came into these lodgings, Addis[2] and I, at beginning of this term – 18, New Inn Hall Street.

Weather cold and raw, chestnut leaves touched with frost and limp. Sun today. Swallows playing over Ch. Ch.[3] meadows with a wavy and hanging flight and shewing their white bellies. Snakes'-heads. Yellow wagtails. Almost think you can hear the lisp of the swallow's wings.

Coaching with W. H. Pater this term. Walked with him on Monday evening last, April 30. Fine evening bitterly cold. 'Bleak-faced Neology in cap and gown': no cap and gown but very bleak. Same evening Hexameron[4] met here: Addis read on the Franciscans: laughter. Thought all the next day of the terrible history of Fra Dolcino. Same day, I believe, Case at one of the cricket grounds saw three Ch. Ch. men laughing loudly at a rat with back broken, a most ghastly sight, flying at the dog. He kicked away the dog, put his heel on the rat's head and killed it, and drove away the crowd of cads. Wonder what would be the just statement of the effects of cruelty to animals, cruel sports, etc.

Little girls singing abt. May Day under the windows yesterday. Never heard this before the other day –

Violante

In the pantry

Gnawing at a mutton bone,

How she gnawed it,

How she clawed it,

When she felt herself alone.

---

[1] The text retains G. M. H.'s abbreviations, e.g., 'fr.' = 'from', 'cd.'= 'could', etc.

[2] William Edward Addis (1844–1917), Snell Exhibitioner at Balliol and one of G. M. H.'s most intimate Oxford friends. See footnote to p. 162 and also Note G, p. 251.   [3] Christ Church, Oxford.

[4] Unidentified Oxford 'paper-reading' or 'essay' club. Cf. below, p. 154.

Reading Maurice de Guérin's Remains, enjoying but without sufficient knowledge of French. This day week brought forward motion in defence of the Fenians at the Balliol Debating Society. Wandered about S. Hinksey that day with most sad distracting scruple, as bad as any single one almost ever was.

May 3. Cold. Morning raw and wet, afternoon fine. Walked then with Addis, crossing Bablock Hythe, round by Skinner's Weir through many fields into the Witney Road. Sky sleepy blue without liquidity. Fr. Cumnor Hill saw St. Philip's and the other spires through blue haze rising pale in a pink light. On further side of the Witney road hills, just fleeced with grain or other green growth, by their dips and waves foreshortened here and there and so differenced in brightness and opacity the green on them, with delicate effect. On left, brow of the near hill glistening with very bright newly turned sods and a scarf of vivid green slanting away beyond the skyline, agst. which the clouds shewed the slightest tinge of rose or purple. Copses in grey-red or grey-yellow – the tinges immediately forerunning the opening of full leaf. Meadows skirting Seven-bridge road voluptuous green. Some oaks are out in small leaf. Ashes not out, only tufted with their fringy blooms. Hedges springing richly. Elms in small leaf, with more or less opacity. White poplars most beautiful in small grey crisp spray-like leaf. Cowslips capriciously colouring meadows in creamy drifts. Bluebells, purple orchis. Over the green water of the river passing the slums of the town and under its bridges swallows shooting, blue and purple above and shewing their amber-tinged breasts reflected in the water, their flight unsteady with wagging wings and leaning first to one side then the other. Peewits flying. Towards sunset the sky partly swept, as often, with moist white cloud, tailing off across which are morsels of grey-black woolly clouds. Sun seemed to make a bright liquid hole in this, its texture had an upward northerly sweep or drift fr. the W. marked softly in grey. Dog violets. Eastward after sunset range of clouds rising in bulky heads moulded softly in tufts or bunches of snow – so it looks – and membered somewhat elaborately, rose-coloured. Notice often imperfect fairy rings. Apple and other fruit trees blossomed beautifully. A.[1] talking about the whole story of the home affairs. His idea was (when he went down three years ago and was all the Long[2] preparing for confession) that 7 yrs. was a moderate time during wh. to fast within the boundaries of life and abstain from communicating. Being not allowed to read he took long walks, and it must have been on one of these that he fainted as he once told me. . . .   •   •   •   •   •   •   •

May 6. Grey. A little time ago on much such another day noticed Trinity gardens. Much distinctness, charm, and suggestiveness abt. the match of white grey sky, solid smooth lawn, firs and yews, dark trees, below, and chestnuts and other brighter-hued trees above, the young green having a fresh moist opaque look and there being in the whole picture an absence of projection, and apprehension of colour. On such a day also last Friday week boated with H. Dugmore to Godstow, but the warm greyness of the day, the river, the spring green, and the cuckoo wanted a canon by wh. to harmonise and round them in – e.g. one of feeling.   •   •   •   •   •   •

June 30. Thunderstorms all day, great claps and lightning running up and down. When it was bright betweentimes great towering clouds behind which the sun put out his shaded horns very clearly and a longish way. Level curds and whey sky after sunset. – Graceful growth of Etzkoltzias[3] or however those unhappy flowers are spelt. Yews and evergreen trees now very thin and putting out their young pale shoots.

July 1. Sharp showers, bright between. Late in the afternoon, the light and shade being brilliant, snowy blocks of cloud were filing over the sky, and under the sun hanging above and along the earth-line were those multitudinous up-and-down crispy sparkling chains with pearly shadows up to the edges. At sunset, wh. was in a grey bank with moist gold dabs and racks, the whole round of skyline had level clouds naturally lead-colour but the

---

[1] W. E. Addis. See Note G, p. 251.   [2] i.e. the Long Vacation.
    [3] Eschscholtzias.

upper parts ruddled, some more, some less, rosy. Spits or beams braided or built in with slanting pellet flakes made their way. Through such clouds anvil-shaped pink ones and up-blown fleece-of-wool flat-topped dangerous-looking pieces.

. . . .

July 11. . . . Oats: hoary blue-green sheaths and stalks, prettily shadow-stroked spikes of pale green grain. Oaks: the organisation of this tree is difficult. Speaking generally no doubt the determining planes are concentric, a system of brief contiguous and continuous tangents, whereas those of the cedar wd. roughly be called horizontals and those of the beech radiating but modified by droop and by a screw-set towards jutting points. But beyond this since the normal growth of the boughs is radiating and the leaves grow some way in there is of course a system of spoke-wise clubs of green – sleeve-pieces. And since the end shoots curl and carry young and scanty leaf-stars these clubs are tapered, and I have seen also the pieces in profile with chiselled outlines, the blocks thus made detached and lessening towards the end. However the star knot is the chief thing: it is whorled, worked round, a little and this is what keeps up the illusion of the tree: the leaves are rounded inwards and figure out ball-knots. Oaks differ much, and much turns on the broadness of the leaf, the narrower giving the crisped and starry and catharine-wheel forms, the broader the flat-pieced mailed or shard-covered ones, in wh. it is possible to see composition in dips, etc., on wider bases than the single knot or cluster. But I shall study them further. See the 19th.

July 17. . . . It was this night I believe but possibly the next that I saw clearly the impossibility of staying in the Church of England, but resolved to say nothing to anyone till three months are over, that is the end of the Long, and then of course to take no step till after my Degree.

July 18. Bright. Sunset over oaks a dapple of rosy clouds blotted with purple, sky round confused pale green and blue with faint horned rays,[1] crimson sparkles through the leaves below. . . .

[1] Cf. poem No. 39, l. 3.

July 19. . . . Alone in the woods and in Mr. Nelthorpe's park, whence one gets such a beautiful view southwards over the country. I have now found the law of the oak leaves. It is of platter-shaped stars altogether; the leaves lie close like pages, packed, and as if drawn tightly to. But these old packs, wh. lie at the end of their twigs, throw out now long shoots alternately and slimly leaved, looking like bright keys. All the sprays but markedly these ones shape out and as it were embrace greater circles and the dip and toss of these make the wider and less organic articulations of the tree.

. . . .

Aug. 23, 1867. Fine and cloudless; fiery sunset. – Some wychelms seem to have leaves smaller, others bigger, than the common elm: . . .

Papa, Mamma, and Milicent[1] went off to Brittany. I went down to call on Mrs. Cunliffe, who was out, and walked a little in Hyde Park, where I noticed a fine oblate chestnut-tree with noble long ramping boughs more like an oak. Then to the chapel of the poor Clares,[2] where I made my resolution "if it is better", but now, Sept. 4, nothing is decided. For the evening to Aunt Kate's. See *infra* May 2 and 11. . . .

Aug. 30. Fair; in afternoon fine; the clouds had a good deal of crisping and mottling. – A round by Plumley.[3] – Stands of ash in a copse: they consisted of two or three rods most gracefully leaved, for each wing or comb finally curled inwards, that is upwards. – Putting my hand up against the sky whilst we lay on the grass I saw more richness and beauty in the blue than I had known of before, not brilliance but glow and colour.[4] It was not transparent and sapphire-like, but turquoise-like, swarming and blushing round the edge of the hand and in the pieces clipped in by the fingers, the flesh being sometimes sunlit, sometimes glassy

---

[1] G. M. H.'s eldest sister (1849–1947). She became an Anglican nun.
[2] i.e. Poor Clares, nuns of the order founded by St. Clare of Assisi.
[3] Village in Devonshire.   [4] Cf. poem No. 37, ll. 73–8.

with reflected light, sometimes lightly shadowed in that violet
one makes with cobalt and Indian red.

. . . .

Ap. 27, 1868. Generally fine betw. hard showers; some hail, wh.
made the evening very cold, a flash of lightning, a clap of thunder,
and a bright rainbow; some grey cloud betw. showers ribbed and
draped and some wild bright big brown flix at the border of a
great rack with blue rising behind – though it was too big in
character to be called flix. To Roehampton into retreat.[1] . . .

May 2. Fine, with some haze, and warm. This day, I think, I
resolved. See *supra* last 23rd August and *infra* May 11.

May 3. Bright, with haze – dark-in-bright –, hot, and like
summer; when cloud formed it was delicately barred. – Cuckoo
singing all day. Oaks out, wych-elms not, except a few leaves.

May 4. Dull; then fine; cold, esp. in wind. – Note the elm here
on one side of beautiful build with one great limb overhanging
the sunk fence into the Park and headed like the one near the
house at Shanklin but when seen fr. the opposite side to this limb
uninteresting or clumsy.

May 5. Cold. Resolved to be a religious.

May 6. Fine but rather thick and with a very cold N.E. wind.

May 7. Warm; misty morning; then beautiful torquoise sky.
Home, after having decided to be a priest and religious but still
doubtful betw. St. Benedict and St. Ignatius. . . .

May 11. Dull; afternoon fine. Slaughter of the innocents.[2] See
above, the 2nd.

. . . .

June 27. Silver mottled clouding, and clearer; else like yesterday.

[1] i.e. to Manresa House, Roehampton, the Jesuit Novitiate which
G. M. H. eventually entered as a novice on September 7, 1868. The present
retreat was undertaken by him as a Catholic layman seeking spiritual
guidance.
[2] This probably refers to the burning of his poems. See below, p. 187,
and also *Journals and Papers of G. M. H.* (2nd edn., 1959), p. 357.

At the Nat. Gallery. That Madonna by Beltraffio. Qy. has not Giotto the instress[1] of loveliness? Mantegna's draperies.

.   .   .   .

July 3. . . . Started with Ed. Bond[2] for Switzerland. We went by Dover and Ostende to Brussels. . . .

July 5. To mass at the cathedral [Cologne]. Then up the Rhine to Mainz. The Rhine hills are shaped in strict planes and coigns.[3] Where the banks are flat mossy or velvet eyots of poplar edged with osier rise plump from the river.

The day was, I think, dull.

Watching from close the motion of a flag in the wind.

July 6. Rainy till lately (5 o'clock), when a low rainbow backed by the Black Forest hills, which were partly dimmed out with wet mist, appeared, and – what I never saw before – rays of shadow crossed it, all its round, and where they crossed it paled the colour. It was a "blue bow". That evening saw a shepherd *leading* his flock through the town.

By railway to Basel. Beautiful view from the train of the hills near Mülheim etc. They were clothed with wood and at the openings in this and indeed all upward too they were charactered by vertical stemming, dim in the distance. Villages a little bare like Brill rise in blocks of white and deep russet tiling. The nearer hills terraced with vineyards deep and vertical, the pale grey shaven poles close on the railway leaning capriciously towards one another. – Here we met the young Englishman who had been to see Charlotte Brontë's school in Brussels. . . .

But Basel at night! with a full moon waking the river and sending up straight beams from the heavy clouds that overhung it. We saw this from the bridge. The river runs so strong that it keeps the bridge shaking. Then we walked about the place and first of all had the adventure of the little Englishwoman with her hat off. We went through great spacious streets and places dead

---

[1] For 'instress' see Introduction, p. xx.
[2] See below, p. 114, footnote 2.
[3] Cf. the word 'quains' on p. 112 and Note B, p. 249.

still and came to fountains of the clearest black water through which pieces of things at the bottom gleamed white. We got up to a height where a bastion-shaped vertical prominence shaded with chestnut trees looked down on the near roofs, which then in the moonlight were purple and velvety and edged along with ridges and chimneys of chalk white. A woman came to a window with a candle and some mess she was making, and then that was gone and there was no light anywhere but the moon. We heard music indoors about. We saw the courtyard of a charming house with some tree pushing to the windows and a fountain. A church too of immensely high front all dead and flush to the top and next to it three most graceful flamboyant windows. Nothing cd. be more taking and fantastic than this stroll.

July 7. Fine morning; rain betw. Basel and Lucerne and in the evening. We saw the Münster and the Museum – where there is a noble dead Christ by the younger Holbein, but the other Holbeins were unimpressive; also a Crucifixion by a German master in which the types of the two thieves, especially the good thief – a young man with a moustache and modern air – were in the wholeness and general scape of the anatomy original and interesting. (The prominence of the peculiar square-shaped drapery etc. in Holbein and his contemporaries is remarkable – e.g. as a determination of German art.) . . .

Swiss trees are, like English, well inscaped[1] – in quains.

. . . .

July 9. Before sunrise looking out of window saw a noble scape of stars – the Plough all golden falling, Cassiopeïa[2] on end with her bright quains pointing to the right, the graceful bends of Perseus underneath her, and some great star whether Capella or not I am not sure risen over the brow of the mountain. Sunrise

[1] For 'inscape', see Introduction, p. xx.

[2] In July the principal stars of this constellation form a sort of flattened W on end – its two base angles ('quains') pointing to the right. For 'quain', which is a dialect form of 'quoin' (= a wedge, corner; cf. 'coign'), see Note B, p. 249.

we saw well: the north landscape was blighty but the south, the important one, with the Alps, clear; lower down all was mist and flue of white cloud, wh. grew thicker as the day went on and like a junket lay scattered on the lakes. The sun lit up the bright acres of the snows at first with pink but afterwards clear white: the snow of the Bernese Highland remained from its distance pinkish all day. – The mountain ranges, as any series or body of inanimate like things not often seen, have the air of persons and of interrupted activity; they are multitudinous too, and also they express a second level with an upper world or shires of snow. – In going down betw. Pilatus and a long streak of cloud the blue sky was greenish. Since I have found this colour is seen in looking fr. the snow to the sky but why I do not understand: can there possibly be a rose hue suppressed in the white (– *purpurea candidior nive*)?

. . . .

July 11. Fine. We took a guide up the Wylerhorn but the top being clouded dismissed him and stayed up the mountain, lunching by a waterfall. Presently after long climbing – for there was a good chance of a clearance – we nearly reached the top, when a cloud coming on thick frightened me back: had we gone on we shd. have had the view, for it cleared quite. Still we saw the neighbouring mountains well. The snow is often cross-harrowed and lies too in the straightest paths as though artificial, wh. again comes fr. the planing. In the sheet it glistens yellow to the sun. How fond of and warped to the mountains it wd. be easy to become! For every cliff and limb and edge and jutty has its own nobility. – Two boys came down the mountain yodelling. – We saw the snow in the hollows for the first time. In one the surface was crisped across the direction of the cleft and the other way, that is across the broader crisping and down the stream, combed: the stream ran below and smoke came fr. the hollow: the edge of the snow hewn in curves as if by moulding planes. – Crowd of mountain flowers – gentians; gentianellas; blood-red lucerne; a deep blue glossy spiked flower like plantain, flowering gradually up the spike, so that at the top it looks like clover or honeysuckle;

rich big harebells glistening black like the cases of our veins when dry and heated fr. without; and others. All the herbage enthronged with every fingered or fretted leaf. – Firs very tall, with the swell of the branching on the outer side of the slope so that the peaks seem to point inwards to the mountain peak, like the lines of the Parthenon, and the outline melodious and moving on many focuses. – I wore my pagharee[1] and turned it with harebells below and gentians in two rows above like double pan-pipes. – In coming down we lost our way and each had a dangerous slide down the long wet grass of a steep slope.

Waterfalls not only skeined but silky too – one saw it fr. the inn across the meadows: at one quain of the rock the water glistened above and took shadow below, and the rock was reddened a little way each side with the wet, wh. sets off the silkiness. . . .

. . . .

July 19, 1868. Sunday, but no Catholics, I found, at Meyringen. The day fine.

Walked up the valley of the Aar, sallow-coloured and torrent, to the Grimsel. The heights bounding the valley soon became a mingle of lilac and green, the first the colour of the rock, the other the grass crestings, and seemed to group above in crops and rounded buttresses, yet to be cut sharp in horizontal or leaning planes below.

We came up with a guide who reminded me of F. John. He took E. B.'s[2] knapsack and on finding the reason why I would not let him take mine said 'Le bon Dieu n'est pas comme ca.' The man probably was a rational Protestant; if a Catholic at least he rationalised gracefully, as they do in Switzerland.

At a turn in the road the foam-cuffs in the river, looked down upon, were of the crispiest endive spraying.

We lunched at Guttannen, where there was that strange party of Americans.

---

[1] Presumably 'puggaree' or 'pugaree'.
[2] Edward Bond, close Oxford friend of G. M. H., Conservative M.P. for E. Nottingham (1895–1906); died 1920.

I was arguing about the planing of rocks and made a sketch of two in the Aar, and after that it was strange, for Nature became Nemesis, so precise they were, and E. B. himself pointed out two which looked, he said, as if they had been sawn. And of the hills themselves it could sometimes be seen, but on the other hand the sides of the valley often descended in trending sweeps of vertical section and so met at the bottom.

At times the valley opened in *cirques*, amphitheatres, enclosing levels of plain, and the river then ran between flaky flat-fish isles made of cindery lily-white stones. – In or near one of these openings the guide cries out 'Voulez-vous une Alp-rose?' and up he springs the side of the hill and brings us each bunches of flowers down.

In one place over a smooth table of rock came slipping down a blade of water looking like and as evenly crisped as fruitnets let drop and falling slack.

We saw Handeck waterfall. It is in fact the meeting of two waters, the right the Aar sallow and jade-coloured, the left a smaller stream of clear lilac foam. It is the greatest fall we have seen. The lower half is hidden in spray. I watched the great bushes of foam-water, the texture of branchings and water-spandrils which makes them up. At their outsides nearest the rock they gave off showers of drops strung together into little quills which sprang out in fans.

On crossing the Aar again there was as good a fall as some we have paid to see, all in jostling foam-bags.

Across the valley too we saw the fall of the Gelmer – like milk chasing round blocks of coal; or a girdle or long purse of white weighted with irregular black rubies, carelessly thrown aside and lying in jutty bends, with a black clasp of the same stone at the top – for those were the biggest blocks, squared, and built up, as it happened, in lessening stories, and the cascade enclosed them on the right and left hand with its foam; or once more like the skin of a white snake square-pied with black.

July 20. Fine.

Walked down to the Rhone glacier. It has three stages – first a smoothly-moulded bed in a pan or theatre of thorny peaks, swells of ice rising through the snow-sheet and the snow itself tossing and fretting into the sides of the rock walls in spray-like points: this is the first stage of the glaciers generally; it is like bright-plucked water swaying in a pail –; second, after a slope nearly covered with landslips of moraine, was a ruck of horned waves steep and narrow in the gut: now in the upper Grindelwald glacier between the bed or highest stage was a descending limb which was like the rude and knotty bossings of a strombus shell –; third the foot, a broad limb opening out and reaching the plain, shaped like the fan-fin of a dolphin or a great bivalve shell turned on its face, the flutings in either case being suggested by the crevasses and the ribs by the risings between them, these being swerved and inscaped strictly to the motion of the mass. Or you may compare the three stages to the heel, instep, and ball or toes of a foot. – The second stage looked at from nearer appeared like a box of plaster of Paris or starch or tooth-powder a little moist, tilted up and then struck and jarred so that the powder broke and tumbled in shapes and rifts.

We went into the grotto and also the vault from which the Rhone flows. It looked like a blue tent and as you went further in changed to lilac. As you come out the daylight glazes the groins with gleaming rosecolour. The ice inside has a branchy wire texture. The man shewed us the odd way in which a little piece of ice will stick against the walls – as if drawn by a magnet.

Standing on the glacier saw the prismatic colours in the clouds, and worth saying what sort of clouds: it was fine shapeless skins of fretted make, full of eyebrows or like linings of curled leaves which one finds in shelved corners of a wood.

I had a trudge over the glacier and a tumble over the side moraine, which was one landslip of limestone. It was neighboured however by hot sweet smells and many flowers – small crimson pinks, the brown tulip-like flower we have seen so often, another which we first saw yesterday like Solomon's seal but rather coarser with a spike of greenish veiny-leaved blossom, etc.

•   •   •   •   •   •   •   •

July 24. Bright.

E. B. started in the night for the Cima di Jazzi; I stayed behind being ill.

At sunset great bulks of brassy cloud hanging round, which changed their colour to bright reds over the sundown and to fruittree-blossom colour opposite: later a honey-brown edged the Dent Blanche and Weisshorn ridge.

Note that a slender race of fine flue cloud inscaped in continuous eyebrow curves hitched on the Weisshorn peak as it passed: this shews the height of this kind of cloud, from its want of shadow etc. not otherwise discoverable.

July 25. But too bright.

Up at two to ascend the Breithorn. Stars twiring[1] brilliantly. Taurus up, a pale light stressily edging the eastern skyline, and lightning mingled with the dawn. In the twilight we tumbled over the moraine and glacier until the sunrise brightly fleshed the snow of the Breithorn before us and then the colour changing through metallic shades of yellow recovered to white.

We were accompanied by a young Mr. Pease of Darlington, his guide Gasser, and ours, Welchen.

From the summit the view on the Italian side was broken by endless ranges of part-vertical dancing cloud, the highest and furthest flaked or foiled like fungus and coloured pink. But, as the Interlaken Frenchman said, the mountain summits are not the places for mountain views, the things do not look high when you are as high as they are; besides Monte Rosa, the Lyskamm, etc. did not make themselves; shape as well as size went: then the cold feet, the spectacles, the talk, and the lunching came in. Even with one companion ecstasy is almost banished: you want to be alone and to feel that, and leisure – all pressure taken off.

．　　．　　．　　．　　．　　．　　．

Feb. —, 1870.[2] One day in the Long Retreat (which ended on Xmas Day) they were reading in the refectory Sister Emmerich's

---

[1] *Sic* (archaic); 'peeping', 'winking'.
[2] Written at Manresa House, Roehampton, London, S.W.

account of the Agony in the Garden[1] and I suddenly began to cry
and sob and could not stop. I put it down for this reason, that if I
had been asked a minute beforehand I should have said that
nothing of the sort was going to happen and even when it did I
stood in a manner wondering at myself not seeing in my reason
the traces of an adequate cause for such strong emotion – the
traces of it I say because of course the cause in itself is adequate for
the sorrow of a lifetime. I remember much the same thing on
Maundy Thursday when the presanctified Host was carried to
the sacristy. But neither the weight nor the stress of sorrow, that
is to say of the thing which should cause sorrow, by themselves
move us or bring the tears as a sharp knife does not cut for being
pressed as long as it is pressed without any shaking of the hand
but there is always one touch, something striking sideways and
unlooked for, which in both cases undoes resistance and pierces,
and this may be so delicate that the pathos seems to have gone
directly to the body and cleared the understanding in its passage.
On the other hand the pathetic touch by itself, as in dramatic
pathos, will only draw slight tears if its matter is not important
or not of import to us, the strong emotion coming from a force
which was gathered before it was discharged: in this way a knife
may pierce the flesh which it had happened only to graze and only
grazing will go no deeper.

The winter was called severe. There were three spells of frost
with skating, the third beginning on Feb. 9. No snow to speak of
till that day. Some days before Feb. 7 I saw catkins hanging. On
the 9th there was snow but not lying on the roads. On the grass it
became a crust lifted on the heads of the blades. As we went down
a field near Caesar's Camp[2] I noticed it before me *squalentem*,[3] coat
below coat, sketched in intersecting edges bearing 'idiom', all
down the slope: – I have no other word yet for that which takes
the eye or mind in a bold hand or effective sketching or in marked

---

[1] In *The Dolorous Passion of Our Lord Jesus Christ; from the Meditations of
Anne Catherine Emmerich* (Eng. trans., 1862). Sister E. was an Augustinian
nun of Westphalia (1774–1824).

[2] An earthwork S. of Wimbledon Common.   [3] Stiff, crusted.

features or again in graphic writing, which not being beauty nor true inscape yet gives interest and makes ugliness even better than meaninglessness. – On the Common the snow was channelled all in parallels by the sharp driving wind and upon the tufts of grass (where by the dark colour shewing through it looked greyish) it came to turret-like clusters or like broken shafts of basalt. – In the Park[1] in the afternoon the wind was driving little clouds of snow-dust which caught the sun as they rose and delightfully took the eyes: flying up the slopes they looked like breaks of sunlight fallen through ravelled cloud upon the hills and again like deep flossy velvet blown to the root by breath which passed all along. Nearer at hand along the road it was gliding over the ground in white wisps that between trailing and flying shifted and wimpled like so many silvery worms to and from one another.

· · · · · · ·

March 12. A fine sunset: the higher sky dead clear blue bridged by a broad slant causeway rising from right to left of wisped or grass cloud, the wisps lying across; the sundown yellow, moist with light but ending at the top in a foam of delicate white pearling and spotted with big tufts of cloud in colour russet between brown and purple but edged with brassy light. But what I note it all for is this: before I had always taken the sunset and the sun as quite out of gauge with each other, as indeed physically they are, for the eye after looking at the sun is blunted to everything else and if you look at the rest of the sunset you must cover the sun, but today I inscaped them together and made the sun the true eye and ace of the whole, as it is. It was all active and tossing out light and started as strongly forward from the field as a long stone or a boss in the knop of the chalice-stem: it is indeed by stalling it so that it falls into scape with the sky.

The next morning a heavy fall of snow. It tufted and toed the firs and yews and went on to load them till they were taxed beyond their spring. The limes, elms, and Turkey-oaks it crisped

[1] The 'Park' was Richmond Park, which still adjoins the Manresa property, now earmarked for a housing estate.

beautifully as with young leaf. Looking at the elms from under-
neath you saw every wave in every twig (become by this the
wire-like stem to a finger of snow) and to the hangers and flying
sprays it restored, to the eye, the inscapes they had lost. They
were beautifully brought out against the sky, which was on one
side dead blue, on the other washed with gold.

. . . .

May 14. Wych-elms not out till today. – The chestnuts down
by St. Joseph's were a beautiful sight: each spike had its own pitch,
yet each followed in its place in the sweep with a deeper and
deeper stoop. When the wind tossed them they plunged and
crossed one another without losing their inscape. (Observe that
motion multiplies inscape only when inscape is discovered, other-
wise it disfigures)

May 18. Great brilliancy and projection: the eye seemed to fall
perpendicular from level to level along our trees, the nearer and
further Park; all things hitting the sense with double but direct
instress . . .

This was later. One day when the bluebells were in bloom I
wrote the following. I do not think I have ever seen anything
more beautiful than the bluebell I have been looking at. I know
the beauty of our Lord by it. It[s inscape][1] is [mixed of] strength
and grace, like an ash [tree]. The head is strongly drawn over
[backwards] and arched down like a cutwater [drawing itself back
from the line of the keel]. The lines of the bell strike and overlie
this, rayed but not symmetrically, some lie parallel. They look
steely against [the] paper, the shades lying between the bells and
behind the cockled petal-ends and nursing up the precision of
their distinctness, the petal-ends themselves being delicately lit.
Then there is the straightness of the trumpets in the bells softened
by the slight entasis and [by] the square splay of the mouth. One
bell, the lowest, some way detached and carried on a longer
footstalk, touched out with the tips of the petals an oval/not like
the rest in a plane perpendicular to the axis of the bell but a little

[1] G. M. H.'s brackets throughout.

atilt, and so with [the] square-in-rounding turns of the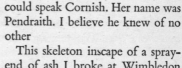
petals. . . . There is a little drawing of this detached bell.
It looks square-cut in the original

Drought up to Corpus Xti (June 16), on evening of which day
thunderstorm.

Aug. 25. A Captain Newman living in the Scilly Isles told my
father he had known an old lady (she is now some years dead) who
could speak Cornish. Her name was
Pendraith. I believe he knew of no
other

This skeleton inscape of a spray-
end of ash I broke at Wimbledon
that summer is worth noticing for
the suggested globe: it is leaf on the
left and keys on the right

Sept. 8. I took my vows[1]

Sept. 9. To Stonyhurst to the seminary

Sept. 24. First saw the Northern Lights. My eye was caught by
beams of light and dark very like the crown of horny rays the sun
makes behind a cloud. At first I thought of silvery cloud until I
saw that these were more luminous and did not dim the clearness
of the stars in the Bear. They rose slightly radiating thrown out
from the earthline. Then I saw soft pulses of light one after
another rise and pass upwards arched in shape but waveringly and
with the arch broken. They seemed to float, not following the
warp of the sphere as falling stars look to do but free though
concentrical with it. This busy working of nature wholly inde-
pendent of the earth and seeming to go on in a strain of time not
reckoned by our reckoning of days and years but simpler and as
if correcting the preoccupation of the world by being preoccupied
with and appealing to and dated to the day of judgment was like
a new witness to God and filled me with delightful fear

.   .   .   .

[1] i.e. first vows at the end of his two years' probation at Manresa House,
Roehampton.

1871

End of March and beginning of April – This is the time to study inscape in the spraying of trees, for the swelling buds carry them to a pitch which the eye could not else gather – for out of much much more, out of little not much, out of nothing nothing: in these sprays at all events there is a new world of inscape. The male ashes are very boldly jotted with the heads of the bloom which tuft the outer ends of the branches. The staff of each of these branches is closely knotted with the places where buds are or have been, so that it is something like a finger which has been tied up with string and keeps the marks. They are in knops of a pair, one on each side, and the knops are set alternately, at crosses with the knops above and the knops below, the bud of course is a short smoke-black pointed nail-head or beak pieced of four lids or nippers. Below it, like the hollow below the eye or the piece between the knuckle and the root of the nail, is a half-moon-shaped sill as if once chipped from the wood and this gives the twig its quaining[1] in the outline. When the bud breaks at first it shews a heap of fruity purplish anthers looking something like unripe elder-berries but these push open into richly-branched tree-pieces coloured buff and brown, shaking out loads of pollen, and drawing the tuft as a whole into peaked quains[1] – mainly four, I think, two bigger and two smaller

. . . .

April 22. But such a lovely damasking in the sky as today I never felt before. The blue was charged with simple instress, the higher, zenith sky earnest and frowning, lower more light and sweet. High up again, breathing through woolly coats of cloud or on the quains and branches of the flying pieces it was the true exchange of crimson, nearer the earth/ against the sun/ it was turquoise, and in the opposite south-western bay below the sun it was like clear oil but just as full of colour, shaken over with

[1] For 'quaining', 'quains', etc., see Note to poem No. 65, line 37, p. 249; also see Note B (p. 249).

slanted flashing 'travellers', all in flight, stepping one behind the other, their edges tossed with bright ravelling,[1] as if white napkins were thrown up in the sun but not quite at the same moment so that they were all in a scale down the air falling one after the other to the ground

. . . .

April 27. . . . Mesmerised a duck with chalk lines drawn from her beak sometimes level and sometimes forwards on a black table. They explain that the bird keeping the abiding offscape of the hand grasping her neck fancies she is still held down and cannot lift her head as long as she looks at the chalk line, which she associates with the power that holds her. This duck lifted her head at once when I put it down on the table without chalk. But this seems inadequate. It is most likely the fascinating instress of the straight white stroke

. . . .

May 9. . . . This day and May 11 the bluebells in the little wood between the College and the highroad and in one of the Hurst Green cloughs. In the little wood/ opposite the light/ they stood in blackish spreads or sheddings like the spots on a snake. The heads are then like thongs and solemn in grain and grape-colour. But in the clough/ through the light/ they came in falls of sky-colour washing the brows and slacks of the ground with vein-blue, thickening at the double, vertical themselves and the young grass and brake fern combed vertical, but the brake struck the upright of all this with light winged transomes. It was a lovely sight. – The bluebells in your hand baffle you with their inscape, made to every sense: if you draw your fingers through them they are lodged and struggle/ with a shock of wet heads; the long stalks rub and click and flatten to a fan on one another like your fingers themselves would when you passed the palms hard across one another, making a brittle rub and jostle like the noise of a hurdle strained by leaning against;[2] then there is the faint honey

[1] Cf. poem No. 49, ll. 1–2.   [2] Cf. poem No. 57, st. 3.

smell and in the mouth the sweet gum when you bite them. But this is easy, it is the eye they baffle. They give one a fancy of pan-pipes and of some wind instrument with stops – a trombone perhaps. The overhung necks – for growing they are little more than a staff with a simple crook but in water, where they stiffen, they take stronger turns, in the head like sheephooks or, when more waved throughout, like the waves riding through a whip that is being smacked – what with these overhung necks and what with the crisped ruffled bells dropping mostly on one side and the gloss these have at their footstalks they have an air of the knights at chess. Then the knot or 'knoop' of buds some shut, some just gaping, which makes the pencil of the whole spike, should be noticed: the inscape of the flower most finely carried out in the siding of the axes, each striking a greater and greater slant, is finished in these clustered buds, which for the most part are not straightened but rise to the end like a tongue and this and their tapering and a little flattening they have make them look like the heads of snakes

• • • • • • •

June 13. A beautiful instance of inscape sided on the slide, that is/ successive sidings[1] of one inscape, is seen in the behaviour of the flag flower from the shut bud to the full blowing: each term you can distinguish is beautiful in itself and of course if the whole 'behaviour' were gathered up and so stalled it would have a beauty of all the higher degree

• • • • • • •

June (Later). The Horned Violet is a pretty thing, gracefully lashed. Even in withering the flower ran through beautiful inscapes by the screwing up of the petals into straight little barrels or tubes. It is not that inscape does not govern the behaviour of things in slack and decay as one can see even in the pining of the skin in the old and even in a skeleton but that horror pre-

[1] i.e. 'modifications'. See *N*, p. 101.

possesses the mind, but in this case there was nothing in itself to shew even whether the flower were shutting or opening

The 'pinion' of the blossom in the comfrey is remarkable for the beauty of the coil and its regular lessening to its centre. Perhaps the duller-coloured sorts shew it best

. . . .

1872

Feb. 23. A lunar halo: I looked at it from the upstairs library window. It was a grave grained sky, the strands rising a little from left to right. The halo was not quite round, for in the first place it was a little pulled and drawn below, by the refraction of the lower air perhaps, but what is more it fell in on the nether left hand side to rhyme the moon itself, which was not quite at full. I could not but strongly feel in my fancy the odd instress of this, the moon leaning on her side, as if fallen back, in the cheerful light floor within the ring, after with magical rightness and success tracing round her the ring the steady copy of her own outline. But this sober grey darkness and pale light was happily broken through by the orange of the pealing of Mitton bells

Another night from the gallery window I saw a brindled heaven, the moon just marked by a blue spot pushing its way through the darker cloud, underneath and on the skirts of the rack bold long flakes whitened and swaled like feathers, below/ the garden with the heads of the trees and shrubs furry grey: I read a broad careless inscape flowing throughout

At the beginning of March they were felling some of the ashes in our grove

. . . .

July 19. The ovary of the blown foxglove surrounded by the green calyx is perhaps that conventional flower in Pointed and other floriated work which I could not before identify. It might also be St. John's-wort

Stepped into a barn of ours, a great shadowy barn, where the hay had been stacked on either side, and looking at the great rudely arched timberframes – principals(?) and tie-beams, which make them look like bold big *A's* with the cross-bar high up – I thought how sadly beauty of inscape was unknown and buried away from simple people and yet how near at hand it was if they had eyes to see it and it could be called out everywhere again. . . .

After the examinations we went for our holiday out to Douglas in the Isle of Man Aug. 3. At this time I had first begun to get hold of the copy of Scotus on the Sentences[1] in the Baddely library and was flush with a new stroke of enthusiasm. It may come to nothing or it may be a mercy from God. But just then when I took in any inscape of the sky or sea I thought of Scotus[2]

.   .   .   .

Aug. 10. I was looking at high waves. The breakers always are parallel to the coast and shape themselves to it except where the curve is sharp however the wind blows. They are rolled out by the shallowing shore just as a piece of putty between the palms whatever its shape runs into a long roll. The slant ruck or crease one sees in them shows the way of the wind. The regularity of the barrels surprised and charmed the eye; the edge behind the comb or crest was as smooth and bright as glass. It may be noticed to be green behind and silver white in front: the silver marks where the air begins, the pure white is foam, the green/ solid water. Then looked at to the right or left they are scrolled over like mouldboards or feathers or jibsails seen by the edge. It is pretty to see the hollow of the barrel disappearing as the white comb on each side runs along the wave gaining ground till the two meet at a pitch and crush and overlap each other

About all the turns of the scaping from the break and flooding of the wave to its run out again I have not yet satisfied myself. The shores are swimming and the eyes have before them a region

---

[1] His Commentary on the *Sentences* of Peter Lombard, known as the *Opus Oxoniense.* See Note N, p. 254.

[2] See Note to poem No. 21 and Introduction, pp. xxiii–xxv.

of milky surf but it is hard for them to unpack the huddling and gnarls of the water and law out the shapes and the sequence of the running: I catch however the looped or forked wisp made by every big pebble the backwater runs over – if it were clear and smooth there would be a network from their overlapping, such as can in fact be seen on smooth sand after the tide is out –; then I saw it run browner, the foam dwindling and twitched into long chains of suds, while the strength of the backdraught shrugged the stones together and clocked them one against another

Looking from the cliff I saw well that work of dimpled foam-laps – strings of short loops or halfmoons – which I had studied at Freshwater years ago

It is pretty to see the dance and swagging of the light green tongues or ripples of waves in a place locked between rocks

. . . .

Dec. 12. A Blandyke.[1] Hard frost, bright sun, a sky of blue 'water'. On the fells with Mr. Lucas.[2] Parlick Pike and that ridge ruddy with fern and evening light. Ground sheeted with taut tattered streaks of crisp gritty snow. Green-white tufts of long bleached grass like heads of hair or the crowns of heads of hair, each a whorl of slender curves, one tuft taking up another – however these I might have noticed any day. I saw the inscape though freshly, as if my eye were still growing, though with a companion the eye and the ear are for the most part shut and instress cannot come. We started pheasants and a grouse with flickering wings. On the slope of the far side under the trees the fern looked ginger-coloured over the snow. When there was no snow and dark greens about, as I saw it just over the stile at the top of the Forty-Acre the other day, it made bats and splinters of smooth caky road-rut-colour

. . . .

[1] Stonyhurst word for a monthly holiday.
[2] Herbert Lucas (1852–1933), Jesuit lecturer and author.

1873

Feb. 24. In the snow flat-topped hillocks and shoulders outlined with wavy edges, ridge below ridge, very like the grain of wood in line and in projection like relief maps. These the wind makes I think and of course drifts, which are in fact snow waves. The sharp nape of a drift is sometimes broken by slant flutes or channels. I think this must be when the wind after shaping the drift first has changed and cast waves in the body of the wave itself. All the world is full of inscape and chance left free to act falls into an order as well as purpose: looking out of my window I caught it in the random clods and broken heaps of snow made by the cast of a broom. The same of the path trenched by footsteps in ankledeep snow across the fields leading to Hodder wood through which we went to see the river. The sun was bright, the broken brambles and all boughs and banks limed and cloyed with white, the brook down the clough pulling its way by drops and by bubbles in turn under a shell of ice

In March there was much snow

April 8. The ashtree growing in the corner of the garden was felled. It was lopped first: I heard the sound and looking out and seeing it maimed there came at that moment a great pang and I wished to die and not to see the inscapes of the world destroyed any more[1]

.   .   .   .

June 16. . . . As I passed the stables later and stayed to look at the peacocks John Myerscough came out to shew me a brood of little peafowl (though it could not be found at that time) and the kindness touched my heart

I looked at the pigeons down in the kitchen yard and so on. They look like little gay jugs by shape when they walk, strutting and jod-jodding with their heads. The two young ones are all white and the pins of the folded wings, quill pleated over quill, are like crisp and shapely cuttleshells found on the shore. The others are dull thundercolour[2] or black-grape-colour except in the white pieings, the quills and tail, and in the shot of the neck. I saw

[1] Cf. poem No. 20.   [2] Cf. poem No. 22, l. 12.

one up on the eaves of the roof: as it moved its head a crush of satin green came and went, a wet or soft flaming of the light

Sometimes I hear the cuckoo with wonderful clear and plump and fluty notes: it is when the hollow of a rising ground conceives them and palms them up and throws them out, like blowing into a big humming ewer – for instance under Saddle Hill one beautiful day and another time from Hodder wood when we walked on the other side of the river[1]

.   .   .   .

July 22. Very hot, though the wind, which was south, dappled very sweetly on one's face and when I came out I seemed to put it on like a gown as a man puts on the shadow he walks into and hoods or hats himself with the shelter of a roof, a penthouse, or a copse of trees, I mean it rippled and fluttered like light linen, one could feel the folds and braids of it – and indeed a floating flag is like wind visible and what weeds are in a current; it gives it thew and fires it and bloods it in. – Thunderstorm in the evening, first booming in gong-sounds, as at Aosta, as if high up and so not reechoed from the hills; the lightning very slender and nimble and as if playing very near but after supper it was so bright and terrible some people said they had never seen its like. People were killed, but in other parts of the country it was more violent than with us. Flashes lacing two clouds above or the cloud and the earth started upon the eyes in live veins of rincing or riddling liquid white, inched and jagged as if it were the shivering of a bright riband string which had once been kept bound round a blade and danced back into its pleating. Several strong thrills of light followed the flash but a grey smother of darkness blotted the eyes if they had seen the fork, also dull furry thickened scapes of it were left in them

.   .   .   .

Aug. 1. To Derby Castle at Douglas [Isle of Man] as last year

.   .   .   .   .   .

Aug. 16. We rose at four, when it was stormy and I saw dun-
[1] Cf. poem No. 60.

coloured waves leaving trailing hoods of white breaking on the beach. Before going I took a last look at the breakers, wanting to make out how the comb is morselled so fine into string and tassel, as I have lately noticed it to be. I saw big smooth flinty waves, carved and scuppled in shallow grooves, much swelling when the wind freshened, burst on the rocky spurs of the cliff at the little cove and break into bushes of foam. In an enclosure of rocks the peaks of the water romped and wandered and a light crown of tufty scum standing high on the surface kept slowly turning round: chips of it blew off and gadded about without weight in the air. At eight we sailed for Liverpool in wind and rain. I think it is the salt that makes rain at sea sting so much. There was a good-looking young man on board that got drunk and sung 'I want to go home to Mamma'. I did not look much at the sea: the crests I saw ravelled up by the wind into the air in arching whips and straps of glassy spray and higher broken into clouds of white and blown away. Under the curl shone a bright juice of beautiful green. The foam exploding and smouldering under water makes a chrysoprase green. From Blackburn I walked: infinite stiles and sloppy fields, for there has been much rain. A few big shining drops hit us aslant as if they were blown off from eaves or leaves. Bright sunset: all the sky hung with tall tossed clouds, in the west with strong printing glass edges, westward lamping with tipsy bufflight, the colour of yellow roses. Parlick ridge like a pale goldfish skin without body. The plain about Clitheroe was sponged out by a tall white storm of rain. The sun itself and the spot of 'session' dappled with big laps and flowers-in-damask of cloud. But we hurried too fast and it knocked me up. We went to the College, the seminary being wanted for the secular priests' retreat: almost no gas, for the retorts are being mended; therefore candles in bottles, things not ready, darkness and despair. In fact being unwell I was quite downcast: nature in all her parcels and faculties gaped and fell apart, *fatiscebat*,[1] like a clod cleaving and holding only by strings of root. But this must often be

* * * * * * *

[1] 'Sank exhausted.'

1874

July 12. I noticed the smell of the big cedar, not just in passing it but always at a patch of sunlight on the walk a little way off. I found the bark smelt in the sun and not in the shade and I fancied too this held even of the smell it shed in the air

July 13. The comet – I have seen it at bedtime in the west, with head to the ground, white, a soft well-shaped tail, not big: I felt a certain awe and instress, a feeling of strangeness, flight (it hangs like a shuttlecock at the height, before it falls), and of threatening

．　．　．　．　．　．　．

July 23. To Beaumont: it was the rector's day. It was a lovely day: shires-long of pearled cloud under cloud, with a grey stroke underneath marking each row; beautiful blushing yellow in the straw of the uncut ryefields, the wheat looking white and all the ears making a delicate and very true crisping along the top and with just enough air stirring for them to come and go gently; then there were fields reaping. All this I would have looked at again in returning but during dinner I talked too freely and unkindly and had to do penance going home. One field I saw from the balcony of the house behind an elmtree, which it threw up, like a square of pale goldleaf, as it might be, catching the light

Our schools at Roehampton ended with two days of examination before St. Ignatius' feast the 31st. I was very tired and seemed deeply cast down till I had some kind words from the Provincial. Altogether perhaps my heart has never been so burdened and cast down as this year. The tax on my strength has been greater than I have felt before: at least now at Teignmouth I feel myself weak and can do little. But in all this our Lord goes His own way

．　．　．　．　．　．　．

Aug. 8. Walking in morning with Fr. Beiderlinden. Pretty farmyard at ——————[1] – thatch casting sharp shadow on whitewash[2]

[1] Gap in MS.　　　　　　　　[2] Cf. poem No. 49, line 3.

in the sun and a village rising beyond, all in a comb; sharp showers, bright clouds; sea striped with purple. In the evening I went by myself up the hills towards Bishopsteignton, by a place a little girl called Ke-am or Ku-am, perhaps she meant Coomb. Before reaching that, just out of Teignmouth, I looked over a hedge down to a row of seven slender rich elms at a bottom between two steep fields: the run of the trees and their rich and handsome leafage charmed and held me. It is a little nearer the sea in the same coomb the little girl spoke of indeed. Then near Bishopsteignton from a hilltop I looked into a lovely coomb that gave me the instress of *Weeping Winifred*, which all the west country seems to me to have: soft maroon or rosy cocoa-dust-coloured handkerchiefs of ploughfields, sometimes delicately combed with rows of green, their hedges bending in flowing outlines and now misted a little by the beginning of twilight ran down into it upon the shoulders of the hills; in the bottom crooked rows of rich tall elms, foreshortened by position, wound through it: some cornfields were still being carried

. . . .

Aug. 17. We went over to Ugbrooke at Lord Clifford's invitation. . . .
– I liked the family: all the children spoke in a very frank and simple way which shewed innocence as well as good breeding. As we drove home the stars came out thick: I leant back to look at them and my heart opening more than usual praised our Lord to and in whom all that beauty comes home[1]

. . . .

Sept. 6. With Wm. Kerr, who took me up a hill behind ours (ours is Mynefyr),[2] a furze-grown and heathy hill, from which I could look round the whole country, up the valley towards Ruthin and down to the sea. The cleave in which Bodfari and Caerwys lie was close below. It was a leaden sky, braided or

[1] Cf. poem No. 9.
[2] Near St. Beuno's College, Tremeirchion, N. Wales.

roped with cloud, and the earth in dead colours, grave but distinct. The heights by Snowdon were hidden by the clouds but not from distance or dimness. The nearer hills, the other side of the valley, shewed a hard and beautifully detached and glimmering brim against the light, which was lifting there. All the length of the valley the skyline of hills was flowingly written all along upon the sky. A blue bloom, a sort of meal, seemed to have spread upon the distant south, enclosed by a basin of hills. Looking all round but most in looking far up the valley I felt an instress and charm of Wales. Indeed in coming here I began to feel a desire to do something for the conversion of Wales. I began to learn Welsh[1] too but not with very pure intentions perhaps. However on consulting the Rector on this, the first day of the retreat, he discouraged it unless it were purely for the sake of labouring among the Welsh. Now it was not and so I saw I must give it up. At the same time my music seemed to come to an end. Yet, rather strangely, I had no sooner given up these two things (which disappointed me and took an interest away – and at that time I was very bitterly feeling the weariness of life and shed many tears, perhaps not wholly into the breast of God but with some unmanliness in them too, and sighed and panted to Him), I had no sooner given up the Welsh than my desire seemed to be for the conversion of Wales and I had it in mind to give up everything else for that; nevertheless weighing this by St. Ignatius' rules of election[2] I decided not to do so

· · · · · · ·

1875

On Feb. 4 and 5 1875 frost. On the 4th I walked with Hughes to Denbigh.

Denbigh is a taking picturesque town. Seen from here, as Henry Kerr says, it is always beautiful. The limekiln under a

[1] See Note C, p. 250.
[2] See *The Spiritual Exercises of St. Ignatius Loyola*, ed. J. Rickaby, p. 149, *et seq.* (or ed. W. H. Longridge, 3rd edn., pp. 125–32).

quarried cliff on this side of the town is always sending out a white smoke and this, and the greyer smoke of Denbigh, creeping upon the hill, what with sun and wind give fairy effects which are always changing

The day was bright, the sun sparkling through a frostfog which made the distance dim and the stack of Denbigh hill, as we came near, dead mealy grey against the light: the castle ruins, which crown the hill, were punched out in arches and half arches by bright breaks and eyelets of daylight. We went up to the castle but not in: standing before the gateway I had an instress which only the true old work gives from the strong and noble inscape of the pointedarch. We went to eat our lunch to a corner opening by a stone stile upon a wilderness by which you get down to the town, under the outer wall, overgrown with ivy, bramble, and some graceful herb with glossy lush green sprays, something like celery

Feb. 7. I asked Miss Jones in my Welsh lesson the Welsh for *fairy*, for we were translating Cinderella. She told me *cĭpenăper* (or perhaps *cĭpernăper*, *Anglice kippernapper*):* the word is nothing but *kidnapper*, moulded, according to their fashion, to give it a Welsh etymology, as she said, from *cĭpio/* to snatch, to whisk away. However in coming to an understanding between ourselves what fairies (she says *fairess* by the way for a she-fairy) and kippernappers were, on my describing them as little people 'that high', she told me quite simply that she had seen them. It was on or near the Holywell road (she indicated the spot). She was going to her grandfather's farm on the hill, not far from where Justice Williams lived, on the slope of the Rhuallt. It was a busy time, haymaking I think. She was going up at five o'clock in the morning, when she saw three little boys of about four years old wearing little frock coats† and odd little caps running and dancing

* She afterwards told me the true Welsh word *tolwyth-teg*. (G. M. H.'s note.)

† She afterwards called the coats long (*llaes*, that is/ trailing; perhaps unconfined by a girdle) and black. The caps or hats were round and black. (G. M. H.'s note.)

before her, taking hands and going round, then going further, still dancing and always coming together, she said. She would take no notice of them but went on to the house and there told them what she had seen and wondered that children could be out so early. 'Why she has seen the kippernappers' her grandmother said to her son, Susannah Jones' father. They were

(Here the extant Journal ends. – Ed.)

SERMON

FOR SUNDAY EVENING NOV. 23 1879 AT BEDFORD LEIGH[1] –
LUKE ii 33. *Et erat pater ejus et mater mirantes super his quae
dicebantur de illo* (text taken at random)

ST. JOSEPH though he often carried our Lord Jesus Christ in his
arms and the Blessed Virgin though she gave him birth and
suckled him at her breast, though they seldom either of them
had the holy child out of their sight and knew more of him far
than all others, yet when they heard what Holy Simeon a stranger
had to say of him the Scripture says they wondered. Not indeed
that they were surprised and had thought to hear something
different but that they gave their minds up to admiration and
dwelt with reverent wonder on all God's doings about the child
their sacred charge. Brethren, see what a thing it is to hear about
our Lord Jesus Christ, to think of him and dwell upon him; it
did good to these two holiest people, the Blessed Virgin and
St. Joseph, even with him in the house God thought fit to give
them lights by the mouth of strangers. It cannot but do good to
us, who have more need of holiness, who easily forget Christ, who
have not got him before our eyes to look at. And though we do
have him before our eyes, masked in the Sacred Host, at mass and
Benediction and within our lips receive him at communion, yet
to hear of him and dwell on the thought of him will do us good.

Our Lord Jesus Christ, my brethren, is our hero, a hero all the
world wants. You know how books of tales are written, that put
one man before the reader and shew him off handsome for the
most part and brave and call him My Hero or Our Hero. Often
mothers make a hero of a son; girls of a sweetheart and good
wives of a husband. Soldiers make a hero of a great general, a
party of its leader, a nation of any great man that brings it glory,
whether king, warrior, statesman, thinker, poet, or whatever it
shall be. But Christ, he is the hero.[2] He too is the hero of a book

---

[1] i.e. St. Joseph's, Bedford Leigh, near Manchester.
[2] Cf. poem No. 18, ll. 109–12, and Nos. 40 and 41.

or books, of the divine Gospels. He is a warrior and a conqueror; of whom it is written he went forth conquering and to conquer. He is a king, Jesus of Nazareth king of the Jews, though when he came to his own kingdom his own did not receive him, and now, his people having cast him off, we Gentiles are his inheritance. He is a statesman, that drew up the New Testament in his blood and founded the Roman Catholic Church that cannot fail. He is a thinker, that taught us divine mysteries. He is an orator and poet, as in his eloquent words and parables appears. He is all the world's hero, the desire of nations. But besides he is the hero of single souls; his mother's hero, not out of motherly foolish fondness but because he was, as the angel told her, great and the son of the Most High and all that he did and said and was done and said about him she laid up in her heart. He is the truelove and the bridegroom of men's souls; the virgins follow him whithersoever he goes; the martyrs follow him through a sea of blood, through great tribulation; all his servants take up their cross and follow him. And those even that do not follow him, yet they look wistfully after him, own him a hero, and wish they dared answer to his call. Children as soon as they can understand ought to be told about him, that they may make him the hero of their young hearts. But there are Catholic parents that shamefully neglect their duty: the grown children of Catholics are found that scarcely know or do not know his name. Will such parents say they left instruction to the priest or the schoolmaster? Why, if they sent them very early to the school they might make that excuse, but when they do not what will they say then? It is at the father's or the mother's mouth first the little one should learn. But the parents may be gossiping or drinking and the children have not heard of their lord and saviour. Those of you, my brethren, who are young and yet unmarried resolve that when you marry, if God should bless you with children, this shall not be but that you will have more pity, will have pity upon your own.

There met in Jesus Christ all things that can make man lovely and loveable. In his body he was most beautiful. This is known

first by the tradition in the Church that it was so and by holy
writers agreeing to suit those words to him/ Thou art beautiful
in mould above the sons of men:[1] we have even accounts of him
written in early times. They tell us that he was moderately tall,
well built and slender in frame, his features straight and beautiful,
his hair inclining to auburn, parted in the midst, curling and
clustering about the ears and neck as the leaves of a filbert, so they
speak, upon the nut. He wore also a forked beard and this as well
as the locks upon his head were never touched by razor or shears;
neither, his health being perfect, could a hair ever fall to the
ground. The account I have been quoting (it is from memory,
for I cannot now lay my hand upon it) we do not indeed for
certain know to be correct, but it has been current in the Church
and many generations have drawn our Lord accordingly either
in their own minds or in his images. Another proof of his beauty
may be drawn from the words *proficiebat sapientia et aetate et gratia
apud Deum et homines* (Luc. ii 52)/ he went forward in wisdom
and bodily frame and favour with God and men; that is/ he
pleased both God and men daily more and more by his growth
of mind and body. But he could not have pleased by growth of
body unless the body was strong, healthy, and beautiful that
grew. But the best proof of all is this, that his body was the
special work of the Holy Ghost. He was not born in nature's
course, no man was his father; had he been born as others are he
must have inherited some defect of figure or of constitution,
from which no man born as fallen men are born is wholly free
unless God interfere to keep him so. But his body was framed
directly from heaven by the power of the Holy Ghost, of whom
it would be unworthy to leave any the least botch or failing in his
work. So the first Adam was moulded by God himself and Eve
built up by God too out of Adam's rib and they could not but be
pieces, both, of faultless workmanship: the same then and much
more must Christ have been. His constitution too was tempered
perfectly, he had neither disease nor the seeds of any: weariness
he felt when he was wearied, hunger when he fasted, thirst when

[1] Ps. xliv. 3; A.V. xlv. 2.

he had long gone without drink, but to the touch of sickness he was a stranger. I leave it to you, brethren, then to picture him, in whom the fulness of the godhead dwelt bodily, in his bearing how majestic, how strong and yet how lovely and lissome in his limbs, in his look how earnest, grave but kind. In his Passion all this strength was spent, this lissomness crippled, this beauty wrecked, this majesty beaten down.[1] But now it is more than all restored, and for myself I make no secret I look forward with eager desire to seeing the matchless beauty of Christ's body in the heavenly light.

I come to his mind. He was the greatest genius that ever lived. You know what genius is, brethren – beauty and perfection in the mind. For perfection in the bodily frame distinguishes a man among other men his fellows: so may the mind be distinguished for its beauty above other minds and that is genius. Then when this genius is duly taught and trained, that is wisdom; for without training genius is imperfect and again wisdom is imperfect without genius. But Christ, we read, advanced in wisdom and in favour with God and men: now this wisdom, in which he excelled all men, had to be founded on an unrivalled genius. Christ then was the greatest genius that ever lived. You must not say, Christ needed no such thing as genius; his wisdom came from heaven, for he was God. To say so is to speak like the heretic Apollinaris, who said that Christ had indeed a human body but no soul, he needed no mind and soul, for his godhead, the Word of God, that stood for mind and soul in him. No, but Christ was perfect man and must have mind as well as body and that mind was, no question, of the rarest excellence and beauty; it was genius. As Christ lived and breathed and moved in a true and not a phantom human body and in that laboured, suffered, was crucified, died, and was buried; as he merited by acts of his human will; so he reasoned and planned and invented by acts of his own human genius, genius made perfect by wisdom of its own, not the divine wisdom only.

A witness to his genius we have in those men who being sent

[1] See note to poem No. 13 (p. 228).

to arrest him came back empty handed, spellbound by his elo-
quence, saying/ Never man spoke like this man.

A better proof we have in his own words, his sermon on the
mount, his parables, and all his sayings recorded in the Gospel.
My brethren, we are so accustomed to them that they do not
strike us as they do a stranger that hears them first, else we too
should say/Never man, etc. No stories or parables are like Christ's,
so bright, so pithy, so touching; no proverbs or sayings are such
jewellery: they stand off from other men's thoughts like stars,
like lilies in the sun; nowhere in literature is there anything to
match the Sermon on the Mount: if there is let men bring it
forward. Time does not allow me to call your minds to proofs
or instances. Besides Christ's sayings in the Gospels a dozen or
so more have been kept by tradition and are to be found in the
works of the Fathers and early writers and one even in the
Scripture itself: It is more blessed, etc.[1] When these sayings are
gathered together, though one cannot feel sure of every one, yet
reading all in one view they make me say/These must be Christ's,
never man etc. One is: Never rejoice but when you look upon
your brother in love. Another is: My mystery is for me and for
the children of my house.

And if you wish for another still greater proof of his genius
and wisdom look at this Catholic Church that he founded, its
ranks and constitution, its rites and sacraments.

Now in the third place, far higher than beauty of the body,
higher than genius and wisdom the beauty of the mind, comes
the beauty of his character, his character as man. For the most
part his very enemies, those that do not believe in him, allow that
a character so noble was never seen in human mould. Plato the
heathen, the greatest of the Greek philosophers, foretold of him;[2]
he drew by his wisdom a picture of the just man in his justice
crucified and it was fulfilled in Christ. Poor was his station,

---

[1] 'It is more blessed to give than to receive.' Acts xx. 35.
[2] In the *Republic*, 361e . . . 'the just man will be flogged, tortured', &c.
Cf. poem No. 5, st. 7, l. 7.

laborious his life, bitter his ending: through poverty, through labour, through crucifixion his majesty of nature more shines. No heart as his was ever so tender, but tenderness was not all: this heart so tender was as brave, it could be stern. He found the thought of his Passion past bearing, yet he went through with it. He was feared when he chose: he took a whip and singlehanded cleared the temple. The thought of his gentleness towards children, towards the afflicted, towards sinners, is often dwelt on; that of his courage less. But for my part I like to feel that I should have feared him. We hear also of his love, as for John and Lazarus; and even love at first sight, as of the young man that had kept all the commandments from his childhood. But he warned or rebuked his best friends when need was, as Peter, Martha, and even his mother. For, as St. John says, he was full both of grace and of truth.

But, brethren, from all that might be said of his character I single out one point and beg you to notice that. He loved to praise, he loved to reward. He knew what was in man, he best knew men's faults and yet he was the warmest in their praise. When he worked a miracle he would grace it with/ Thy faith hath saved thee, that it might almost seem the receiver's work, not his. He said of Nathanael that he was an Israelite without guile; he that searches hearts said this, and yet what praise that was to give! He called the two sons of Zebedee Sons of Thunder, kind and stately and honourable name! We read of nothing thunderlike that they did except, what was sinful, to wish fire down from heaven on some sinners, but they deserved the name or he would not have given it, and he has given it them for all time. Of John the Baptist he said that his greater was not born of women. He said to Peter/ Thou art Rock/ and rewarded a moment's acknowledgment of him[1] with the lasting headship of his Church. He defended Magdalen and took means that the story of her generosity should be told for ever. And though he bids *us* say we are unprofitable servants, yet he himself will say to each of us/ Good and faithful servant, well done.

[1] Cf. poem No. 5, st. 29, ll. 7–8.

And this man whose picture I have tried to draw for you, brethren, is your God. He was your maker in time past; hereafter he will be your judge. Make him your hero now. Take some time to think of him; praise him in your hearts. You can over your work or on your road praise him, saying over and over again/ Glory be to Christ's body; Glory to the body of the Word made flesh; Glory to the body suckled at the Blessed Virgin's breasts; Glory to Christ's body in its beauty; Glory to Christ's body in its weariness; Glory to Christ's body in its Passion, death and burial; Glory to Christ's body risen; Glory to Christ's body in the Blessed Sacrament; Glory to Christ's soul; Glory to his genius and wisdom; Glory to his unsearchable thoughts; Glory to his saving words; Glory to his sacred heart; Glory to its courage and manliness; Glory to its meekness and mercy; Glory to its every heartbeat, to its joys and sorrows, wishes, fears; Glory in all things to Jesus Christ God and Man. If you try this when you can you will find your heart kindle and while you praise him he will praise you – a blessing etc.

THE PRINCIPLE OR FOUNDATION

*An Address based on the opening of 'The Spiritual Exercises' of
St. Ignatius Loyola*[1]

[*Editor's note.* – The 'Principle and Foundation' (as it should be termed) begins: 'Man was created to praise, reverence, and serve God our Lord, and thereby to save his soul. And the other things on the face of the earth were created for man's sake, and to help him in the following out of the end for which he was created.' Having asked 'Why did God create?' and contrasted the purpose and general adequacy of inanimate creatures with the relative inadequacy of Man, the preacher concludes:]

But what we have not done yet we can do now, what we have done badly hitherto we can do well henceforward, we can repent our sins and BEGIN TO GIVE GOD GLORY. The moment we do this we reach the end of our being, we do and are what we were made for, we make it worth God's while to have created us. This is a comforting thought: we need not wait in fear till death; any day, any minute we bless God for our being or for anything, for food, for sunlight, we do and are what we were meant for, made for – things that give and mean to give God glory. This is a thing to live for. Then make haste so to live.

For IF YOU ARE IN SIN YOU ARE GOD'S ENEMY, you cannot love or praise him. You may say you are far from hating God; but if you live in sin you are among God's enemies, you are under Satan's standard and enlisted there; you may not like it, no wonder; you may wish to be elsewhere; but there you are, an enemy to God. It is indeed better to praise him than blaspheme, but the praise is not a hearty praise; it cannot be. You cannot mean your praise if while praise is on the lips there is no reverence in the mind; there can be no reverence in the mind if there is no obedience, no sub-mission, no service. And there can be no obeying God while you

[1] See Note D, p. 251.

disobey him, no service while you sin. Turn then, brethren, now and give God glory. You do say grace at meals and thank and praise God for your daily bread, so far so good, but thank and praise him now for everything. When a man is in God's grace and free from mortal sin, then everything that he does, so long as there is no sin in it, gives God glory and what does not give him glory has some, however little, sin in it. It is not only prayer that gives God glory but work. Smiting on an anvil, sawing a beam, whitewashing a wall, driving horses, sweeping, scouring, everything gives God some glory if being in his grace you do it as your duty. To go to communion worthily gives God great glory, but to take food in thankfulness and temperance gives him glory too. To lift up the hands in prayer gives God glory, but a man with a dungfork in his hand, a woman with a sloppail, give him glory too. He is so great that all things give him glory if you mean they should. So then, my brethren, live.

COMMENTS ON THE SPIRITUAL EXERCISES OF ST. IGNATIUS LOYOLA

On *Principium sive Fundamentum*[1]

'HOMO creatus est' – Aug. 20 1880: during this retreat, which I am making at Liverpool, I have been thinking about creation and this thought has led the way naturally through the exercises hitherto. I put down some thoughts. – We may learn that all things are created by consideration of the world without or of ourselves the world within. The former is the consideration commonly dwelt on, but the latter takes on the mind more hold. I find myself both as man and as myself something most determined and distinctive, at pitch, more distinctive and higher pitched than anything else I see; I find myself with my pleasures and pains, my powers and my experiences, my deserts and guilt, my shame and sense of beauty, my dangers, hopes, fears, and all my fate, more important to myself than anything I see. And when I ask where does all this throng and stack of being, so rich, so distinctive, so important, come from/ nothing I see can answer me. And this whether I speak of human nature or of my individuality, my selfbeing. For human nature, being more highly pitched, selved, and distinctive than anything in the world, can have been developed, evolved, condensed, from the vastness of the world not anyhow or by the working of common powers but only by one of finer or higher pitch and determination than itself and certainly than any that elsewhere we see, for this power had to force forward the starting or stubborn elements to the one pitch required. And this is much more true when we consider the mind; when I consider my selfbeing, my consciousness and feeling of myself, that taste of myself, of *I* and *me* above and in all things, which is more distinctive than the taste of ale or alum, more distinctive than the smell of walnutleaf or camphor, and is

[1] See preceding extract and Note D, on p. 251.

incommunicable by any means to another man (as when I was a child I used to ask myself: What must it be to be someone else?).[1] Nothing else in nature comes near this unspeakable stress of pitch, distinctiveness, and selving, this selfbeing of my own. Nothing explains it or resembles it, except so far as this, that other men to themselves have the same feeling. But this only multiplies the phenomena to be explained so far as the cases are like and do resemble. But to me there is no resemblance: searching nature I taste *self* but at one tankard, that of my own being. The development, refinement, condensation of nothing shews any sign of being able to match this to me or give me another taste of it, a taste even resembling it.

One may dwell on this further. We say that any two things however unlike are in something like. This is the one exception: when I compare my self, my being-myself, with anything else whatever, all things alike, all in the same degree, rebuff me with blank unlikeness; so that my knowledge of it, which is so intense, is from itself alone, they in no way help me to understand it. And even those things with which I in some sort identify myself, as my country or family, and those things which I own and call mine, as my clothes and so on, all presuppose the stricter sense of *self* and *me* and *mine* and are from that derivative.

From what then do I with all my being and above all that taste of self, that selfbeing, come? Am I due (1) to chance? (2) to myself, as selfexistent? (3) to some extrinsic power?

(1) Chance in name no one acknowledges as a cause or principle or explanation of being. But to call things positive facts and refuse further explanation is to explain them by chance. What then is chance proper, not chance as we use it for causes unknown or causes beside a present purpose? – Chance applies only to things possible; what must be does not come by chance and what cannot be by no chance comes. Chance then is the ἐνέργεια,[2] the stress, of the intrinsic possibility which things have. *A* chance is an event come about by its own intrinsic possibility. And as

---

[1] With this and the whole passage cf. the poems Nos. 22, 34, etc.
[2] Gk. – action, operation, energy.

mere possibility, passive power, is not power proper and has no
activity it cannot of itself come to stress, cannot instress itself.[1]
And in fact chance existence is a selfexistence. Chance is in-
credible or impossible by this *a priori* consideration, but more
strikingly is it incredible from experience. It is never verified and
the more examined the less is it verified, the more is it out of the
question. For if it is a chance for anything at any given instant to
exist and exist as so-and-so it is so for the next. These chances are
equal and in any finite time it is infinitely unlikely that it should
continue being and being what it was, for there are infinite
instants. It is incredible then that its continued existence should be
due to chance. If you say that its being is the mental flush of a
string of broken existences at very small average intervals, this is
incredible because monstrous. Moreover its nature should quite
change, for its parts might chance elsewhere and the parts of other
things here, and the variation will be infinite. The most plausible,
if anything is plausible here, is that virgin matter is due to chance,
other things not. But as this does not affect the present case it may
be let alone. No man then can believe that his being is due to
chance.

(2) Can I then be selfexistent and even in some way necessary? –
This is clearly not true of my body and that crowd of being in me
spoken of above, but may it be true of some part of it or some-
thing in it, *aliquid ejus*, the soul, the mind and its consciousness?

The mind and all my being is finite. This is plain in its outward
and inward operations. In its outward, for there is a resistance in
the body and things outside the body which it cannot overcome;
there is a degree of effort, pain, weariness to which it yields. And
in the inward; it has a finite insight, memory, grasp of appre-
hension, power of calculation, invention, force of will.

Nothing finite can exist of itself. For being finite it is limited
and determined in time and space, as the mind is limited and
determined to particular dates of time and place by the body.
And apart from the body it is determined. I say apart from the
body because it may be maintained that the mind has no bound

[1] Cf. poems No. 5, st. v, l. 7 and No. 28, l. 7.

from space nor even from time, for it may exist after death and may have existed before birth. Nevertheless it is finite in its own being, as said above, and determined. Its faculties compared one with another and compared with those of other minds are determined; they might be more, they might be less, they might be otherwise; they are then determined and distinctive. It is plain it might have more perfection, more being. Nevertheless the being it has got has a great perfection, a great stress, and is more distinctive and higher selved, than anything else I see, except other such minds, in nature. Now to be determined and distinctive is a perfection, either self-bestowed or bestowed from without. In anything finite it cannot be self-bestowed; nothing finite can determine its own being, I mean its being as a whole; nothing finite can determine what itself shall, in the world of being, be. For to determine is a perfection, greater than and certainly never less than, the perfection of being determined. It is a function of a nature, even if it should be the whole function, the naturing, the selving of that nature. It always in nature's order is after the nature it is of. Nothing finite then can either begin to exist or eternally have existed of itself, because nothing can in the order of time or even of nature act before it exists or exercise function and determination before it has a nature to 'function' and determine, to selve and instress, with; how much less then when the very determination is what the determiner itself is to be and the selving what its self shall be like! And this is above all true of that inmost self of mine which has been said to be and to be felt to be, to taste, more distinctive than the taste of clove or alum, the smell of walnutleaf or hart'shorn, more distinctive, more selved, than all things else and needing in proportion a more exquisite determining, selfmaking, power.

But is it as a last alternative possible that, though neither my body nor the faculties and functions of my soul exist of themselves, there should be one thing in the soul or mind, as if compounded or selved-up with these, which does? a most spiritual principle in some manner the form of the mind as the mind or the soul is said to be of the body; so that my mind would be one selving or pitch of a great universal mind, working in other minds too besides mine, and even in all other things, according to their natures and powers and becoming conscious in man. And this would be that very/ distinctive self that was spoken of. Here we touch the *intellectus agens* of the Averrhoists and the doctrine of the Hegelians and others.

Whether anything of this sort can be true or not, alike I find that I myself can not be selfexistent. I may treat the question from the side of my being, which is said to be compounded, selved-up, or identified with this universal mind, or from the side of the universal mind itself. And first from my side.

The universal mind being identified not only with me but also with all other minds cannot be the means of communicating what is individual in me to them nor in them to me. I have and every other has, as said above, my own knowledge and powers, pleasures, pains, merit, guilt, shame, dangers, fortunes, fates: we are not chargeable for one another. But these things and above all my shame, my guilt, my fate are the very things in feeling, in tasting, which I most taste, that selftaste which nothing in the world can match. The universal cannot taste this taste of self as I taste it,[1] for it is not to it, let us say/ to him, that the guilt or shame, the fatal consequence, the fate, comes home; either not at all or not altogether. If not at all, then he is altogether outside of my self, my personality/ one may call it, my *me*. If not altogether, if for instance there is something done or willed which I am wholly chargeable with and answerable for and he only so far as I am a part of him, a function or selving of his, then only so far is he answerable and chargeable, and this difference may make the difference of mortal and venial sin and of a happy or unhappy fate. Put it thus: suppose my little finger could have a being of its own, a personal being, without ceasing to be my finger and my using it and feeling in it; if now I hold it in the candleflame the pain of the burning, though the selfsame feeling of pain, experienced by me in my finger and by my finger in itself, will be nevertheless unlike in us two, for to my finger it is the scorching

[1] Cf. poem No. 44, ll. 9-14.

of its whole self, but to me the scorching only of one finger. And beyond this, taking it morally, if I have freely put my finger into the flame and the finger is unwilling, but unable to resist, then I am guilty of my folly and self-mutilation, but my finger is innocent; if on the other hand my finger is willing, then it is more guilty than I, for to me the loss of a finger is but mutilation, but to my finger itself it is selfmurder. Or if again it were selfsacrifice the sacrifice would be nobler in the finger, to which it was a holocaust, than in me, in whom it was the consuming of a part only. Though then I most intimately share my finger's feeling of pain, for indeed it is to me and to it one and the same, I do not share its feeling of self at all and share little, if I share any, of its guilt or merit, fortune and fate. So then the universal mind is outside of my inmost self and not within it; nor does it share my state, my moral standing, or my fate. And for all that this universal being may be at work in mine it leaves me finite: I am selfexistent none the more for any part the selfexistent plays in me. . . .

SELECTED LETTERS

I

TO C. N. LUXMOORE[1]

(Extract)

Oak Hill, Hampstead, N.W.
May 7, 1862.

Dear Luxmoore,

In the first place many thanks for your long and refreshing letter, for which I am not ungrateful though I may have delayed or rather been unable to answer it. Before proceeding to other matters I must endeavour to dispossess your mind of an extraordinary but firmly-seated idea that I wish to give you the cut which appears to have been smouldering on for a long time, and occasionally breaks out in your letters to Karslake and to me. If I could shew you the first page of one of your letters to me, written immediately after you left, I think you would see that all your misconceptions are of your own making, this said page being a tissue of curious contradictions. I will not send you 'a long and really untenable defence', as you advise, – I do not need one; Examinations speak for themselves. Before answering your questions I would remark that you were the very first who ever to my knowledge made Pelides (*i.e.* the son of Peleus, *i.e.* Achilles) a friend of Orestes (the son of Agamemnon)! A most extraordinary friendship! Can the classical Luxmoore mean Pylades by this funnily misplaced hero? However, you ask whether I am 'still cock of the walk at Elgin'. Why no. I am no longer an Elginite – I am a dayboarder. Fancy that of me! But it arose thus. Last quarter while working for the Exhibition I petitioned Dyne[2] for a private room to work in, representing to him the great disadvantage I was at compared with my rivals and indeed the

[1] C. N. Luxmoore (1844–1936); later a great friend of G. M. H.'s brother Arthur, under whom he studied painting.

[2] Rev. J. B. Dyne, D.D., Head Master of Highgate, 1838–1874.

whole sixth (for even the Grove-Bankites have their quiet sixth-
form room to hold three), in this respect. I alone in fact was forced
to work for the exhibition and keep order etc. at once, and in a
noisy room. He quite readily and ungrudgingly (though to be
sure Mrs. Rich pays him for her rooms, and he has no right to
do what he likes with them) granted me one of her rooms – the
sitting room, but Mrs. Chapple exchanged it for the bedroom.
Dyne added unasked that I might have a fire every evening; so I
was really quiet and comfortable for a little time. So far so good,
but shortly afterwards I got nearly expelled, deprived of the
testimonial which enables one to try for the ex. and degraded to
the bottom of the prefects for the most trifling ludicrous little
thing which I cannot relate at present and actually was turned
out of the room and had to make 6 apologies to avoid the other
punishments being inflicted. Dyne and I had a terrific altercation.
I was driven out of patience and cheeked him wildly, and he
blazed into me with his riding-whip. However Nesfield[1] and
Mrs. C. soon gave me back my room on their own responsi-
bility, repenting, I believe, of their shares in my punishment.
Shortly after this Bord's cards were discovered but happily in that
matter I was found irreproachable, but not so in the next case,
when like a fool I seized one of the upstairs candles on Sunday
night when they had taken ours away too soon and my room
was denied me for a week. Nesfield presently offered it me back
as a favour, but in such a way that I could not take it. Before,
however, it was time for me to resume possession I was in a worse
row than ever about absolutely nothing, with the chill off, and
an accident. Clarke,[2] my co-victim, was flogged, struck off the
confirmation list and fined £1; I was deprived of my room for
ever, sent to bed at half past nine till further orders, and ordered
to work *only* in the school room, not even in the school library
and might not sit on a window sill on the staircase to read. Dyne
had repeatedly said he hoped I might not be at the top of the
school after the exam., so you may suppose, when he took these

---

[1] J. C. Nesfield (1836–1919), author of several widely-used English text-
books.   [2] See Note E, p. 251.

last measures, I drew my own conclusions. Next – was late on
Sunday; I was exemplary on other days but took Sunday as a
'day of rest' too literally, consequently the fifth time, Dyne
having heard, sent me to bed at nine and for the third time this
quarter threatened expulsion, deprivation. . . .

II

TO A. W. M. BAILLIE[1]

(Extracts)

Blunt House, Croydon, S.
Sept. 10, 1864.

Dear Baillie,[2]

Your letter has been sent to me from Hampstead. It has just
come, and I do a rare thing with me, begin at once on an answer.
I have just finished *The Philippics* of Cicero and an hour remains
before bedtime; no one except Wharton would begin a new book
at that time of night, so I was reading *Henry IV*, when your letter
was brought in – a great enjoyment.

The letter-writer on principle does not make his letter only an
answer; it is a work embodying perhaps answers to questions put
by his correspondent but that is not its main motive. Therefore
it is as a rule not well to write with a received letter fresh on you.
I suppose the right way is to let it sink into you, and reply after a
day or two. I do not know why I have said all this.

Do you know, a horrible thing has happened to me. I have
begun to *doubt* Tennyson. (Baillejus ap. Hopk.) It is a great
argumentum, a great clue, that our minds jump together even if it
be a leap into the dark. I cannot tell you how amused and I must

---

[1] See Note F, p. 251.
[2] G. M. H. usually put the salutation into the first line, thus
   'Dearest Bridges, – Many thanks. . . . '
Here and throughout I have adopted the more regular form. (Ed.)

say pleased and comforted by this coincidence I am. A little explanation first. You know I do not mistrust my judgment as soon as you do; I say it to the praise of your modesty. Therefore I do not think myself 'getting into my dotage' for that, and I will shew why. I think (I am assuming a great deal in saying this I fear) I may shew, judging from my own mind, how far we are both of us right in this, and on what, if I may use the word, more *enlightened* ground we may set our admiration of Tennyson. I have been thinking about this on and off since I read *Enoch Arden* and the other new poems, so that my judgment is more digested than if the ideas had only struck me while answering you. I was shaken too you know by Addis, which makes a good deal of difference.

I am meditating an essay, perhaps for the *Hexameron*,[1] on some points of poetical criticism, and it is with reference to this a little that I have composed my thoughts on Tennyson. I think then the language of verse may be divided into three kinds. The first and highest is poetry proper, the language of inspiration. The word inspiration need cause no difficulty. I mean by it a mood of great, abnormal in fact, mental acuteness, either energetic or receptive, according as the thoughts which arise in it seem generated by a stress and action of the brain, or to strike into it unasked.[2] This mood arises from various causes, physical generally, as good health or state of the air or, prosaic as it is, length of time after a meal. But I need not go into this; all that it is needful to mark is, that the poetry of inspiration can only be written in this mood of mind, even if it only last a minute, by poets themselves. Everybody of course has like moods, but not being poets what they then produce is not poetry. The second kind I call *Parnassian*. It can only be spoken by poets, but is not in the highest sense poetry. It does not require the mood of mind in which the poetry of inspiration is written. It is spoken *on and from the level* of a poet's mind, not, as in the other case, when the inspiration, which is the gift of genius, raises him above himself. For I think it is the case with genius that it is not when quiescent so very much above mediocrity as the difference between the two might lead us to think, but that it has the power and privilege of rising from that level to a height utterly far from mediocrity: in other words that its greatness is *that it can be* so great. You will understand. *Parnassian* then is that language which genius speaks as fitted to its exaltation, and place among other genius, but does not sing (I have been betrayed into the whole hog of a metaphor) in its flights. Great men, poets I mean, have each their own dialect as it were of Parnassian, formed generally as they go on writing, and at last, – this is the point to be marked, – they can see things in this Parnassian way and describe them in this Parnassian tongue, without further effort of inspiration. In a poet's particular kind of Parnassian lies most of his style, of his manner, of his mannerism if you like. But I must not go farther without giving you instances of Parnassian. I shall take one from Tennyson, and from *Enoch Arden*, from a passage much quoted already and which will be no doubt often quoted, the description of Enoch's tropical island.[1]

> The mountain wooded to the peak, the lawns
> And winding glades high up like ways to Heaven,
> The slender coco's drooping crown of plumes,
> The lightning flash of insect and of bird,
> The lustre of the long convolvuluses
> That coil'd around the stately stems, and ran
> Ev'n to the limit of the land, the glows
> And glories of the broad belt of the world,
> All these he saw.

Now it is a mark of Parnassian that one could conceive oneself writing it if one were the poet. Do not say that *if* you were Shakespear you can imagine yourself writing Hamlet, because that is just what I think you *cannot* conceive. In a fine piece of inspiration every beauty takes you as it were by surprise, not of course that you did not think the writer could be so great, for that is not it, – indeed I think it is a mistake to speak of people admiring Shakespear more and more as they live, for when the judgment is

[1] ll. 572–80.

ripe and you have read a good deal of any writer including his best things, and carefully, then, I think, however high the place you give him, that you must have rated him equally with his merits however great they be; so that all after admiration cannot increase but keep alive this estimate, make his greatness stare into your eyes and din it into your ears, as it were, but not make it greater, – but to go on with the broken sentence, every fresh beauty could not in any way be predicted or accounted for by what one has already read. But in Parnassian pieces you feel that if you were the poet you could have gone on as he has done, you see yourself doing it, only with the difference that if you actually try you find you cannot write his Parnassian. Well now to turn to the piece above. The glades being 'like ways to Heaven' is, I think, a new thought, it is an inspiration. Not so the next line, that is pure Parnassian. If you examine it the words are choice and the description is beautiful and unexceptionable, but it does not *touch* you. The next is more Parnassian still. In the next lines I think the picture of the convolvuluses does touch; but only the picture: the words are Parnassian. It is a very good instance, for the lines are undoubtedly beautiful, but yet I could scarcely point anywhere to anything more idiomatically Parnassian, to anything which I more clearly see myself writing *qua* Tennyson, than the words

> The glows
> And glories of the broad belt of the world.

What Parnassian is you will now understand, but I must make some more remarks on it. I believe that when a poet palls on us it is because of his Parnassian. We seem to have found out his secret. Now in fact we have not found out more than this, that when he is not inspired and in his flights, his poetry does run in an intelligibly laid down path. Well, it is notorious that Shakespear does not pall, and this is because he uses, I believe, so little Parnassian. He does use some, but little. Now judging from my own experience I should say no author palls so much as Wordsworth; this is because he writes such an 'intolerable deal of' Parnassian.

If with a critical eye and in a critical appreciative mood you read a poem by an unknown author or an anonymous poem by a known, but not at once recognisable, author, and he is a real poet, then you will pronounce him so at once, and the poem will seem truly inspired, though afterwards, when you know the author, you will be able to distinguish his inspirations from his Parnassian, and will perhaps think the very piece which struck you so much at first mere Parnassian. You know well how deadened, as it were, the critical faculties become at times, when all good poetry alike loses its clear ring and its charm; while in other moods they are so enlivened that things that have long lost their freshness strike you with their original definiteness and piquant beauty.

I think one had got into the way of thinking, or had not got out of the way of thinking, that Tennyson was always new, *touching*, beyond other poets, not pressed with human ailments, never using Parnassian. So at least I used to think. Now one sees he uses Parnassian; he is, one must see it, what we used to call Tennysonian. But the discovery of this must not make too much difference. When puzzled by one's doubts it is well to turn to a passage like this. Surely your maturest judgment will never be fooled out of saying that this is divine, terribly beautiful – the stanza of *In Memoriam*[1] beginning with the quatrain

> O Hesper o'er the buried sun,
>   And ready thou to die with him,
>   Thou watchest all things ever dim
> And dimmer, and a glory done.

I quote from memory. Inconsequent conclusion: Shakespear is and must be utterly the greatest of poets.

Just to end what I was saying about poetry. There is a higher sort of Parnassian which I call *Castalian*, or it may be thought the lowest kind of inspiration. Beautiful poems may be written wholly in it. Its peculiarity is that though you can hardly conceive yourself having written in it, if in the poet's place, yet it is too

[1] CXXI. 'Sad Hesper . . .'

characteristic of the poet, too so-and-so-all-over-ish, to be quite inspiration. E.g.

> Yet despair
> Touches me not, though pensive as a bird
> Whose vernal coverts winter hath laid bare.

This is from Wordsworth[1], beautiful, but rather too essentially Wordsworthian, too persistently his way of looking at things. The third kind is merely the language of verse as distinct from that of prose, Delphic, the tongue of the Sacred *Plain*, I may call it, used in common by poet and poetaster. Poetry when spoken is spoken in it, but to speak it is not necessarily to speak poetry. I may add there is also *Olympian*. This is the language of strange masculine genius which suddenly, as it were, forces its way into the domain of poetry, without naturally having a right there. Milman's poetry is of this kind I think, and Rossetti's *Blessed Damozel*. But unusual poetry has a tendency to seem so at first. . . .

Read if you can a paper on *The ethics of friendship* in the September *Cornhill*. It is good and worth reading. Do you read *The Mutual Friend*? The reviews will most likely be unkindly severe on it. Dickens' literary history is melancholy to me, yet to take that view of him which is taken or will be by some people is not just or balanced. You must also read, if you have not done so, Matthew Arnold on *The literary influence of Academies* in the August *Cornhill*. Much that he says is worth attention, but, as is so often the case, in censuring bad taste he falls into two flagrant pieces of bad taste himself. I am coming to think much of taste myself, good taste and moderation, I who have sinned against them so much. But there is a prestige about them which is indescribable.

What do you think? It occurred to me that the story of *Floris in Italy* is dramatic, and all of a sudden I began to turn it into a

[1] Sonnet beginning 'Jones! when from Calais...' (1802). In 1827 the end was changed to

> 'Yet despair
> I feel not: happy am I as a Bird:
> Fair seasons yet will come, and hopes as fair.'

play. It is a great experiment. I shall alter the plot to suit require-
ments a little. I fancy there is a fascination about the dramatic
form. Beside this I have done very little since I wrote last, except
three verses, a fragment, being a description of Io (transformed
into a heifer). It sounds odd.

I have been reading the twelve first (which is it? The first twelve
then) books of the *Odyssey*, and have begun to receive Homer in
earnest. How great his dramatic power is! Do you know, I am
going, not at once of course, to reach Petronius Arbiter. I am
though.

You must be tired of Parnassian by this time. I must however
add a few words left out. A great deal of Parnassian lowers a
poet's average, and more than anything else lowers his fame I fear.
This is in the main what is meant by artificial poetry; it is all
Parnassian. When one reads Pope's Homer with a critical eye one
sees, artificial as it is, in every couplet that he was a great man,
but no doubt to an uncritical humour and an uncritical flippant
modernist it does offer a great handle. . . .

III

TO E. H. COLERIDGE[1]

Balliol College, Oxford.
Jan. 22, 1866.

Dear Coleridge,

I never wrote to congratulate you on your best essay wh. I
meant to do. I was sincerely proud of you, and I had half thought
beforehand it might be so.

I have thought often since you were here of what you said
about the particular shape in wh. the doctrine of eternal punish-
ment presented itself with offence to you. You said you know yr.
repugnance was to view the issues of eternity as depending on
anything so trivial and inadequate as life is. I do understand the

[1] 1846-1920: grandson of S. T. Coleridge, he was at Balliol College
from 1866 to 1870.

point of view. But I think the answer wh. I gave then comes at once – that in fact the argument tells the other way, because it is incredible and intolerable if there is nothing which is the reverse of trivial and will correct and avenge the triviality of this life. To myself all this trivialness is one of the strongest reasons for the opposite belief and is always in action more or less. Of course it is plain too that the belief in the future of theology destroys the triviality in proportion to its intensity. I think certainly that strong beliefs make ordinary goings on look more ridiculously trivial than they wd. otherwise, but then the trivialness is one to wh. oneself does not belong and fr. wh. one longs to bring other people. However this is to the same effect as what I said before; but I have thought of something wh. will weigh perhaps more as not being merely a reversal of yr. argument. I think that the trivial-ness of life is, and personally to each one, ought to be seen to be, done away with by the Incarnation – or, I shd. say the difficulty wh. the trivialness of life presents ought to be. It is one adorable point of the incredible condescension of the Incarnation (the greatness of which no saint can have ever hoped to realise) that our Lord submitted not only to the pains of life, the fasting, scourging, crucifixion etc, or the insults, as the mocking, blind-folding, spitting etc, but also to the mean and trivial accidents of humanity. It leads one naturally to rhetorical antithesis to think for instance that after making the world He shd. consent to be taught carpentering, and, being the eternal Reason, to be cate-chised in the theology of the Rabbins. It seems therefore that if the Incarnation cd. *versari inter*[1] trivial men and trivial things it is not surprising that our reception or non-reception of its benefits shd. be also amidst trivialities.

Buchanan (Buchannan?)[2] had no further message for you than that he was here. I see too that Ball[3] is up. Believe me always yr. affectionate friend,

Gerard Hopkins.

[1] 'be, take place, among . . .'

[2] T. R. Buchanan, a brilliant Balliol man who became a barrister and M.P. for the Western Division of Edinburgh.

[3] F. J. Ball of Pembroke College; later Rector of East Mersea.

IV

TO THE REV. DR. JOHN H. NEWMAN[1]

Oak Hill, Hampstead, N.W.
Aug. 28, 1866.

Reverend Sir,

I address you with great hesitation knowing that you are in the midst of yr. own engagements and because you must be much exposed to applications from all sides. I am anxious to become a Catholic, and I thought that you might possibly be able to see me for a short time when I pass through Birmingham in a few days, I believe on Friday. But I feel most strongly the injustice of intruding on yr. engagements or convenience and therefore, if that is the case, I shall think it a favour if you will kindly let me know that you are unable to see me. I do not want to be helped to any conclusions of belief, for I am thankful to say my mind is made up, but the necessity of becoming a Catholic (although I had long foreseen where the only consistent position wd. lie) coming upon me suddenly has put me into painful confusion of mind about my immediate duty in my circumstances. I wished also to know what it wd. be morally my duty to hold on certain formally open points, because the same reasoning which makes the Tractarian ground contradictory wd. almost lead one also to shrink from what Mr. Oakley calls a minimising Catholicism. I say this much to take fr. you any hesitation in not allowing me to come to Birmingham if duties shd. stand in the way: you will understand that by God's mercy I am clear as to the sole authority of the Church of Rome. While much in doubt therefore as to my right to trouble you by this application, I wd. not deny at the same time that I shd. feel it the greatest privilege to see you. If it were so, I shd. hope not to detain you long. I may perhaps in some way introduce myself by reminding you of an

---

[1] Then at the Birmingham Oratory, which he founded in 1847. He was created Cardinal in 1879.

intimate college friend of mine, William Addis,[1] who once had the pleasure of spending an hour with you at the Oratory; I think also he has written to you since: I have little doubt that in not a very long time he will become a Catholic. If I shd. be so happy as to hear before Friday that you cd. spare time to see me, I shd. hope to be at Birmingham that day and sleep there, or if you had any convenient time in the two or three weeks after that I shd. like to come over fr. Rochdale where I shall be staying at Dr. Molesworth's. But in ending I wd. again say that I beg you will have no hesitation, as I have no doubt you will not, in declining to see me if you think best.

Believe me, Reverend Sir, your obedient servant,

Gerard M. Hopkins.

V

TO THE REV. DR. JOHN H. NEWMAN

18 New Inn Hall Street, Oxford.
St. Theresa (15 Oct.) 1866.

Very Reverend Father,

I have been up at Oxford just long enough to have heard fr. my father and mother in return for my letter announcing my conversion. Their answers are terrible: I cannot read them twice. If you will pray for them and me just now I shall be deeply thankful. But what I am writing for is this – they urge me with the utmost entreaties to wait till I have taken my degree – more than half a year. Of course it is impossible, and since it is impossible to wait as long as they wish it seems to me useless to wait at all. Wd. you therefore wish me to come to Birmingham at once, on Thursday, Friday, or Saturday? You will understand why I have any hesitation at all, namely because if immediately

---

[1] William E. Addis (1844–1917) was received into the R.C. Church just before G. M. H. See Letters V and XXVII, and also Note G, p. 251.

after their letters urging a long delay I am received without any, it will be another blow and look like intentional cruelty. I did not know till last night the rule about *communicatio in sacris*[1] – at least as binding catechumens, but I now see the alternative thrown open, either to live without Church and sacraments or else, in order to avoid the Catholic Church, to have to attend constantly the services of that very Church. This brings the matter to an absurdity and makes me think that any delay, whatever relief it may be to my parents, is impossible. I am asking you then whether I shall at all costs be received at once.

Strange to say of four conversions mine is the earliest and yet my reception will be last. I think I said that my friend William Garrett was converted and received shortly after hearing of my conversion; just before term began another friend, Alexander Wood, wrote to me in perplexity, and when I wrote back to his surprise telling him I was a convert he made up his own mind the next morning and is being received today; by a strange chance he met Addis in town and Addis, who had put off all thought of change for a year, was by God's mercy at once determined to see a priest and was received at Bayswater the same evening – Saturday. All our minds you see were ready to go at a touch and it cannot but be that the same is the case with many here. Addis' loss will be deep grief to Dr. Pusey I think: he has known him so long and stayed with him at Chale in a retreat.

I shall ask F. William Neville to open and answer this in your absence.

Monsignor Eyre seemed to say that I ought not to make my confession by means of a paper as I have been used to do. Will you kindly say whether you wd. prefer it so or not?

Believe me, dear Father, your affectionate son in Christ,

Gerard M. Hopkins.

P.S. And if you shd. bid me be received at once will you kindly name the day? The liberality of the college authorities will throw no hindrance in the way.

[1] Rule forbidding Catholics to co-operate in worship with non-Catholics.

VI

TO HIS FATHER[1]

Oxford.

Oct. 16 [1866]

My dear Father,

I must begin with a practical immediate point. The Church strictly forbids all communion in sacred things with non-Catholics. I have only just learnt this, but it prevents me going to chapel, and so yesterday I had to inform the Dean of Chapel. Today the Master sent for me and said he cd. not grant me leave of absence without an application from you. As the College last term passed a resolution admitting Catholics and took a Catholic into residence it has no right to alter its principle in my case. I wish you therefore not to give yourself the pain of making this application, even if you were willing: I am of age moreover and am alone concerned. If you refuse to make the application, the Master explains that he shall lay my case before the common-room. In this case there is very little doubt indeed that the Fellows wd. take the reasonable course and give me leave of absence fr. chapel, and if not, I am quite contented: but in fact I am satisfied as to the course our Fellows will take and the Master will at the last hesitate to lay the matter before them perhaps even. I want you therefore to write at once, if you will, – not to the Master who has no right to ask what he does, but to me, with a refusal: no harm will follow.

The following is the position of things with me. You ask me to suspend my judgment for a long time, or at the very least more than half a year, in other words to stand still for a time. Now to stand still is not possible, thus: I must either obey the Church or disobey. If I disobey, I am not suspending judgment but deciding, namely, to take backward steps fr. the grounds I have already come to. To stand still if it were possible might be justifiable, but to go back nothing can justify. I must therefore obey the Church by ceasing to attend any service of the Church of England. If I am

[1] See note L, p. 253.

to wait then I must either be altogether without services and sacraments, which you will of course know is impossible, or else I must attend the services of the Church – still being unreceived. But what can be more contradictory than, in order to avoid joining the Church, attending the services of that very Church? Three of my friends, whose conversions were later than mine, Garrett, Addis, and Wood, have already been received, but this is by the way. Only one thing remains to be done: I cannot fight against God Who calls me to His Church: if I were to delay and die in the meantime I shd. have no plea why my soul was not forfeit. I have no power in fact to stir a finger: it is God Who makes the decision and not I.

But you do not understand what is involved in asking me to delay and how little good you wd. get from it. I shall hold as a Catholic what I have long held as an Anglican, that literal truth of our Lord's words by which I learn that the least fragment of the consecrated elements in the Blessed Sacrament of the Altar is the whole Body of Christ born of the Blessed Virgin, before which the whole host of saints and angels as it lies on the altar trembles with adoration. This belief once got is the life of the soul and when I doubted it I shd. become an atheist the next day. But, as Monsignor Eyre says, it is a gross superstition unless guaranteed by infallibility. I cannot hold this doctrine confessedly except as a Tractarian or a Catholic: the Tractarian ground I have seen broken to pieces under my feet. What end then can be served by a delay in wh. I shd. go on believing this doctrine as long as I believed in God and shd. be by the fact of my belief drawn by a lasting strain towards the Catholic Church?

About my hastiness I wish to say this. If the question which is the Church of Christ? cd. only be settled by laborious search, a year and ten years and a lifetime are too little, when the vastness of the subject of theology is taken into account. But God must have made his Church such as to attract and convince the poor and unlearned as well as the learned. And surely it is true, though it will sound pride to say it, that the judgment of one who has seen both sides for a week is better than his who has seen only one for a lifetime. I am surprised you shd. say fancy and aesthetic tastes have led me to my present state of mind: these wd. be better satisfied in the Church of England, for bad taste is always meeting one in the accessories of Catholicism. My conversion is due to the following reasons mainly (I have put them down without order) – (i) simple and strictly drawn arguments partly my own, partly others', (ii) common sense, (iii) reading the Bible, especially the Holy Gospels, where texts like 'Thou art Peter' (the evasions proposed for this alone are enough to make one a Catholic) and the manifest position of St. Peter among the Apostles so pursued me that at one time I thought it best to stop thinking of them, (iv) an increasing knowledge of the Catholic system (at first under the form of Tractarianism, later in its genuine place), which only wants to be known in order to be loved – its consolations, its marvellous ideal of holiness, the faith and devotion of its children, its multiplicity, its array of saints and martyrs, its consistency and unity, its glowing prayers, the daring majesty of its claims, etc. etc. You speak of the claims of the Church of England, but it is to me the strange thing that the Church of England makes no claims: it is true that Tractarians make them for her and find them faintly or only in a few instances borne out for them by her liturgy, and are strongly assailed for their extravagances while they do it. Then about applying to Mr. Liddon and the Bp. of Oxford. Mr. Liddon writes begging me to pause: it wd. take too long to explain how I did not apply to him at first and why it wd. have been useless. If Dr. Pusey is in Oxford tomorrow I will see him, if it is any satisfaction to you. The Bishop is too much engaged to listen to individual difficulties and those who do apply to him may get such answers as young Mr. Lane Fox did, who gave up £30,000 a year just lately to become a Catholic. He wrote back about a cob which he wanted to sell to the Dean of some place and wh. Lane Fox was to put his own price on and ride over for the Bishop to the place of sale. In fact Dr. Pusey and Mr. Liddon were the only two men in the world who cd. avail to detain me: the fact that they were Anglicans kept me one, for arguments for the Church of England I had long ago felt there were none that wd. hold water, and when that influence gave way everything was gone.

You are so kind as not to forbid me your house, to which I have no claim, on condition, if I understand, that I promise not to try to convert my brothers and sisters. Before I can promise this I must get permission, wh. I have no doubt will be given. Of course this promise will not apply after they come of age. Whether after my reception you will still speak as you do now I cannot tell.

You ask me if I have had no thought of the estrangement. I have had months to think of everything. Our Lord's last care on the cross was to commend His mother to His Church and His Church to His mother in the person of St. John. If even now you wd. put yourselves into that position wh. Christ so unmistakeably gives us and ask the Mother of sorrows to remember her three hours' compassion at the cross, the piercing of the sword prophecied by Simeon, and her seven dolours, and her spouse Joseph, the lily of chastity, to remember the flight into Egypt, the searching for his Foster-Son at twelve years old, and his last ecstacy with Christ at his death-bed, the prayers of this Holy Family wd. in a few days put an end to estrangements for ever. If you shrink fr. doing this, though the Gospels cry aloud to you to do it, at least for once – if you like, only once – approach Christ in a new way in which you will at all events feel that you are exactly in unison with me, that is, not vaguely, but casting yourselves into His sacred broken Heart and His five adorable Wounds. Those who do not pray to Him in His Passion pray to God but scarcely to Christ. I have the right to propose this, for I have tried both ways, and if you will not give one trial to this way you will see you are prolonging the estrangement and not I.

After saying this I feel lighter-hearted, though I still can by no means make my pen write what I shd. wish. I am your loving son.

Gerard M. Hopkins.

P.S. I am most anxious that you shd. not think of my future. It is likely that the positions you wd. like to see me in wd. have no attraction for me, and surely the happiness of my prospects depends on the happiness to me and not on intrinsic advantages. It is possible even to be very sad and very happy at once and the time that I was with Bridges, when my anxiety came to its height, was I believe the happiest fortnight of my life. My only strong wish is to be independent.

If you are really willing to make the application to the Master, well and good; but I do not want you to put yourself to pain. I have written a remonstrance to him.

Many thanks to Arthur for his letter.

VII

TO A. W. M. BAILLIE
(Extract)

The Oratory,
[Edgbaston].
Feb. 12, 1868.

My dear Baillie,

Though my unwillingness to write letters, important or unimportant, now amounts to a specific craze I see quite fixedly that not to do so is virtually to see and hear no more of you. But even now that I have just begun I seem suddenly to have everything to say and an impatience to do little else than to communicate myself εἰς ἄπειρον.[1] I am very much obliged to you for your letters for many reasons, and you must remember that I normally need the spur. I will answer yr. questions before anything else. About *Ecce Homo*,[2] I am ashamed to be in the position I am but the truth is I have not read it: somehow the very kind of notoriety it had made me not care and it was also the case that I had no time hardly for anything but schools reading when it came out.

[1] *ad infinitum.*

[2] Published in 1856, by [Sir] J. R. Seeley, it made considerable stir as a contribution to 'Neology' or liberal theology.

I see that I ought to have and I will when I can. . . . I have not
yet read Ruskin's new book:[1] the title is perhaps vulgar. Ruskin
is full of follies but I get more and more sympathetic with 'the
true men' as agst. the Sophistik (observe I say K – it is not the
same thing as sophistical), Philistine, Doctrinaire, Utilitarian,
Positive, and on the whole Negative (as Carlyle wd. put it) side,
and prefer to err with Plato. This reminds me to say that I find
myself in an even prostrate admiration of Aristotle and am of the
way of thinking, so far as I know him or know about him, that he
is the end-all and be-all of philosophy. But I shd. be sorry to bore
you with philosophy, of which you no doubt have had enough
what with reading for fellowships: with me on the contrary an
interest in philosophy is almost the only one I can feel myself
quite free to indulge in still.

I have begun learning the violin: I am glad I have.

I must say that I am very anxious to get away from this place.
I have become very weak in health and do not seem to recover
myself here or likely to do so. Teaching is very burdensome,
especially when you have much of it: I have. I have not much
time and almost no energy – for I am always tired – to do any-
thing on my own account. I put aside that one sees and hears
nothing and nobody here. Very happily Challis of Merton is now
here; else the place were without reservation 'damned, shepherd'.
(This is not swearing.) I ought to make the exception that the
boys are very nice indeed. I am expecting to take orders and soon,
but I wish it to be secret till it comes about. Besides that it is the
happiest and best way it practically is the only one. You know I
once wanted to be a painter. But even if I could I wd. not I think,
now, for the fact is that the higher and more attractive parts of
the art put a strain upon the passions which I shd. think unsafe
to encounter. I want to write still and as a priest I very likely can
do that too, not so freely as I shd. have liked, e.g. nothing or
little in the verse way, but no doubt what wd. best serve the

[1] *Time and Tide, by Weare and Tyne; Twenty-five Letters to a Working
Man of Sunderland on the Laws of Work.* First edition, 1867; second edition,
January 1868.

cause of my religion. But if I am a priest it will cause my mother, or she says it will, great grief and this preys on my mind very much and makes the near prospect quite black. The general result is that I am perfectly reckless about things that I shd. otherwise care about, uncertain as I am whether in a few months I may not be shut up in a cloister, and this state of mind, though it is painful coming to, when reached gives a great and real sense of freedom. Do you happen to know of any tutorship I cd. take for a few months after Easter? as I am anxious to leave this place then and also not to leave it without having secured something to live upon till, as seems likely, I take minor orders. . . .

Have you read the *Pervigilium Veneris*? It is about equal to the Atys and, I think, as beautiful as or more beautiful than anything of the same length in Latin.

Believe me always your affectionate friend,

Gerard M. Hopkins.

VIII

TO MISS KATE HOPKINS[1]

Stonyhurst,
April 25, 1871.

My dear Katie,

Many thanks for your letter, which I was delighted to get. When it first came to hand I stood balancing in my mind who it could be from, there was such a younglyladyship and grownupdom about the address, until I remembered that you were older than you used to be. As for me I will say no more than this, that I have prescribed myself twenty four hourglasses a day (which I take even during sleep, such is the force of habit) and that even this does not stop the ravages of time.

What month in the year it may be at Hampstead I will not be sure; with us it is a whity-greeny January. What with east winds,

---

[1] 1856–1933: second daughter in the Hopkins family. She had considerable artistic gifts and was 'a sort of humourist'.

cloud, and rain I think it will never be spring. If we have a bright afternoon the next morning it is winter again.

We were all vaccinated the other day. The next day a young Portug[u]ese came up to me and said 'Oh misther 'Opkins, do *you* feel the cows in *yewer* arm?' I told him I felt the horns coming through. I do I am sure. I cannot remember now whether one ought to say the calf of the arm or the calf of the leg. My shoulder is like a shoulder of beef. I dare not speak above a whisper for fear of bellowing – there now, I was going to say I am obliged to speak low for fear of lowing. I dream at night that I have only two of my legs in bed. I think there is a split coming in both of my slippers. Yesterday I could not think why it was that I would wander about on a wet grass-plot: I see now. I chew my pen a great deal. The long and short of it is that my left forequarter is swollen and painful (I meant to have written arm but I cowld not). Besides the doctor has given us medicine, so that I am in a miserable way just now.

From cows I will turn to lambs. Our fields are full of them. When they were a little younger and nicer and sillier they wd. come gambolling up to one as if one were their mother. One of them sucked my finger and my companion took another up in his arms. The ewes then came up and walked round us making suspicious sheep's eyes at us, as people say. Now, when they are not sucking the breast (to do which they make such terrific butts and digs at the old dam that two of them together will sometimes lift her off her hind legs) they spend their time in bounding and spinning round as if they were tumblers. The same thing is I daresay to be seen (and earlier than this) about Hampstead: still as many of these lambs are ours I cannot pass it by and must tell you of it in black and white.

One thing made me very sad the day we were vaccinated. I was coming away: I left a number of my companions in a room in the infirmary – some had come from the doctor and others were waiting for their turn – all laughing and chatting. As I came down one of the galleries from the room I saw one of our young men standing there looking at a picture. I wondered why he stayed by himself and did not join the rest and then afterwards I remembered that he had had the smallpox and was deeply marked with it and all his good looks gone which he would have had and he did not want to face the others at that time when they were having their fun taking safe precautions against catching what it was too late for him to take any precautions against.

I want to know two things by the next person who writes – first some particulars from Arthur[1] about the American yacht Sappho which seems to have had such great successes last year and next whether it is true that the cuckoo has come unusually early this year, as I heard said. It has not come here yet and I do not know if it will.

With best love to all believe me your loving brother
                                                    Gerard M. Hopkins.

IX

TO ROBERT BRIDGES[2]
Stonyhurst, Whalley, Lancashire.
August 2, 1871.

My dear Bridges,

Our holidays have begun, so I will write again. I feel inclined to begin by asking whether you are secretary to the International as you seem to mean me to think nothing too bad for you but then I remember that you never relished 'the intelligent artisan'. I must tell you I am always thinking of the Communist future. The too intelligent artisan is master of the situation I believe. Perhaps it is what everyone believes, I do not see the papers or hear strangers often enough to know. It is what Carlyle has long threatened and foretold. But his writings are, as he might himself say, 'most inefficacious-strenuous heaven-protestations, caterwaul, and Cassandra-wailings'. He preaches obedience but I do not think he has done much except to ridicule instead of strengthening the hands of the powers that be. Some years ago when he published his *Shooting Niagara*[3] he did make some

---

[1] See note 2 on p. 179.
[2] See Note H, p. 251.   [3] *Macmillan's Magazine*, 1867.

practical suggestions but so vague that they should rather be called 'too dubious moonstone-grindings and on the whole impracticable-practical unveracities'. However I am afraid some great revolution is not far off. Horrible to say, in a manner I am a Communist.[1] Their ideal bating some things is nobler than that professed by any secular statesman I know of (I must own I live in bat-light and shoot at a venture). Besides it is just. – I do not mean the means of getting to it are. But it is a dreadful thing for the greatest and most necessary part of a very rich nation to live a hard life without dignity, knowledge, comforts, delight, or hopes in the midst of plenty – which plenty they make. They profess that they do not care what they wreck and burn, the old civilisation and order must be destroyed. This is a dreadful look out but what has the old civilisation done for them? As it at present stands in England it is itself in great measure founded on wrecking. But they got none of the spoils, they came in for nothing but harm from it then and thereafter. England has grown hugely wealthy but this wealth has not reached the working classes; I expect it has made their condition worse. Besides this iniquitous order the old civilisation embodies another order mostly old and what is new in direct entail from the old, the old religion, learning, law, art, etc and all the history that is preserved in standing monuments. But as the working classes have not been educated they know next to nothing of all this and cannot be expected to care if they destroy it. The more I look the more black and deservedly black the future looks, so I will write no more.

I can hardly believe that this is August and your letter dated May. True there has been here and I believe elsewhere no summer between. There seems some chance now. In a fortnight we are going, also for a fortnight, to Inellan in Argyleshire on the Clyde. After that I expect to pay my people a short visit down near Southampton, where they have taken a cottage. None of them are turned Catholics: I do not expect it. –

Believe me your affectionate friend   Gerard Hopkins S. J.

[1] In his next letter to R. B. he says: 'I have little reason to be Red: it was the red Commune that murdered five of our Fathers lately.' (B, p. 29.)

X

TO HIS MOTHER

Stonyhurst.
March 5, 1872.

My dearest Mother,

I cannot tell how I have overpassed your birthday and only been recalled to it now too late by seeing the date March 3 on a letter but you must believe that I am very sorry. I wish you many happy returns of it: they cannot begin to come into effect for nearly a year, so that it is still quite a valid wish. I enclose three northcountry primroses, our firstlings of this mildest of early springs: I think they must be early for anywhere. They will no doubt look fagged but they must be taken symbolically and they are hedge primroses, not from the garden.

My cold that was is off but I am on with a new one worse. It has however given notice.

When you next meet Miss Rossetti give her my kind remembrances and do not forget. I am most glad to hear of the success and appreciation of her book.[1] I did see a review of it somewhere. Miss Christina also has comparatively lately published some stories in prose, I find.[2] But she has been, I am afraid, thrown rather into the shade by her brother. I have not read his book.[3] From the little I have seen and gathered of it I daresay he has more range, force, and interest, and then there is the difference between a man and a woman, but for pathos and pure beauty of art I do not think he is her equal: in fact the simple beauty of her work cannot be matched.

Thank Kate for her letter. No one knows (as Fr. Gallwey said and of me) where I may break out next – but let them look out below.

Believe me your loving son

Gerard Hopkins.

[1] *A Shadow of Dante*, etc., by Maria Francesca Rossetti (1871).
[2] *Commonplace and Other Stories* (1870).
[3] *Poems*, by Dante Gabriel Rossetti (1870).

XI

TO HIS FATHER

St. Beuno's,
St. Asaph,
North Wales.
Aug. 29, 1874.

My dearest Father,

I came here yesterday, to begin my studies in theology. I had expected to have another year's teaching at Roehampton, but now my ordination and profession will be earlier. The house stands on a steep hillside, it commands the long-drawn valley of the Clwyd to the sea, a vast prospect, and opposite is Snowdon and its range, just now it being bright visible but coming and going with the weather. The air seems to me very fresh and wholesome. Holidays till the 2nd of October. After that hours of study very close – lectures in dogmatic theology, moral ditto, canon law, church history, scripture, Hebrew and what not. I have half a mind to get up a little Welsh: all the neighbours speak it. I have said nothing about the house. It is built of limestone, decent outside, skimping within, Gothic, like Lancing College done worse. The staircases, galleries, and bopeeps are inexpressible: it takes a fortnight to learn them. Pipes of affliction convey lukewarm water of affliction to some of the rooms, others more fortunate have fires. The garden is all heights, terraces, Excelsiors, misty mountain tops, seats up trees called Crows' Nests, flights of steps seemingly up to heaven lined with burning aspiration upon aspiration of scarlet geraniums: it is very pretty and airy but it gives you the impression that if you took a step farther you would find yourself somewhere on Plenlimmon, Conway Castle, or Salisbury Craig. With best love to detachments stationed at Hampstead believe me your loving son

Gerard M. Hopkins S.J.

XII

TO ROBERT BRIDGES

St. Beuno's College,
St. Asaph, N. Wales.
Feb. 20, 1875.

My dearest Bridges,

The above address shews how impossible it is for me to execute your kind and welcome wish by calling at Maddox Street. There was never any moral difficulty, I could have got leave to spend more than an hour and a half with you, but a long crow-flight is between us – one over which the crowquill, to follow the lead of my own thoughts, does not carry. But if you had sent me such an invitation last year, when I really was at Roehampton, what a pleasure it would have been and what a break in the routine of rhetoric, which I taught so badly and so painfully![1]

You will wonder what I do under the sign of those Welsh saints. Study theology – for four years from last September. We live on a hillside of the beautiful valley of the Clwyd, but now the other side of the valley vanishes in mist and the ground is deep in snow.

Feb. 22 – It was yesterday waistdeep in the drifts.

I have quite forgotten what I may have said in my last letter. What you write about yourself interests me of course but is beyond me: I have had no time to read even the English books about Hegel, much less the original, indeed I know almost no German. (However I think my contemporary Wallace of Balliol has been translating him.) I do not afflict myself much about my ignorance here, for I could remove it as far as I should much care to do, whenever it became advisable, hereafter, but it was with sorrow I put back Aristotle's Metaphysics in the library some time ago feeling that I could not read them now and so probably should never. After all I can, at all events a little, read Duns Scotus[2]

[1] From Sept. 1873 to Aug. 1874 he was 'professor of rhetoric' at Manresa House. See *N*, pp. 221-48.

[2] See Introduction, p. xxiii.

and I care for him more even than Aristotle and more *pace tua* than a dozen Hegels. However this is me, not you. But it explains why I can do nothing more than say how much I like to hear about you and how glad I am you are as you say, nearer the top than the bottom of Hegel's or anybody else's bottomless pit.

I wd. have answered more promptly but I saw that you would not be in London for some little time. The close pressure of my theological studies leaves me time for hardly anything: the course is very hard, it must be said. Nevertheless I have tried to learn a little Welsh, in reality one of the hardest of languages.*

Believe me always your affectionate friend

Gerard M. Hopkins S.J.

> * Hebrew is part of our curriculum.

XIII

TO ROBERT BRIDGES

Stonyhurst College,
Blackburn (or Whalley).
May 13, 1878.

Dearest Bridges,

Remark the above address. After July I expect to be stationed in town – 111 Mount Street, Grosvenor Square.

I hope your bad cold is gone.

I am very glad to hear the Rondeliers have come to see the beauty of your poetry. I have little acquaintance with their own. I have read a rondeau or rondel by Marzials[1] in the *Athenaeum* beginning and ending 'When I see you': it was very graceful and shewing an art and finish rare in English verse. This makes me the more astonished about *Flop flop*. Is his name Spanish, Provençal, or what? Barring breach of confidence I wish I could have seen his letter and that of the habitually joyous.[2] I think that school is too artificial and exotic to take root and last, is it not?

I enclose you my Eurydice,[3] which the *Month* refused. It is my

[1] Theophilus Julius Henry Marzials, a minor poet.
[2] Edmund W. Gosse (1849–1928), poet, critic, and essayist. Knighted in 1925.   [3] Poem No. 18.

only copy. Write no bilgewater about it: I will presently tell you what that is and till then excuse the term. I must tell you I am sorry you never read the Deutschland[1] again.

Granted that it needs study and is obscure, for indeed I was not over-desirous that the meaning of all should be quite clear, at least unmistakeable, you might, without the effort that to make it all out would seem to have required, have nevertheless read it so that lines and stanzas should be left in the memory and super-ficial impressions deepened, and have liked some without ex-hausting all. I am sure I have read and enjoyed pages of poetry that way. Why, sometimes one enjoys and admires the very lines one cannot understand, as for instance 'If it were done when 'tis done' sqq.,[2] which is all obscure and disputed, though how fine it is everybody sees and nobody disputes. And so of many more passages in Shakespere and others. Besides you would have got more weathered to the style and its features – not really odd. Now they say that vessels sailing from the port of London will take (perhaps it should be/ used once to take) Thames water for the voyage: it was foul and stunk at first as the ship worked but by degrees casting its filth was in a few days very pure and sweet and wholesomer and better than any water in the world. However that maybe, it is true to my purpose. When a new thing, such as my ventures in the Deutschland are, is presented us our first criticisms are not our truest, best, most homefelt, or most lasting but what come easiest on the instant. They are barbarous and like what the ignorant and the ruck say. This was so with you. The Deutschland on her first run worked very much and unsettled you, thickening and clouding your mind with vulgar mud-bottom and common sewage (I see that I am going it with the image) and just then unhappily you *drew off* your criticisms all stinking (a necessity now of the image) and bilgy, whereas if you had let your thoughts cast themselves they would have been

---

[1] Poem No. 5. – In an earlier letter G. M. H. had written: 'I cannot think of altering anything. Why shd. I? I do not write for the public. You are my public and I hope to convert you.' (B, p. 46.)

[2] *Macbeth*, I, vii. 1.

clearer in themselves and more to my taste too. I did not heed them therefore, perceiving they were a first drawing-off. Same of the Eurydice – which being short and easy please read more than once.

Can you tell me who that critic in the *Athenaeum* is that writes very long reviews on English and French poets, essayists, and so forth in a style like De Quincey's, very acute in his remarks, provoking, jaunty, and (I am sorry to say) would-be humorous? He always quotes Persian stories (unless he makes them up) and talks about Rabelæsian humour.[1]

My brother's pictures,[2] as you say, are careless and do not aim high, but I don't think it would be much different if he were a batchelor. But, strange to say – and I shd. never even have suspected it if he had not quite simply told me – he has somehow in painting his pictures, though nothing that the pictures express, a high and quite religious aim; however I cannot be more explanatory.

Your bodysnatch story is ghastly, but so are all bodysnatch stories. My grandfather was a surgeon, a fellow-student of Keats', and once conveyed a body through Plymouth at the risk of his own.

Believe me your affectionate friend

Gerard M. Hopkins S.J.

[Postscript.]

May 21, 1878.

Please remember me very kindly to your mother.

To do the Eurydice any kind of justice you must not slovenly read it with the eyes but with your ears, as if the paper were declaiming it at you. For instance the line 'she had come from a

---

[1] It was W. Theodore Watts-Dunton (1832–1914).

[2] Arthur Hopkins (1847–1930), the third son, won a gold medal at the R.A. Member of the R.W.S. and for 25 years on the staff of *The Graphic*, he was also, like his younger brother Everard, a contributor of black-and-white illustrations to *Punch*.

'cruise training seamen' read without stress and declaim is mere
Lloyd's Shipping Intelligence; properly read it is quite a different
thing. Stress is the life of it.

XIV
TO R. W. DIXON[1]

Stonyhurst College,
Blackburn.
June 4, 1878.

Very Rev. Sir,

I take a liberty as a stranger in addressing you, nevertheless
I did once have some slight acquaintance with you. You will not
remember me but you will remember taking a mastership for
some months at Highgate School, the Cholmondeley School,
where I then was. When you went away you gave, as I recollect,
a copy of your book *Christ's Company* to one of the masters, a
Mr. Law if I am not mistaken. By this means coming to know its
name I was curious to read it, which when I went to Oxford I did.
At first I was surprised at it, then pleased, at last I became so fond
of it that I made it, so far as that could be, a part of my own mind.
I got your other volume and your little Prize Essay[2] too. I intro-
duced your poems to my friends and, if they did not share my
own enthusiasm, made them at all events admire. And to shew
you how greatly I prized them, when I entered my present state
of life, in which I knew I could have no books of my own and
was unlikely to meet with your works in the libraries I should
have access to, I copied out *St. Paul, St. John, Love's Consolation*,
and others from both volumes and keep them by me.

What I am saying now I might, it is true, have written any
time these many years back, but partly I hesitated, partly I was
not sure you were yet living; lately however I saw in the *Athenaeum*
a review of your historical work newly published and since have
made up my mind to write to you – which, to be sure, is an
impertinence if you like to think it so, but I seemed to owe you
something or a great deal, and then I knew what I should feel

[1] See Note I, p. 252.   [2] The Arnold Prize Essay for 1858.

myself in your position – if I had written and published works the extreme beauty of which the author himself the most keenly feels and they had fallen out of sight at once and been (you will not mind my saying it, as it is, I suppose, plainly true) almost wholly unknown; then, I say, I should feel a certain comfort to be told they had been deeply appreciated by some one person, a stranger, at all events and had not been published quite in vain. Many beautiful works have been almost unknown and then have gained fame at last, as Mr. Wells'[1] poem of *Joseph*, which is said to be very fine, and his friend Keats' own, but many more must have been lost sight of altogether. I do not know of course whether your books are going to have a revival, it seems not likely, but not for want of deserving. It is not that I think a man is really the less happy because he has missed the renown which was his due, but still when this happens it is an evil in itself and a thing which ought not to be and that I deplore, for the good work's sake rather than the author's.

Your poems had a medieval colouring like Wm. Morris's and the Rossetti's and others but none seemed to me to have it so unaffectedly. I thought the tenderness of *Love's Consolation* no one living could surpass nor the richness of colouring in the 'wolfsbane' and other passages (it is a mistake, I think, and you meant henbane) in that and *Mark and Rosalys* nor the brightness of the appleorchard landscape in *Mother and Daughter*.[2] And the Tale of Dauphiny and 'It is the time to tell of fatal love' (I forget the title) in the other book[3] are purer in style, as it seems to me, and quite as fine in colouring and drawing as Morris's stories in the *Paradise*, so far as I have read them, fine as those are. And if I were making up a book of English poetry I should put your ode to Summer next to Keats' on Autumn and the Nightingale and Grecian Urn. I do not think anywhere two stanzas so crowded with the pathos of nature and landscape could be found (except perhaps there are some in Wordsworth) as the little song of the Feathers of the

[1] Charles Wells, author of *Joseph and His Brethren* (1824), reissued 1876.
[2] All in *Christ's Company* (1861).
[3] *Historical Odes* (1863).

Willow: a tune to it came to me quite naturally. The extreme delight I felt when I read the line 'Her eyes like lilies shaken by the bees' was more than any single line in poetry ever gave me and now that I am older I could not be so strongly moved by it if I were to read it for the first time. I have said all this, and could if there were any use say more, as a sort of duty of charity to make up, so far as one voice can do, for the disappointment you must, at least at times, I think, have felt over your rich and exquisite work almost thrown away. You will therefore feel no offence though you may surprise at my writing.

I am, Very Rev. Sir, your obedient servant

Gerard M. Hopkins S.J.

(I am, you see, in 'Christ's Company').

XV

TO R. W. DIXON

Stonyhurst, Blackburn.
June 13, 1878.

Very Reverend and Dear Sir, Pax Christi,

I am very glad now to think I followed my impulse and wrote to you, since my writing could affect you so much and draw out so kind an answer.

I suppose it is me that you remember at Highgate: I did get a prize for an English poem,[1] I do not well remember when; it may have been while you were there. In those days I knew poor Philip Worsley[2] the poet; he had been at school at Highgate himself; and spent some time at Elgin House (I suppose as Dr. Dyne's guest) when I was a boarder there; indeed he read over and made criticisms on my successful poem: I recollect that he knew you (perhaps you may have made the acquaintance then, but all these facts I recall detachedly, and cannot group them) and said you would praise Keats by the hour – which might well be:

[1] *The Escorial* (1860). See *Poems*, 3rd Edn., No. 1.
[2] 1835–66. Published *Poems and Translations*, 1863; new edn. 1875.

Keats' genius was so astonishing, unequalled at his age and scarcely surpassed at any, that one may surmise whether if he had lived he would not have rivalled Shakspere.

When I spoke of fame I was not thinking of the harm it does to men as artists: it may do them harm, as you say, but so, I think, may the want of it, if 'Fame is the spur that the clear spirit doth raise To shun delights and live laborious days' – a spur very hard to find a substitute for or to do without. But I meant that it is a great danger in itself, as dangerous as wealth every bit, I should think, and as hard to enter the kingdom of heaven with. And even if it does not lead men to break the divine law, yet it gives them 'itching ears' and makes them live on public breath. (You have yourself said something of this – about 'seeking for praise in all the tides of air' in an ode, that 'on Departing Youth',[1] I think.) Mr. Coventry Patmore, whose fame again is very deeply below his great merit, seems to have said something very finely about the loss of fame in his lately published odes (*The Hidden Eros*)[2] – I speak from an extract in a review.

What I do regret is the loss of recognition belonging to the work itself. For as to every moral act, being right or wrong, there belongs, of the nature of things, reward or punishment, so to every form perceived by the mind belongs, of the nature of things, admiration or the reverse. And the world is full of things and events, phenomena of all sorts, that go without notice, go unwitnessed. I think you have felt this, for you say, I remember, in one of the odes: 'What though the white clouds soar Unmarked from the horizon-shore?' or something like that.[3] And if we regret this want of witness in brute nature much more in the things done with lost pains and disappointed hopes by man. But since there is always the risk of it, it is a great error of judgment to have lived for what may fail us. So that if Mr. Burne Jones

[1] 'What has been lost save beating ears
    That sought for praise in all the tides of air, . . .'
[2] G. M. H. means *The Unknown Eros* (1877). For Patmore see Note K, p. 253.
[3] 'Sympathy: An Ode' (*H.O.*). See above, poem No. 15, ll. 11–12.

works for a man who is to arise ages hence he works for what the burning of his pictures or the death of his admirer may for ever cut off. However he in particular has surely many vehement admirers living and even men who have the ear of the public – detractors too no doubt, but who has not? that comes with admiration.

I am happy to think you have an admirer in Mr. Rossetti (Gabriel Rossetti, I suppose): indeed if he read you it could not be otherwise. And I take the same for granted of Mr. Burne Jones.

Let me recommend you, if you have not seen them, my friend Dr. Bridges' poems – not his first little volume of roundels and so forth, now so much the fashion, for I have not read it and he is ashamed of it and does not wish to be known by it, but a set of sonnets, a tiny anonymous work no bigger than a short pamphlet of two dozen pages, they are called *The Growth of Love* and are to be continued some day. They are strict in form and affect Miltonic rhythms (which are caviare to the general, so that his critics, I believe, think him rough) and seem to me, but I am prepossessed, very beautiful – dignified, both manly and tender, and with a vein of quaintness. In imagery he is not rich but excels in phrasing, in sequence of phrase and sequence of feeling on feeling. Milton is the great master of sequence of phrase. By sequence of feeling I mean a dramatic quality by which what goes before seems to necessitate and beget what comes after, at least after you have heard it it does – your own poems illustrate it, as 'Yes, one time in the church I think you mean' or 'It makes me mad' and 'It makes me very sad to think of all the bitterness he had'.[1] This little work is published by Pickering and costs only a shilling, I think.

June 15 – This letter has run to a greater length than the little time at my disposal makes justifiable. – It is sad to think what disappointment must many times over have filled your heart for the darling children of your mind. Nevertheless fame whether won or lost is a thing which lies in the award of a random,

[1] 'La Faerie, or Lovers' World' (*Christ's Company*), stanzas 36 and 31.

reckless, incompetent, and unjust judge, the public, the multitude. The only just judge, the only just literary critic, is Christ, who prizes, is proud of, and admires, more than any man, more than the receiver himself can, the gifts of his own making. And the only real good which fame and another's praise does is to convey to us, by a channel not at all above suspicion but from circumstances in this case much less to be suspected than the channel of our own minds, some token of the judgment which a perfectly just, heedful, and wise mind, namely Christ's, passes upon our doings. Now such a token may be conveyed as well by one as by many. Therefore, believing I was able to pass a fair judgment as people go, it seemed in the circumstances a charity to tell you what I thought. For disappointment and humiliations embitter the heart and make an aching in the very bones. As far as I am concerned I say with conviction and put it on record again that you have great reason to thank God who has given you so astonishingly clear an inward eye to see what is in visible nature and in the heart such a deep insight into what is earnest, tender, and pathetic in human life and feeling as your poems display.

Believe me, dear sir, very sincerely yours
Gerard Hopkins S.J.

My address will be after next month 111 Mount Street, Grosvenor Square, London W., where I am to be stationed. But a letter to Stonyhurst would find me.

XVI

TO R. W. DIXON

111 Mount Street,
Grosvenor Square, W.
Oct. 5 1878.

Very Reverend and Dear Sir,

A visit to Great Yarmouth and pressure of work have kept me from answering before yr. very kind letter, and my reply will now not be written at once but as I shall find leisure.

I hope, to begin with, you have quite recovered from the effects of your accident. I escaped from such a one with very little hurt not long ago in Wales, but I witnessed a terrible and fatal coach-accident years ago in the Vale of Maentwrog.

I have forgotten not only what I said about 'Fr. Prout' but even that I ever read him. I always understood that he was a very amusing writer. I do remember that I was a very conceited boy.

I have quite lost sight of Mr. Lobb; I do not even know whether he is alive or dead. The truth is I had no love for my schooldays and wished to banish the remembrance of them, even, I am ashamed to say, to the degree of neglecting some people who had been very kind to me. Of Oxford on the other hand I was very fond. I became a Catholic there. But I have not visited it, except once for three quarters of an hour, since I took my degree. We have a church and house there now.

Oct. 6 – The other day Dr. Bridges told me he had in vain tried to get yr. volumes of poems, for want of knowing the publisher. I promised I wd. enquire of you. Was it not Smith and Elder?

I quite agree with what you write about Milton. His verse as one reads it seems something necessary and eternal (so to me does Purcell's music). As for 'proper hue',[1] now it wd. be priggish, but I suppose Milton means *own hue* and they talk of *proper colours* in heraldry; not but what there is a Puritan touch about the line even so. However the word must once have had a different feeling. The Welsh have borrowed it for *pretty*; they talk of birds singing 'properly' and a little Welsh boy to whom I shewed the flowers in a green house exclaimed 'They *are* proper!' – Milton seems now coming to be studied better, and Masson is writing or has written his life at prodigious length. There was an interesting review by Matthew Arnold in one of the Quarterlies of 'a French critic on Milton' – Scherer I think. The same M. Arnold says Milton and Campbell are our two greatest masters of *style*. Milton's art is incomparable, not only in English literature but, I

[1] Dixon had written: 'I remember Burne Jones once saying that he thought one line of Milton's the worst that was ever written. It was – "Celestial rosy red, love's proper hue." [*P. L.* viii, 619.]'

shd. think, almost in any; equal, if not more than equal, to the finest of Greek or Roman. And considering that this is shewn especially in his verse, his rhythm and metrical system, it is amazing that so great a writer as Newman should have fallen into the blunder of comparing the first chorus of the *Agonistes* with the opening of *Thalaba*[1] as instancing the gain in smoothness and correctness of versification made since Milton's time – Milton having been not only ahead of his own time as well as all after-times in verse-structure but these particular choruses being his own highwater mark. It is as if you were to compare the Pana-thenaic frieze and a teaboard and decide in the teaboard's favour.

I have paid a good deal of attention to Milton's versification and collected his later rhythms: I did it when I had to lecture on rhetoric some years since. I found his most advanced effects in the *Paradise Regained* and, lyrically, in the *Agonistes*. I have often thought of writing on them, indeed on rhythm in general; I think the subject is little understood.

You ask, do I write verse myself. What I had written I burnt before I became a Jesuit and resolved to write no more, as not belonging to my profession, unless it were by the wish of my superiors; so for seven years I wrote nothing but two or three little presentation pieces which occasion called for. But when in the winter of '75 the Deutschland was wrecked in the mouth of the Thames and five Franciscan nuns, exiles from Germany by the Falck Laws, aboard of her were drowned I was affected by the account and happening to say so to my rector he said that he wished someone would write a poem on the subject. On this hint I set to work and, though my hand was out at first, produced one. I had long had haunting my ear the echo of a new rhythm which now I realised on paper. To speak shortly, it consists in scanning by accents or stresses alone, without any account of the number of syllables, so that a foot may be one strong syllable or it may be many light and one strong. I do not say the idea is altogether new; there are hints of it in music, in nursery rhymes and popular jingles, in the poets themselves, and, since then, I

[1] Poem by Robert Southey (1801).

have seen it talked about as a thing possible in critics. Here are instances – 'Díng, dóng, béll; Pússy's ín the wéll; Whó pút her ín? Líttle Jóhnny Thín. Whó púlled her óut? Líttle Jóhnny Stóut.' For if each line has three stresses or three feet it follows that some of the feet are of one syllable only. So too 'Óne, twó, Búckle my shóe' *passim*. In Campbell you have 'Ánd their fléet alóng the déep próudly shóne' – 'Ít was tén of Ápril mórn bý the chíme' etc; in Shakspere 'Whý shd. *this* désert bé?' corrected wrongly by the editors; in Moore a little melody I cannot quote; etc. But no one has professedly used it and made it the principle throughout, that I know of. Nevertheless to me it appears, I own, to be a better and more natural principle than the ordinary system, much more flexible, and capable of much greater effects.[1] However I had to **mark the** stresses in blue chalk, and this and my rhymes carried on from one line into another and certain chimes suggested by the Welsh poetry I had been reading (what they call *cynghanedd*) and a great many more oddnesses could not but dismay an editor's eye, so that when I offered it to our magazine the *Month*, though at first they accepted it, after a time they withdrew and dared not print it. After writing this I held myself free to compose, but cannot find it in my conscience to spend time upon it; so I have done little and shall do less. But I wrote a shorter piece on the Eurydice, also in 'sprung rhythm', as I call it, but simpler, shorter, and without marks, and offered the *Month* that too, but they did not like it either. Also I have written some sonnets and a few other little things; some in sprung rhythm, with various other experiments – as 'outriding feet', that is parts of which do not count in the scanning (such as you find in Shakspere's later plays, but as a licence, whereas mine are rather calculated effects); others in the ordinary scanning *counterpointed* (this is counterpoint: 'Hóme to his móther's hóuse *private* retúrned'[2] and 'Bút to vánquish by wísdom héllish wíles'[3] etc); others, one or two, in common uncounterpointed rhythm. But even the impulse to write is wanting, for I have no thought of publishing.

[1] See Note A, p. 249.
[2] *Paradise Regained*, iv. 639.   [3] *Ibid.*, i. 175.

I should add that Milton is the great standard in the use of counterpoint. In *Paradise Lost* and *Regained*, in the last more freely, it being an advance in his art, he employs counterpoint more or less everywhere, markedly now and then; but the choruses of *Samson Agonistes* are in my judgment counterpointed throughout; that is, each line (or nearly so) has two different coexisting scansions. But when you reach that point the secondary or 'mounted rhythm', which is necessarily a sprung rhythm, overpowers the original or conventional one and then this becomes superfluous and may be got rid of; by taking that last step you reach simple sprung rhythm. Milton must have known this but had reasons for not taking it.

I read Arnold's *Essays in Criticism* at Oxford and got Maurice de Guérin's Journal in consequence, admired it, but for some reason or other never got far in it. I should be glad to read it now if I had time. But I have no time for more pressing interests. I hear confessions, preach, and so forth; when these are done I have still a good deal of time to myself, but I find I can do very little with it. . . .

> Believe me, dear Sir, very sincerely yours
>   Gerard Hopkins.
>   Oct. 10

•   •   •   •   •   •   •

[*Editor's Note:* On October 19, 1879, Canon R. W. Dixon wrote:—

'Should you be angry that I sent your *Loss of the Eurydice*, or part of it, to one of the Carlisle Papers, giving your name, and a line or two of introduction from myself?'

The next two letters give G. M. H.'s characteristic reaction.]

XVII

TO R. W. DIXON

St. Joseph's, Bedford Leigh,
near Manchester.
Oct. 24 1879.

Reverend and Dear Sir,

I have left Oxford and am appointed to Liverpool (St. Francis Xavier's, Salisbury Street). I am uncertain how long I shall be at Leigh. The place is very gloomy but our people hearty and devoted.

I cannot be quite sure from your words whether you have sent the verses to the paper or only were thinking of sending; I suppose however that they are sent. If it is too late to recall them the matter can not be helped. I am troubled about it because it may come to the knowledge of some of ours and an unpleasant construction be put upon it. It would be easy to explain it to the Provincial, but not so easy to guard myself against what others might say. However we have no house at or near Carlisle, so that I daresay it may pass without notice taken. You, I know, acted out of pure kindness, but publication of my lines except by the ordinary channels cannot serve me. You would not, I hope, think I secretly wished to steal a march upon my superiors: that would be in me a great baseness. I believe after all that no great harm will have been done, since Carlisle papers are not likely to have more than a local circulation; but do not send them any more pieces.

The learned Fr. Joseph Stevenson,[1] who joined our body two years ago very late in life, and his friend the Rev. Mr. Sole, late of Oscot, also an antiquary, by my persuasion made themselves acquainted with the first volume of your history (I have not looked at it myself, I have no time for study, at least at Oxford I had

[1] 1806–95: well-known archivist and editor.

none) and reported to me highly of its learning and spirit. I hope it is going on well.

Believe me affectionately your friend

Gerard M. Hopkins S.J.

XVIII

TO R. W. DIXON

St. Joseph's, Bedford Leigh.
Oct. 31, 1879.

My dear Canon,

Pray do not send the piece to the paper: I cannot consent to, I forbid its publication. You must see that to publish my manuscript against my expressed wish is a breach of trust. Ask any friend and he will tell you the same.

Moreover this kind of publication is very unlikely to do the good that you hope and very likely to do the harm that I fear. For who ever heard of fame won by publication in a local paper, and of one piece? If everything of its intrinsic goodness gravitated to fame your poems wd. long since have been famous. Were Tennyson, putting aside marks of style by which he might be recognised, to send something to the *Nineteenth Century* or best circulated London magazine *without his name* it wd. be forgotten in a month: now no name and an unknown name is all one. But what is not near enough for public fame may be more than enough for private notoriety, which is what I dread.

You say truly that our Society fosters literary excellence. Why then it may be left to look to its own interests. It could not approve of unauthorised publication, for all that we publish must be seen by censors first.

Then again if you were to print my piece you would surely not mutilate it. And yet you must; for with what grace could you, a clergyman of the Church of England, stand godfather to some of the stanzas in that poem? And besides I want to alter the last stanza.

Nov. 1 – This letter, which the pressure of parish work has delayed, will now, I daresay, be too late and the Eurydice may have appeared. You will see that your warmhearted but much mistaken kindness will be unavailing: if the paper takes the piece (which it is sure to misprint) few will read it and of those few fewer will scan it, much less understand or like it. (To be sure the scanning is plain enough, but people cannot, or they will not, take in anything however plain that departs from what they have been taught and brought up to expect: I know from experience). Indeed I am in hopes that the matter may even escape the notice of our own people.[1]

Believe me affectionately your friend

Gerard Hopkins S.J.

XIX

TO A. W. M. BAILLIE

8 Salisbury Street,
Liverpool.
May 22, 1880.

Dearest Baillie,

I do not know how it is, when your letters give me so much pleasure to get, I am so slow in answering them. At least I can say my Liverpool work is very harassing and makes it hard to write. Tonight I am sitting in my confessional, but the faithful are fewer than usual and I am unexpectedly delivered from a sermon which otherwise I should have had to be delivered of. Here comes someone.

You say it is something of an affectation for me to run up the Lancashire people and run down 'Oxonians' – unpleasant word, let us say the Oxford ones. I do not remember quite what I said; are you sure it was, as you assume, of Gown, not Town I was

[1] The next letter begins: 'I am very glad that all has blown over and no harm done.'

speaking? Now I do like both. Not to love my University would be to undo the very buttons of my being and as for the Oxford townspeople I found them in my 10 months' stay[1] among them very deserving of affection – though somewhat stiff, stand-off, and depressed. And in that stay I saw very little of the University. But I could not but feel how alien it was, how chilling, and deeply to be distrusted. I could have wished, and yet I could not, that there had been no one that had known me there. As a fact there were many and those friendly, some cordially so, but with others I cd. not feel at home. With the Lancastrians it is the reverse; I felt as if [I] had been born to deal with them. Religion, you know, enters very deep; in reality it is the deepest impression I have in speaking to people, that they are or that they are not of my religion. And then it is sweet to be a little flattered and I can truly say that except in the most transparently cringing way I seldom am. Now these Lancashire people of low degree or not of high degree are those who most have seemed to me to welcome me and make much of me. This is, I suppose, what was on my mind.

If you have set to work in earnest on the fascinating study of hieroglyphics, or rather, of Egyptian, perhaps you will come to translate texts, and then you will do it better than they do in the Biblical Archaeological Society and that slipshod publication, the 'Ancient Texts' I think it is called. I have been reading the first Egyptian volume of the issue (the right name is 'Records of the Past', I find) and the translations are a very bad business. Allowance must be made for a little known language but, making it, still they are bad. The most curious thing in this volume is called the Travels of an Egyptian: it is in reality, as it would appear, a sarcastic criticism, and meant to be published too, on a journal or account of his Syrian travels by a man calling himself, and laying a great stress on being, a Mohar, whatever a Mohar is. The critic, just like a modern Reviler or Athenaeum, asks why he makes no mention of such and such places, quoting a learned string of names. He also ridicules his pomposity and wd. seem to parody his style. Altogether it is condemned modern in spirit

[1] i.e. as a priest, actually from Dec. 1878 to Aug. 1879.

and levels all up or all down surprisingly. I daresay you have read it in the original.

June 9 – I had written a great deal more, about this place (to which I came on Dec. 30), but have suppressed it all after keeping it by me and reading it with my head first on one side, then on the other, at various distances and in various lights, many times over. I do not think I can be long here; I have been long nowhere yet. I am brought face to face with the deepest poverty and misery in my district. On this theme I could write much, but it would do no good.

What you write of Apuleius is interesting. But when you have a parish you can no longer read nor have intellectual interests. . . .

By the by when I was at Oxford Pater was one of the men I saw most of.

June 18 – This is a dull letter, but you can answer it by a livelier one.

What do you think of Wagner? I heard a concert of his music in the winter. He loses greatly, I fancy, off the stage. The Germans call him the Master of Masters and Hartmann the greatest of philosophers and the last new thing everywhere the greatest that ever was. This is a barbarous business of greatest this and supreme that that Swinburne and others practise. What is the thing that has been? The same that shall be. Everything is vanity and vexation of spirit.

Believe me your affectionate friend
Gerard M. Hopkins S.J.

P.S. What is the origin of *wean*?[1] Some people say *wee'un*, but I do not think it can be so. The common people in this town talk of 'a little weany bit'.

I see with sorrow that it is *half a year* since you wrote. Return good for evil.

. . . .

[1] i.e. a young child: a contraction of *wee ane* (Abbott).

XX
TO R. W. DIXON
(Extract)

Manresa House,
Roehampton, S.W.
Dec. 1, 1881.

(the very day 300 years ago of Father Campion's martyrdom.)
My dear Friend,

I am heartily glad you did not make away with, as you say you thought of doing, so warm and precious a letter as your last.[1] It reached me on the first break or day of repose in our month's retreat; I began answering it on the second, but could not finish; and this is the third and last of them.

When a man has given himself to God's service, when he has denied himself and followed Christ, he has fitted himself to receive and does receive from God a special guidance, a more particular providence. This guidance is conveyed partly by the action of other men, as his appointed superiors, and partly by direct lights and inspirations. If I wait for such guidance, through whatever channel conveyed, about anything, about my poetry for instance, I do more wisely in every way than if I try to serve my own seeming interests in the matter. Now if you value what I write, if I do myself, much more does our Lord. And if he chooses to avail himself of what I leave at his disposal he can do so with a felicity and with a success which I could never command. And if he does not, then two things follow: one that the reward I shall nevertheless receive from him will be all the greater; the other that then I shall know how much a thing contrary to his will and even to my own best interests I should have done if I had taken things into my own hands and forced on publication.

[1] In this letter (November 4th) Dixon had written: 'Surely one vocation cannot destroy another: and such a Society as yours will not remain ignorant that you have such gifts as have seldom been given by God to man.'

This is my principle and this in the main has been my practice: leading the sort of life I do here it seems easy, but when one mixes with the world and meets on every side its secret solicitations, to live by faith is harder, is very hard; nevertheless by God's help I shall always do so.

Our Society values, as you say, and has contributed to literature, to culture; but only as a means to an end. Its history and its experience shew that literature proper, as poetry, has seldom been found to be to that end a very serviceable means. We have had for three centuries often the flower of the youth of a country in numbers enter our body: among these how many poets, how many artists of all sorts, there must have been! But there have been very few Jesuit poets and, where they have been, I believe it would be found on examination that there was something exceptional in their circumstances or, so to say, counterbalancing in their career. For genius attracts fame and individual fame St. Ignatius[1] looked on as the most dangerous and dazzling of all attractions. There was a certain Fr. Beschi[2] who in Southern Hindustan composed an epic which has become one of the Tamul classics and is spoken of with unbounded admiration by those who can read it. But this was in India, far from home, and one can well understand that fame among Hindu pundits need not turn the head of an Italian. In England we had Fr. Southwell[3] a poet, a minor poet but still a poet; but he wrote amidst a terrible persecution and died a martyr, with circumstances of horrible barbarity: this is the counterpoise in his career. Then what a genius was Campion[4] himself! was not he a poet? perhaps a great one, if he had chosen. His History of Ireland, written in hiding and hurrying from place to place, Mr. Simpson in his

[1] See Note D, p. 251.

[2] Costanzo Giuseppe Beschi's *Tem-bav-ani* (an epic on the legends of St. Joseph and the Gospel narratives) was published in three vols., 1851–1853.

[3] 1561–1595: author of *St. Peter's Complaint*, *The Burning Babe* and other devotional poems.

[4] 1540–1581. See *Edmund Campion*, by Evelyn Waugh (1936).

Life says, and the samples prove it, shews an eloquence like Shakspere's; and in fact Shakspere made use of the book. He had all and more than all the rhetoric of that golden age and was probably the most vigorous mind and eloquent tongue engaged in theological strife then in England, perhaps in Europe. It seems in time he might have done anything. But his eloquence died on the air, his genius was quenched in his blood after one year's employment in his country. Music is more professional than poetry perhaps and Jesuits have composed and well, but none has any fame to speak of. We had one painter who reached excellence, I forget his name, he was a laybrother; but then he only painted flower pieces. You see then what is against me, but since, as Solomon says, there is a time for everything, there is nothing that does not some day come to be, it may be that the time will come for my verses. . . .

XXI

TO ROBERT BRIDGES

Stonyhurst College,
Blackburn.
Feb. 3 1883.

Dearest Bridges,

I cd. not venture to ask that our library should subscribe half a sovereign for an *édition de luxe* of a new book[1] by an almost unknown author; still less could I expect, nor shd. I like, you to present me, that is our library, with a copy. Here then is a downright deadlock and there is nothing for it but for me to wait for the second edition and then, like Brewer in the *Mutual Friend*, 'see how things look'.

Many thanks for the anthems. I remember now that I heard the first at Magdalen. Did you remark that the first 9 notes of the Hallelujah are, with a slight change, the beginning of *Cease your funning?* . . .

[1] R. B.'s *Prometheus the Firegiver*.

[Here follows the comment on 'Have fair fallen', given below in the notes to *Henry Purcell*, p. 231.]

I quite understand what you mean about gentlemen and 'damfools'; it is a very striking thing and I could say much on the subject. I shall not say that much, but I say this: if a gentleman feels that to be what we call a gentleman is a thing essentially higher than without being a gentleman to be ever so great an artist or thinker or if, to put it another way, an artist or thinker feels that were he to become in those ways ever so great he wd. still essentially be lower than a gentleman that was no artist and no thinker – and yet to be a gentleman is but on the brim of morals and rather a thing of manners than of morals properly – then how much more must art and philosophy and manners and breeding and everything else in the world be below the least degree of true virtue. This is that chastity of mind which seems to lie at the very heart and be the parent of all other good, the seeing at once what is best, the holding to that, and the not allowing anything else whatever to be even heard pleading to the contrary. Christ's life and character are such as appeal to all the world's admiration, but there is one insight St. Paul gives us of it which is very secret and seems to me more touching and constraining than everything else is:[1] This mind, he says, was in Christ Jesus – he means as man: being in the form of God – that is, finding, as in the first instant of his incarnation he did, his human nature informed by the godhead – he thought it nevertheless no snatching-matter for him to be equal with God, but annihilated himself, taking the form of servant; that is, he could not but see what he was, God, but he would see it as if he did not see it, and be it as if he were not and instead of snatching at once at what all the time was his, or was himself, he emptied or exhausted himself so far as tliat was possible, of godhead and behaved only as God's slave, as his creature, as man, which also he was, and then being in the guise of man humbled himself to death, the death of the cross. It is this holding of himself back, and not snatching at the truest and highest good, the good that

[1] Philippians ii. 5–11.

was his right, nay his possession from a past eternity in his other nature, his own being and self, which seems to me the root of all his holiness and the imitation of this the root of all moral good in other men. I agree then, and vehemently, that a gentleman, if there is such a thing on earth, is in the position to despise the poet, were he Dante or Shakspere, and the painter, were he Angelo or Apelles, for anything in him that shewed him *not* to be a gentleman. He is in the position to do it, I say, but if he is a gentleman perhaps this is what he will not do. Which leads me to another remark.

The quality of a gentleman is so very fine a thing that it seems to me one should not be at all hasty in concluding that one possesses it. People assume that they have it, take it quite for granted, and claim the acknowledgment from others: now I should say that this also is 'no snatching-matter'. And the more a man feels what it means and is – and to feel this is certainly some part of it – the more backward he will be to think he can have realised in himself anything so perfect. It is true, there is nothing like the truth and 'the good that does itself not know scarce is'; so the perfect gentleman will know that he is the perfect gentleman. But few can be in the position to know this and, being imperfect gentlemen, it will perhaps be a point of their gentlemanliness, for a gentleman is modest, to feel that they are not perfect gentlemen.

By the by if the English race had done nothing else, yet if they left the world the notion of a gentleman, they would have done a great service to mankind.

As a fact poets and men of art are, I am sorry to say, by no means necessarily or commonly gentlemen. For gentlemen do not pander to lust or other basenesses nor, as you say, give themselves airs and affectations nor do other things to be found in modern works. And this adds a charm to everything Canon Dixon writes, that you feel he is a gentleman and thinks like one. But now I have prosed my prose and long enough.

Believe me your affectionate friend

Gerard M. Hopkins S.J.

XXII

TO ROBERT BRIDGES

University College,
Stephen's Green, Dublin.
Nov. 11, 1884.

Dearest Bridges,

My heavy examination work is now some while over and I have begun to lecture: it is time therefore that I shd. write; indeed I have done so once, but the letter did not please and this is its recast.

I was very glad you gave me some word of your married life; I wish it had been more. I have a kind of spooniness and delight over married people, especially if they say 'my wife', 'my husband', or shew the wedding ring.

I shall read *Eros and Psyche* with the greatest joy; so let civilisation execute its daily eggtrick over the book with the usual adroitness as far as the south side of Stephen's Green.

Mr. Tom Arnold[1] (but I dreamt I told you this before) asked me to write a short notice of Canon Dixon for a new edition of his handbook of English literature. I did it, but whether it was time enough (for he was in the press) and short enough (for he was under pressure) I have not heard.[2]

I have some musical matters to speak of. Stainer has written a capital Treatise on Harmony which has earned him the heartfelt thanks of people as ignorant as myself (I cannot say his Novello-Primer of the same earned them) and of others, I believe, not ignorant at all. For instance Sir Robert Stewart,[3] learned musician of this city, much given to Purcell, Handel, and Bach, says it is the most scientific treatment he has seen. Though his theory is not final, it is a great step forward and has quite a daylight, a *grand*

---

[1] 1823–1900: second son of Arnold of Rugby, Professor of English Literature in University College, Dublin, since 1882.

[2] G. M. H.'s long footnote appeared in the 5th edn. (1885).

[3] Professor of Music in the University of Dublin.

jour, of sense. I am sure Stainer must be very nice to know and meet.

I have a great light on the matter of harmony myself, new, I need not say (framed on the model of Mr. Pecksniff's 'pagan, I regret to say'); true, I hope.

You saw and liked some music of mine to Mr. Patmore's *Crocus*.[1] The harmony came in the end to be very elaborate and difficult. I sent it through my cousin to Sir Frederick Gore Ouseley[2] for censure and that censure I am awaiting.

Before leaving Stonyhurst I began some music, Gregorian, in the natural scale of A, to Collins' *Ode to Evening*. Quickened by the heavenly beauty of that poem I groped in my soul's very viscera for the tune and thrummed the sweetest and most secret catgut of the mind. What came out was very strange and wild and (I thought) very good. Here I began to harmonise it, and the effect of harmony well in keeping upon that strange mode (which, though it is, as far as notes go, the same as the descending minor, has a character of which the word minor gives you little notion) was so delightful that it seems to me (and I think you would find the same) as near a new world of musical enjoyment as in this old world we could hope to be. To the novelty of effect the rhythm and a continued suspense natural to the mode and easy to carry further contribute too. It is meant for a solo and a double choir singing in unison, the organ or a string band bearing all the harmony. It is in three movements, something like a glee, the third returning to the first.

If this letter is dull the writer was so and wearifully tired. So goodnight, and goodnight to Mrs. Bridges or (what is more beautiful) to your wife:

I am your affectionate friend

Gerard M. Hopkins S.J.

Nov. 12 – You asked me some time since if I would write you a short paper on English scanning. I should like to do this if you still want it, but all that we Jesuits publish (even anonymously)

[1] 'The Year', *Poems* (Oxford), p. 57.
[2] Professor of Music at Oxford, 1855–1889.

must be seen by censors and this is a barrier which I do not know how anything of mine on a large scale would ever pass. In this particular case no doubt there would be no difficulty.

XXIII

TO ROBERT BRIDGES

University College,
Stephen's Green, Dublin.
May 17 1885.

Dearest Bridges,

I must write something, though not so much as I have to say. The long delay was due to work, worry, and languishment of body and mind – which must be and will be; and indeed to diagnose my own case (for every man by forty is his own physician or a fool, they say; and yet again he who is his own physician has a fool for his patient – a form of epigram, by the bye, which, if you examine it, has a bad flaw), well then to judge of my case, I think that my fits of sadness, though they do not affect my judgment, resemble madness. Change is the only relief, and that I can seldom get.

I saw that *Ulysses*[1] was a fine play, the action and interest well centred, the characters finely drawn and especially Penelope, the dialogue throughout good; nevertheless, perhaps from my mood of mind, I could not take to it, did not like it, beyond a dry admiration. Not however to remain in a bare Doctor Felldom on the matter, I did find one fault in it which seems indeed to me to be the worst fault a thing can have, unreality. I hope other people will think otherwise, but the introduction in earnest of Athene gave me a distaste I could not recover from. With *Prometheus* it was not the same. Three kinds of departure from truth I understand and agree to in a play – first in a History those changes and conventions without which, as in other works of art, the facts could not be presented at all; secondly a plot of fiction: though

[1] R. B.'s *The Return of Ulysses*.

the facts never actually happened they are a picture of life and a sample of the sort of facts that do – those also subject to their own changes and conventions; lastly an allegory, where things that neither do nor could be mask and mean something that is. To this last class *Prometheus*, as I take it, belongs; moreover it was modelled on the Greek and scarcely meant for acting. But *Ulysses* is to act; and in earnest, not allegorically, you bring in a goddess among the characters: it revolts me. Then, not un-naturally, as it seemed to me, her speech is the worst in the play: being an unreality she must talk unreal. Believe me, the Greek gods are a totally unworkable material; the merest frigidity, which must chill and kill every living work of art they are brought into. Even if we put aside the hideous and, taken as they stand, unspeakable stories told of them, which stories nevertheless are as authentic as their names and personalities – both are equally imaginary; if you do not like that, both equally symbolical –, putting these out of sight and looking only at their respectable side, they are poor ignoble conceptions ennobled bodily only (as if they had bodies) by the artists, but once in motion and action worthless – not gentlemen or ladies, cowards, loungers, without majesty, without awe, antiquity, foresight, character; old bucks, young bucks, and Biddy Buckskins. What did Athene do after leaving Ulysses? Lounged back to Olympus to afternoon nectar. Nothing can be made of it. May 21, 1885. The background of distance and darkness and doom which a tragedy should always have is shut out by an Olympian drop-scene; the characters from men become puppets, their bloodshed becomes a leakage of bran. (This, upon my word, is to ply the lash and to be unpardonable.)[1] I see the nobility of the rest, but this one touch to my eye spoils all; it looks to me like fine relief all daubed and creamed over with heavy whitewash.

I do not wonder at those ladies reading *Nero*[2] through at a sitting. It *is* very interesting and I feel quite the same. You offered to send me a correcter copy: I shd. be glad if you now would.

[1] For G. M. H.'s further comment on this theme in a letter to Dixon, see Note J, p. 252.   [2] Part I (1884).

I must add there was another fault I had to find with *Ulysses* and it was to the same effect and same defect, of unreality; I mean the archaism of the language, which was to my mind overdone. I hold that by archaism a thing is sicklied o'er as by blight. Some little flavours, but much spoils, and always for the same reason – it destroys earnest: we do not speak that way; therefore if a man speaks that way he is not serious, he is at something else than the seeming matter in hand, *non hoc agit, aliud agit*. I believe you agree with me in principle; if so I think that your practice in that play is beyond what your principle allows. But slight changes would satisfy me. The example of Shakspere (by a 'corrupt following', for it is an absurd fallacy – like a child having to repeat the substance of something it has been told and saying *you* and *I* wherever the speaker said *you* and *I*, whereas it should say *I* where he said *you* and so on) has done ever so much harm by his very genius, for poets reproduce the diction which in him was modern and in them is obsolete. But you know all this.

How did Michael Field[1] in the end go off?

It is too bad that I shd. so abuse *Ulysses* after your encouragement of *St. Winefred*.[2] But how cd. you think such a thing of me as that I shd. in cold blood write 'fragments of a dramatic poem'? – I of all men in the world. To me a completed fragment, above all of a play, is the same unreality as a prepared impromptu. No, but we compose fragmentarily and what I had here and there done I finished up and sent as samples to see if I cd. be encouraged to go on – and I was encouraged; that is by your last, for before I thought you thought they wd. not do. There is a point with me in matters of any size when I must absolutely have encouragement as much as crops rain; afterwards I am independent. However I am in my ordinary circumstances unable, with whatever encouragement, to go on with *Winefred* or anything else. I have after long silence written two sonnets, which I am touching: if ever anything was written in blood one of these was.[3]

---

[1] The pen-name of Katharine Bradley and her niece Edith Cooper, who from 1884 produced together numerous lyrics and verse dramas.

[2] Dramatic fragment – poem No. 58.   [3] See note to No. 41, p. 239.

Of two metrical criticisms you made on the fragments one I did not well understand, the other was a misunderstanding on your part.

About the music I shd. like to write at some length. But for the present I only say first, how could you think I shd. be offended at your criticism or remarks or wanted you to express yourself so modestly? May 28, 1885. Next I am much obliged for the quotations from Purcell, but could not get my household musician to play the one in open score nor have had time or opportunity of running after professionals, besides that for myself I have kept away some time now from the piano. Thirdly the bass solo you give me to shew the variety Purcell could command by the modern system – well of that beautiful passage I have to say that it illustrates the wellknown variety of the minor as we now understand it, a variety for which Purcell particularly prized it, but that that variety I did not need the illustrating of and, ahem, I can send you an illustration of my own which as it seems to me is happy in that way – made long ago. Then of course I admire and surely I could produce – it requires no more knowledge than I have already got for at least the simpler effects and in fact modulation even to remote keys and so on is not difficult to do; it may be to explain – could produce and have produced modulations, but in the two first verses of the *Battle of the Baltic*[1] (which has some eleven) I wanted to see what could be done (and for how long I could go on) without them. ——[2] of course thought they cd. not be done without even for that length and I do not dispute the judgment; I scarcely had myself heard my second verse – for that is the great difficulty, in reality my only, and I fear my insuperable, one, that I cannot play. But nevertheless Palestrina and the old madrigal writers and others did produce masterpieces – and Hullah says actually final in their kind, that is which you cannot develope by modern science; you can only change the school and kind – without modulations, but employing the modes; without

[1] Setting of Campbell's poem, 'with pianoforte accompaniment, ... for two choirs singing in unison, the first choir consisting of the British, the second of the Danes.' See *N*, 2nd edn., App. 11. [2] Name deleted by R. B.

even the authentic cadence: I wish I cd. study them. Then 'do I mean to rival Purcell and Mozart?' No. Even given the genius, a musician must be that and nothing else, as music now is; at least so it has been with all the great musicians. But I did aim at two things not in themselves unattainable, if to me far easier things were not now unattainable. But of these, if ever, hereafter.

Believe me your affectionate friend

Gerard M. Hopkins S.J.

XXIV

TO COVENTRY PATMORE

University College,
St. Stephen's Green, Dublin.
June 4 1886.

My dear Mr. Patmore,

I have been meaning and meaning to write to you, to return the volumes of Barnes' poems you lent me and for other reasons, and partly my approaching examination work restrained me, when last night there reached me from Bell's the beautiful new edition of your works. I call it beautiful and think it is the best form upon the whole for poetry and works of pure literature that I know of and I thank you for your kindness in sending it. And I hope the bush or the bottle may do what little in a bush or bottle lies to recommend the liquor to the born and the unborn. But how slowly does the fame of excellence spread! And crooked eclipses and other obscure causes fight against its rise and progress.

Your poems are a good deed done for the Catholic Church and another for England, for the British Empire, which now trembles in the balance held in the hand of unwisdom. I remark that those Englishmen who wish prosperity to the Empire (which is not all Englishmen or Britons, strange to say) speak of the Empire's mission to extend freedom and civilisation in India and elsewhere. The greater the scale of politics the weightier the influence of a

¹ See Note K, p. 253.

great name and a high ideal. It is a terrible element of weakness that now we are not well provided with the name and ideal which would recommend and justify our Empire. 'Freedom': it is perfectly true that British freedom is the best, the only successful freedom, but that is because, with whatever drawbacks, those who have developed that freedom have done so with the aid of law and obedience to law. The cry then shd. be Law and Freedom, Freedom and Law. But that does not please: it must be Freedom only. And to that cry there is the telling answer: No freedom you can give us is equal to the freedom of letting us alone: take yourselves out of India, let us first be free of you. Then there is civilisation. It shd. have been Catholic truth. That is the great end of Empires before God, to be Catholic and draw nations into their Catholicism. But our Empire is less and less Christian as it grows. There remains that part of civilisation which is outside Christianity or which is not essentially Christian. The best is gone, still something worth having is left. How far can the civilisation England offers be attractive and valuable and be offered and insisted on as an attraction and a thing of value to India for instance? Of course those who live in our civilisation and belong to it praise it: it is not hard, as Socrates said, among the Athenians to praise the Athenians; but how will it be represented by critics bent on making the worst of it or even not bent on making the best of it? It is good to be in Ireland to hear how enemies, and those rhetoricians, can treat the things that are unquestioned at home. I know that to mere injustice and slander innocence and excellence themselves stand condemned, but since there is always in mankind some love of truth and admiration for good (only that the truth must be striking and the good on a great scale) what marked and striking excellence has England to shew to make her civilisation attractive? Her literature is one of her excellences and attractions and I believe that criticism will tend to make this more and more felt; but there must be more of that literature, a continued supply and in quality excellent. That is why I hold that fine works of art, and especially if, like yours, they[1] are

[1] *F* has 'that'.

not only ideal in form but deal with high matter as well, are really a great power in the world, an element of strength even to an empire. But now time and tediousness forbid me to write more on this.

It has struck me since I was at Hastings that, if it is not impertinent of me to say it, Miss Patmore[1] might gain by taking some lessons from some painter. It is true she does what no painter can either do or teach but it is also true there are other things she might with advantage learn. For in fact everyone is the better for teaching: it is universally true. It struck me that she was hampered by want of some mechanical knowledge, as in the use of washes for background, and she tends, I think, to use bodycolour in a way which would be considered vicious. This has naturally arisen from her circumstances; for in the delicate detail in which she so wonderfully excells the use of bodycolour is legitimate and even necessary and naturally she extended a practice with which she was familiar to a new field. I will send Barnes's poems back in a few days.

Believe me your sincere friend
Gerard M. Hopkins S.J.[2]

XXV

TO COVENTRY PATMORE

Glenaveena, Howth.
Whitsunday (May 20) 1888.

Dear Mr. Patmore,

This is to express the hope that your attack of quinsy has passed or is passing off and to say that my paper on the *Angel*[3] is really in hand and when finished will be printed without difficulty: there is more difficulty about getting it finished. If it is to be printed at all however it is a pity it cannot be somewhere where it would have more readers. It treats of the matters your letter

[1] C.P.'s fourth child, Bertha.
[2] A short postscript has been omitted.
[3] A projected review of Patmore's *The Angel in the House.*

touches on. But about the 'tyke' you did not altogether under-
stand me. If I had said you had less than anyone else of the
Bohemian, though that is not the same thing, the meaning would
have been plainer. As there is something of the 'old Adam' in all
but the holiest men and in them at least enough to make them
understand it in others, so there is an old Adam of barbarism,
boyishness, wildness, rawness, rankness, the disreputable, the
unrefined in the refined and educated. It is that that I meant by
tykishness (a tyke is a stray sly unowned dog) and said you have
none of; and I did also think that you were without all sympathy
for it and must survey it when you met with it wholly from
without. Ancient Pistol is the typical tyke, he and all his crew are
tykes, and the tykish element undergoing dilution in Falstaff and
Prince Hal[1] appears to vanish, but of course really exists, in
Henry V as king. I thought it was well to have ever so little of it
and therefore it was perhaps a happy thing that you were en-
trapped into the vice of immoderate smoking, for to know one
yields to a vice must help to humanise and make tolerant.

Since I wrote last I have had a piece of good luck which also
has something to do with you. I made another attempt on my
tune to the Crocus.[2] I set it in strict counterpoint (or as strict as
the case allowed of) as a madrigal in canon at the octave, a most
difficult task, and after much labour sent it to my friend Sir Robert
Stewart to correct. He gave it a very good mark, but suggested
some changes in the rhythm chiefly. I have made them, but to
touch a composition of this sort is like touching a house of cards;
one piece pulls down another, so the alterations cost a good deal
of trouble more. And this is only the first verse: the two others
are still to do. When all is done it ought to be sung by an un-
accompanied choir. I hope in the end it may be: the attempt was
daring (like verse in intricate metre) and Sir Robert's verdict
amounted to saying that it was successful.

I am very sincerely yours

Gerard M. Hopkins.

[1] MS. 'Hall'.   [2] See above, p. 201. See N, 2nd edn., p. 489.

XXVI

TO ROBERT BRIDGES

University College,
St. Stephen's Green, Dublin.
Sept. 25 1888.

Dearest Bridges,

I am sorry to hear of our differing so much in taste: I was hardly aware of it. (It is not nearly so sad as differing in religion). I feel how great the loss is of not reading, as you say; but if I did read I do not much think the effect of it would be what you seem to expect, on either my compositions or my judgments.

I *must* read something of Greek and Latin letters and lately I sent you a sonnet, on the Heraclitean Fire,[1] in which a great deal of early Greek philosophical thought was distilled; but the liquor of the distillation did not taste very Greek, did it? The effect of studying masterpieces is to make me admire and do otherwise. So it must be on every original artist to some degree, on me to a marked degree. Perhaps then more reading would only *refine my singularity*, which is not what you want. . . .

But not on my criticisms either, I suspect. Wide reading does two things – it extends knowledge and it adjusts the judgment. Now it is mostly found that a learned judgment is less singular than an unlearned one and oftener agrees with the common and popular judgment, with which it coincides as a fine balance or other measure does with the rule of thumb. But, so far as I see, where we differ in judgment, my judgments are less singular than yours; I agree more than you do with the mob and with the *communis criticorum*. Presumably I shd. agree with these still more if I read more and so differ still more from you than now. Who for instance is singular about Dryden,[2] you or I? These considerations are very general, but so far as they go they appear to be reasonable.

To return to composition for a moment: what I want there, to

[1] See poem No. 49.   [2] G. M. H. admired Dryden; R. B. did not.

be more intelligible, smoother, and less singular, is an audience. I think the fragments I wrote of *St. Winefred*, which was meant to be played, were not hard to understand. My prose I am sure is clear and even flowing. This reminds me that I have written a paper for an Irish magazine the *Lyceum*, organ of this College, one may say. I was asked and I rewrote something I had by me and it is to appear next month. And yet I bet you it will not: my luck will not allow it. But if it does, I then bet you it is intelligible, though on an obstruse subject, Statistics and Free Will – and I mean very intelligible. (This, by the bye, is a badly made logical bed; for I can only win one wager by losing the other. But never mind.)

I send an improved version of my war-song,[1] less open to the objections made, and am your affectionate friend

Gerard Hopkins.

XXVII

TO ROBERT BRIDGES

Univ. Coll., Stephen's Green,
Dublin.
Oct. 19 '88.

Dearest Bridges,

You remark, I am glad to find, a 'lambness' in my last letter: now in the present I shall have somewhat as schoolboys say, to 'lamb in'. But first of various matters.

My little Paper on *Statistics and Free Will* obeyed the general law and did not appear; so I win that wager, if you remember. The editor made some objections which involved recasting it: I have partly done so, and when it is all recast he will no doubt find others. But meantime I get into print in a way I would not. My father wrote a little book on Numbers,[2] the numbers one to

[1] *Poems*, 3rd Edn., No. 118.
[2] *The Cardinal Numbers*, by Manley Hopkins (1887). For G. M. H.'s father see Note L, p. 253.

ten, a sketchy thing, raising points of interest in a vast, an infinite subject: the *Saturday* lately had a paper on this book, making great game of it from end to end (of it and the article), including something I had contributed to it; however I was not named. Last week same Review has an article 'The American Poet', a comment on Gosse, who lately said, it seems, there *is* no American poet – great poet, he means, or poet proper perhaps. It ends 'After all, the whole affair is a fluke. Great poets are the results of exquisitely rare and incalculable combinations of causes, and nobody would be to blame if there were not a great poet for another century. This country does not seem likely to have another in a hurry [take that], nor have we observed him mewing his mighty youth in France, Germany, Italy, or Spain. Perhaps he is at school in Bolivia at this moment, or he may be at Johns Hopkins University, Baltimore, and his Christian name may be "Gifted".' It is an allusion to that same 'Gifted Hopkins' the humorist 'who died of his own jocosity' that, if you remember, was meant the time before.[1] But if Lang[2] wrote this paper too, then, putting together that very fact that he then did *not* mean me with the fact that Gosse (you told me) admires my muse and the one that being imprudent he may have said so and others, I do not know but I may say to myself, O my soul, perhaps This Is Fame. But I don't want it and beg you will not expose me to it; which you can easily forbear from doing now that you disapprove of my γένος[3] as vicious, and surely you shd. not vitiate taste. And at any rate I shall never cease to deplore that unhappy letter of mine you read sitting leagues and parasangs of country lanes next to Lang that morning: how could I foresee it was so dangerous to write to a remote world's-end place like Yattendon? But indeed you have told me there is plenty of intellectual life there.

Next, music. I am glad to find it is only there we are so far apart. But the contrary is true: there we agree well enough and the rift is elsewhere. I agree to your musical strictures and almost invite your rebukes and if I do not do so heartily it is because a perfect organisation for crippling me exists and the one for

[1] See Note M, p. 253. [2] Andrew Lang (1844–1912). [3] 'kind', genus'.

'encouragemental purposes' (modern English) is not laid down yet. I agree that for contrapuntal writing we shd. read the great masters and study the rules, both. The great masters unhappily I cannot read (unless very little), but the rules I do carefully study, and just on account of the great formality of the art of music it happens that mere adherence to them, without study of examples from the masters, produces – given faculty – results of some interest and value. (I like not that last sentence: it is too much in the manner of the magazines I read and too far entirely from Doughty and the Mighty Dead.) And my madrigal in canon, so far as it has gone, is strict and Sir Robert Stewart (a demon for rule) says it is correct and that it might even have been freer. But, as you say, you have not seen it and now that I have no piano I cannot go on with it. This morning I gave in what I believe is the last batch of examination-work for this autumn (and if all were seen, fallen leaves of my poor life between all the leaves of it), and but for that want I might prance on ivory this very afternoon. I have had to get glasses, by the bye: just now I cannot be happy either with or without them. The oculist says my sight is very good and my eye perfectly healthy but that like Jane Nightwork[1] I am old. And, strange to say, I have taken to drawing again. Perverse Fortune or something perverse (try me): why did I not take to it before? And now enough, for I must whet myself, strop myself, be very bitter, and will secrete and distil a good deal beforehand.

However with no more stropping than the palm of my hand and chopping at a hair, no but at the 'broth of goldish flue'[2] (how well now does the pleasing modern author come in in his own illustration and support!), I can deal with one matter, the sonnet on St. Alphonsus.[3] I am obliged for your criticisms, 'contents of which noted', indeed acted on. I have improved the sestet (in itself I do not call the first version 'cheeky', the imagery as applied to God Almighty being so familiar in the Scripture and the Fathers: however I have not kept it). But now I cannot quite understand nor so far as I understand agree with the difficulty you

[1] 2 *Hen. IV*, iii. 2.   [2] Poem No. 48, l. 1.   [3] Poem No. 50.

raise about the continents and so on. It is true continents are partly made by 'trickling increment'; but what is on the whole truest and most strikes us about them and mountains is that they are made what now we see them by trickling *de*crements, by detrition, weathering and the like.* And at any rate whatever is markedly featured in stone or what is like stone is most naturally said to be hewn, and to *shape*, itself, means in old English to hew and the Hebrew *bara/* to create, even, properly means to hew. But life and living things are not naturally said to be hewn: they grow, and their growth is by trickling increment.

I will not now interpret the thought of the sestet. It is however, so far as I can see, both exâct and pregnant.

I am altogether at a loss to see your objection to *exploit* and to *so we say*. You will allow – would, I shd. think, urge on me – that where the ὄνομα κύριον¹ has nothing flat or poor about it it is the best word to use in poetry as in prose, better I mean than its paraphrase. Now *exploit* is the right word, it is κύριον, there is no other for the thing meant but *achievement*, which is not better, and it is a handsome word in itself: why then should I not say it? Surely I should. By 'regular indoors work' I understand you to mean a drawing finished at home with the eye no longer on the object, something poorly thrown in to fill up a blank the right filling of which is forgotten. But 'so we say' is just what I have to say and want to say (it was made out of doors in the Phoenix Park with my mind's eye on the first presentment of the thought): I mean 'This is what we commonly say, but we are wrong'. The line now stands 'Glory is a flame off exploit, so we say' and I think it must so stand.

I am warming myself at the flame of a little exploit of my own done last night. I could not have believed in such a success nor

---

* By the bye, some geologists say the last end of all continents and dry land altogether is to be washed into the sea and that when all are gone 'water will be the world', as in the Flood, and will still be deep and have to spare. (G. M. H.'s note.)

¹ Strict, literal name for a thing; exact word: a term from Aristotle's *Poetics*.

that life had this pleasure to bestow. Somebody had tried to take me in and I warned him I wd. take him in at our next meeting. Accordingly I wrote him a letter from 'the son of a respected livery and bait stables in Parteen [suburb of Limerick] oftentimes employed by your Honoured Father' asking for an introduction to one of the Dublin newspapers 'as Reporter, occasional paregraphs or sporting inteligence'. The sentence I think best of was one in which I said (or he) could 'give any color which may be desired to reports of speeches or Proceedings subject to the Interests of truth which must always be the paremount consideration'. It succeeded beyond my wildest hopes and action is going to be taken. The letter is even to be printed in the *Nation* as a warning to those who are continually applying in the like strain; but before this takes place I must step in.

It is as you say about Addis.[1] But why should you be glad? Why at any rate should you burst upon me that you are glad, when you know that I cannot be glad?

It seems there is something in you interposed between what shall we say? the Christian and the man of the world which hurts, which is to me like biting on a cinder in bread. Take the simplest view of this matter: he has made shipwreck, I am afraid he must even be in straits: he cannot support himself by his learned writings; I suppose he will have to teach. But this is the least. I hope at all events he will not pretend to marry, and especially no one he has known in his priestly life. Marriage is honourable and so is the courtship that leads to marriage, but the philanderings of men vowed to God are not honourable nor the marriages they end in. I feel the same deep affection for him as ever, but the respect is gone. I would write to him if I had his address, which, I am sorry to say, is still or was lately somewhere at Sydenham; for after bidding farewell to his flock he had not the grace to go away.

This is enough for the time and I will put off the lambing to another season. With kindest remembrances to Mrs. Bridges and Mrs. Molesworth, I am your affectionate friend

Gerard M. Hopkins.

[1] See above, Letters IV and V, and Note G, p. 251.

XXVIII

TO HIS MOTHER

University College,
Dublin.
May 5, 1889.

My dearest Mother,

I am grieved that you should be in such anxiety about me and I am afraid my letter to my father, which you must now have seen and ought, it seems to me, to have had before this morning's letter was sent, can not much have relieved you. I am now in careful hands. The doctor thoroughly examined me yesterday. I have some fever; what, has not declared itself. I am to have perfect rest, and to take only liquid food. My pains and sleeplessness were due to suspended digestion, which has now been almost cured, but with much distress. There is no hesitation or difficulty about the nurses, with which Dublin is provided, I dare say, better than any place, but Dr. Redmond this morning said he must wait further to see the need: for today there is no real difference; only that I feel better.

You do not mention how Mary is.

I am and I long have been sad about Lionel[1], feeling that his visits must be few and far between and that I had so little good of this one, though he and I have so many interests in common and shd. find many more in company. I cd. not send him my Paper,[2] for it had to be put aside.

It is an ill wind that blows nobody good. My sickness falling at the most pressing time of the University work, there will be the devil to pay. Only there is no harm in saying, that gives *me* no trouble but an unlooked for relief. At many such a time I have been in a sort of extremity of mind, now I am the placidest soul in the world. And you will see, when I come round, I shall be better for this.

[1] Lionel Charles Hopkins (1854–1952), a brother of G. M. H.
[2] On the Argei.

I am writing uncomfortably and this is enough for a sick man.
I am your loving son
   Best love to all.

Gerard.

SECTION C

EDITOR'S NOTES

(a) NOTES ON THE POEMS

ABBREVIATIONS USED

R. B. – Dr Robert Bridges, Editor of First Edition of the *Poems* of Gerard Manley Hopkins (hereafter 'G. M. H.'), 1918.

3rd Edn. – *Poems of G. M. H.*, edited by W. H. Gardner (Oxford University Press, 1948; 5th impression, 1956).

B. – *Letters of G. M. H. to R. B.*, edited by Claude Colleer Abbott (O.U.P., 1935; 2nd edition, 1955).

D. – *Correspondence of G. M. H. and R. W. Dixon*, edited by Claude Colleer Abbott (O.U.P., 1935; 2nd edition, 1956).

N. – *Note-books and Papers of G. M. H.*, edited by Humphry House (O.U.P., 1937). (Re-issue as two vols., 1959.)

F. – *Further Letters of G. M. H.*, edited by Claude Colleer Abbott (O.U.P., 1938; 2nd edition, 1956 [refs. to this edn.]).

(Arch. = archaic; obs. = obsolete; dial. = dialect; archit. = architecture; engin. = engineering).

FOUR EARLY POEMS (1865–1866)

1–2. These two poems are from neatly pencilled drafts in an Oxford note-book and are dated '1865'. We cannot be sure that they were ever finally revised.

3. 'HEAVEN-HAVEN.' First rough drafts belong to 1864. Like Nos. 2 and 4, it indicates the turn of the poet's mind and heart towards the priesthood.

4. 'THE HABIT OF PERFECTION.' Jan. 1866. Originally called 'The Kind Betrothal'. Line 24, *unhouse, &c.*: the 'tabernacle' of the altar (Catholic) 'houses' the consecrated Host ('the Lord').

POEMS (1876–1889)

5. 'THE WRECK OF THE DEUTSCHLAND.' For G. M. H.'s own account of the inception of this poem and the new 'Sprung Rhythm' in which it is composed see (first) Letter XVI (p. 187), Letter XIII (p. 177) and Author's Preface (p. 7).

As G. M. H. said, 'this poem is an ode and not primarily a narrative … the principal business is lyrical'. (*B*, p. 49.) The shipwreck, with its dramatic episode of the 'tall nun' (stanzas 12–28), becomes the node round which the poet harmonizes his faith in God and his painful feelings about the problem of suffering – the tragic aspect of human life. The wreck of the *Deutschland* is the symbol of the whole world's plight since the Fall of Man – symbol of man's inevitable shipwreck in this earthly existence (st. 11). This inescapable tragic agony is at once symbolized, explained, and mitigated by the Passion of Christ, which was directly due to the Fall and to 'man's malice' (stanzas 6–9, 22; but the *key* to the symbolism is in st. 29). Life is a period of trial and purgation (stanzas 21, 27). We, like Christ, must accept the pain and offer ourselves as a sacrifice (stanzas 22–24); like Him, we must be prepared to 'succeed by failure' (stanzas 27, 31). To offset this loss and defeat is Christ's 'proffer' of salvation (stanzas 4, 28); the outcome, for the faithful, is the Heavenly Reward (stanzas 23, 26–8, 35), and of this beatitude the faithful have a vision and foretaste in the beauties of nature and the joys of living, which are intensified by the concomitant pain (stanzas 5, 26). The joys and sorrows are harmonized by the poet's faith in the paradoxical nature of God, who is at once a stern master and a fond father (stanzas 1–3, 9, 21). Returning to the theme of the opening stanzas, the poem rises to a great hymn of submission and praise to God the Father and Christ (stanzas 32–34), and concludes with a plea to the drowned nun for intercessory prayers for the conversion of England (st. 35).

Rhythm: In Part the First the opening line of each stanza has *two* strong stresses, e.g. stanza 1 (my scansion):

'Thou mastering me

God! Giver of breath and bread;

In Part the Second the first line of each stanza has *three* strong stresses, e.g. stanza 11:

'Sóme find me a swórd; sóme'

In lines 2–8 of each stanza throughout the poem the distribution of the stresses is: 3—4—3—5—5—4—6. 'There are no outriding feet in the *Deutschland*.' (*B*. p. 45).

Stanza 1, l. 6, 'álmost únmade'; l. 8, *finger*. See note on st. 3, l. 8. St. 2, l. 2, *láshed ród*: see Note A, p. 249; l. 5. 'I may add for your greater interest and edification that what refers to myself in the poem is all strictly and literally true and did all occur; nothing is added for poetical padding.' (G. M. H. in *B*, p. 47.) *hōur*, thus in MS.

St. 3, l. 4, *spell*, period of stress; l. 8, cf. *N*, p. 337: 'elevating grace, which lifts the receiver from one cleave of being to another and to a vital act in Christ: this is truly God's finger touching the very vein of personality, which nothing else can reach and man can respond to by no play whatever, by bare acknowledgment only, the counter-stress which God alone can feel ("subito probas eum"), the aspiration in answer to his inspiration. Of this I have written . . . somewhere else long ago.' As the late Humphry House suggested, this may refer to st. 1 as well as st. 3.

St. 4, l. 7, *voel*, Welsh for 'bare hill'; mutation of Moel, the name of a mountain near St. Beuno's College, N. Wales, where G. M. H. was then studying Theology. Meaning is that the 'well' is fed by long, twisted (i.e. 'roped') runnels of rainwater down and within the mountain sides. This is the link with the first 'metaphysical' image (ll. 1–4): as the body decays, faith is built up to a calm 'poise' by co-operation with Divine grace.

St. 5, l. 7, *instressed, stressed*: God's nature, though a mystery, can and must 'come to stress' in us, be impressed upon our being, through an 'illumination' or an act of faith; it must then be dwelt upon, actualized and kept at stress by our own readiness to respond to further grace (as in l. 8); moreover the truth of all this must be *stressed*, emphasized.

Stanzas 6–9. The general meaning is: Though the 'divine principle' and God's purpose towards man had been vaguely apprehended in previous ages, the true mystical paradox of God's mastery and mercy (His final Self-revelation to man through the mystery of suffering) dates only from Christ's Incarnation and Passion, which were necessitated by the sins of mankind. The Redemption has sensitized men's hearts to the finger of God, to the 'immortal beauty' of Sacrifice.

St. 10, l. 5, *crāsh Pául*, i.e. the conversion of Saul (St. Paul); l. 6, *Austin*, St. Augustine of Hippo (354–430), whose conversion was gradual.

St. 11, l. 8, *cringe*, cf. obs. meanings (1) 'fall', (2) 'cause to cringe or cower'.

St. 12, l. 7, *bay*, archit. metaphor; cf. *N*, p. 125: 'opposite bays of the sky'; l. 8, *reeve*, cf. the nautical sense, 'rope together'.

St. 14, l. 3, *combs*, crests, shifting ridges (cf. st. 4, ll. 1–4). Note the 'linked rhyme':

'leeward / drew her D——'

So also in stanzas 31 and 35. – l. 4, *Kentish Knock*, sandbank in the Thames estuary; l. 7, *whorl*, the screw-propeller, which was lost; l. 8, *wind*, (naut.) steer.

St. 16, l. 8, *burl*, rounded toss (cf. *buck*).

St. 18, l. 5, *after*, almost 'in pursuit of'; l. 8, *this glee*, &c.: though sad, the poet's heart feels joy too, because of the nun's fortitude and faith.

St. 19, l. 1, *Sister*, &c. From *The Times*, Dec. 11, 1875: 'Five German nuns ... clasped hands and were drowned together, the chief sister, a gaunt woman 6 ft. high, calling out loudly and often "O Christ, come quickly!" till the end came.' – l. 3, *hawling*, thus in MSS.; l. 6, *fetch* (arch.) 'stratagem', 'device'.

St. 20, l. 5, *Gertrude*, Catholic saint and mystic (*c*. 1256–*c*. 1302) of Eisleben, Germany, birthplace of Luther.

St. 21, l. 5, *Orion*, cf. the constellation named after the giant hunter (myth.); l. 6, *unchancelling*, taken with 'Orion' could mean 'driving the nuns from their sanctuary (chancel)'; some see a coinage from Fr. 'chanceler', 'to be unsteady', so that the epithet suggests God's unwavering justice.

St. 22, l. 1, *finding*, 'discovery' and emblematic figure; *sake*, highest common factor of 'He died for oúr sake, we suffer for Hís sake'; so *finding* suggests also 'means of finding Christ'. For G. M. H.'s explanation of 'sake' see note to No. 22. – Line 8, *rose-flake*, the red rose is the traditional emblem of martyrdom.

St. 23, l. 3, *gnarls* ... *niche*, &c., Christ's five wounds, reproduced in the stigmata received by St. Francis, form the *Lovescape* of l. 4, the very essence or the *inscape* of Love.

St. 25, l. 2, *arch*, &c., cf. Gk. ἀρχή, first cause, i.e. the Holy Spirit; l. 5, *the men*, &c. See Matthew, viii, 25.

St. 26, l. 8, *The treasure*, &c. See 1 Corinthians, ii, 9.

St. 29, l. 2, *single eye*, cf. 'When the eye is single, thy whole body is full of light, &c.' (Luke, xi. 34.)

St. 30, l. 5. Feast of the Immaculate Conception of the Blessed Virgin, Dec. 8; ll. 6–7, the nun, also a virgin, had given Christ a new birth ('of a brain').

     / ×× × / ×× ××× / ×× /×××

St. 31, l. 6: 'Finger of a tender of, O of a feathery delicacy....' (Thus in MS.)

St. 32, l. 2, *Yore-flood*, the Deluge, or perhaps the primal waters of Genesis i. 2. – l. 5, *Stanching ... mind*. 'Stanch' means 'make firm', 'stop flow of', 'allay a craving' – a general idea which is strengthened by *quenching*. I take 'motionable mind' to be the mind of Man which is restless, like the ocean, within the bounds set for it by God ('the wharf of it ... granite'). – l. 8, *bodes but abides*, 'knows what will happen but does not therefore forestall the free acts of men'. (R. R. Boyle, S.J.).

St. 33, ll. 3–4, i.e. even those lingering in Purgatory may benefit by God's love; l. 8, *fetched*, (obs.) 'reached'; i.e. Christ, the giant, reached the 'uttermost mark' (l. 6).

St. 34, l. 8, 'A released shówer let flásh....

    / ×××× / ×× × /×× ×·

St. 35, l. 3, 'Remember us in the roads, the heaven-haven of the

  × /

Reward'. Lines 4–8 are heavily loaded with strong syllables, to produce the effect of climax.

6. 'PENMAEN POOL.' St. 3, l. 2, *Giant's stool*, the mountain Cadair Idris.

8. 'GŎD'S GRANDEUR. Standard rhythm counterpointed.' Dated 1877. The first line is to be read thus:

'The wórld is chárged with the grandeur of Gód.'

(Five stresses.) Also line 5, *Generations*, thus in MS. (see Author's Preface, p. 9). – l. 2, *foil*: 'I mean foil in its sense of leaf or tinsel. ... Shaken goldfoil gives off broad glares like sheet lightning and also, and this is true of nothing else, owing to its zigzag dints and creasings and network of small many cornered facets, a sort of fork lightning too.' (*B*, pp. 168–9.)

9. 'THE STARLIGHT NIGHT. Standard rhythm opened and counterpointed. St. Beuno's, 1877.' For 'opened' cf. the 'sprung leadings' (i.e. ll. 1 and 9) of No. 10. – l. 4, *delves*, plural of obs. 'delf', mine, pit. Earlier version has 'diamond wells'. – l. 6, *whitebeam ... abeles*, trees with leaves that turn up their silvery undersides in a wind. – l. 12, *barn*, cf. Matt. xiii 30.

10. 'SPRING. (Standard rhythm, opening with sprung leadings.) May 1877.'

11. 'THE LANTERN OUT OF DOORS. (Standard rhythm, with one sprung leading and one line counterpointed.)' St. Beuno's, 1877. Accents in lines 13 and 14 and the note 'companion to No. 26' (=No. 27 in this ed.) in autograph. – l. 5, 'Mén go bý me ...'; ll. 9–10: of the curious verb 'wind eye after' G. M. H. says: 'I mean that the eye winds/ only in the sense that its focus or point of sight winds and that coincides with a point of the object and winds with that. For the object, a lantern passing further and further away and bearing now east now west of one right line, is truly and properly described as winding.' (*B*, p. 66).

12. 'THE SEA AND THE SKYLARK. Standard rhythm; in parts sprung and in others counterpointed, Rhyl, May '77.' In a letter of 1882 G. M. H. explained the images in ll. 4–8: the 'new-skeined score' is the lark's song 'which from his height gives the impression of something falling to the earth and not vertically quite but trickingly or wavingly, something as a skein of silk ribbed by having been tightly wound on a narrow card or a notched holder or as twine or fishing tackle unwinding from a *reel* or *winch* or as pearls strung on a horsehair: the laps or folds are the notes or short measures and bars of them. The same is called a *score* in the musical sense of score and this score is "writ upon a liquid sky trembling to welcome it", only not horizontally. The lark in wild glee *races the reel round*, paying or dealing out and down the turns of the skein or *coil* right to the earth *floor*, the ground, where it lies in a heap, as it were, or rather is all wound off on to another winch, reel, bobbin or spool in Fancy's eye, by the moment the bird touches earth and so is ready for a fresh unwinding at the next flight. ... *Crisp* means almost *crisped*, namely with notes.' (*B*, p. 164).

13. 'THE WINDHOVER. (Falling paeonic rhythm, sprung and out-riding.) St. Beuno's May 30, 1877.' In 1879 G. M. H. described this poem as 'the best thing I ever wrote'. Each line has five main metrical stresses. For the difference between 'outriding feet' and the smoother paeons ($/\times \times \times$) see note to No. 15. In the MSS, the outrides are marked by nether loops:

'I cáught this mórning mórning's mínion, king-
    dom of dáylight's dáuphin, dapple-dáwn-drawn Fálcon,
      in his ríding . . .'

The other marked outrides are: l. 3, 'rólling level únderneath him steady aír (stresses so marked); l. 6, 'skate's heel'; l. 8, 'achieve of'; l. 11, 'lovelier . . . dangerous'; l. 12, 'No wónder of it' – Line 2. Cf. the Dauphin's praise of his horse in *Henry V*, III. vii. l. 11: '*le cheval volant,* the Pegasus, *qui a les narines de feu!* When I bestride him I soar, I am a hawk: he trots the air.' Line 10, 'AND', thus in MS.; l. 14, 'Fall, gáll themsélves, and gásh góld-vermílion' (stresses so marked).

Line 4, *rung, &c.* Cf. (1) a technical term of the riding-school, 'to ring on the rein' – said of a horse that circles at the end of a long rein held by its trainer, and (2) 'to ring' (falconry), i.e. to rise in spirals. – ll. 9–14: The sestet has often been read as a direct apostrophe to the windhover straightforwardly summing up the Falcon-theme (the unthinking creature perfectly expressing its selfhood and *raison d'être* in spontaneous characteristic action); but many critics have discovered herein a pregnant ambiguity and symbolism, which may be epitomized as follows: 'May the human equivalents of this bird's heroic graces and beautifully disciplined *physical* activity be combined, and brought to a much higher *spiritual* activity in my own being, just as they were once so transmuted in Christ ("O mý cheva-líer"). It is the law of things that all characteristic natural action or "selving", however humble it may be, gives off flashes of divine beauty; how much more then should characteristically Christ-like action (e.g. conscientious toil and willing sacrifice) give glory and be pleasing to Christ our Lord!' – Line 9: the comma after *plume* appears in both autographs in 'A' and is authentic. Its omission from R. B.'s later transcript ('B') was accidental; l. 10, *Buckle!* This presumably imperative verb is the crux of the poem. Here are the various meanings which have been considered apposite: (1) the arch. 'prepare for action; come to grips, engage the enemy'; (2) 'clasp, enclose, bring together' as under one discipline; and (3) the more common meanings, 'to give way, bend, collapse, under stress or pressure'. In its complex 'discipline – fight – fall' connotations, *Buckle!* links the joyful mastery of the octave with the quiet resignation of 'Fall, gall themselves' in l. 14. As a Jesuit, G. M. H. was always intensely preoccupied with Christ's Kingship, soldiership (see Nos. 40 and 50), and Crucifixion (No. 5, st. 7), and with his own 'imitation of Christ', as witness above, pp. 198–9, and also:

(a) 'Christ our Lord ... was doomed to succeed by failure: his plans were baffled, his hopes dashed, and his work was done by being broken off undone.' (*D*. pp. 137–8.)

(b) 'In his Passion all this strength was spent, this lissomness crippled, this beauty wrecked, this majesty beaten down.' (From the sermon quoted above, p. 139.)

Line 10, *from thée then*, a stress on *thee* seems essential; ll. 12–14, *shéer plod, &c.*, cf. the sermon quoted above (b): '... through poverty, through labour, through crucifixion his majesty of nature more shines.' (p. 140) and also above, Letter XXI, p. 198: 'Christ Jesus ... annihilated himself, taking the form of servant, &c.'; l. 12, *sillion* (arch.), strip of arable land, furrow; ll. 13–14, cf. 'Glory be to Christ's body in its weariness ... in its Passion, death and burial'. (Sermon, p. 142.)

14. 'PIED BEAUTY. Curtal Sonnet: sprung paeonic rhythm. St. Beuno's, Tremeirchion. Summer '77.' Line 2, *brinded*, (arch.) brindled; l. 4, *Fresh-firecoal, &c.*, cf. 'Chestnuts as bright as coals or spots of vermilion'. (Jnl., Sept. 17, '68.)

15. 'HURRAHING IN HARVEST. Sonnet (sprung and outriding rhythm. Take notice that the outriding feet are not to be confused with dactyls or paeons, though sometimes the line might be scanned either way. The strong syllable in an outriding foot has always a great stress and after the outrider follows a short pause. The paeon is easier and more flowing). Vale of Clwyd, Sept. 1, 1877.' Later G. M. H. wrote: 'An outriding

foot is, by a sort of contradiction, a recognized extra-metrical effect; it is and it is not part of the metre; not part of it, not being counted, but part of it by producing a calculated effect which tells in the general success.' (*B*, p. 45.) The 'outriding' effect is common before the caesural pause in Shakespeare's later blank verse, e.g.:

'For góodness dáres not chéck thee; wear thóu thy wróngs,
(*Macb.*, IV. iii. 33).

'The Hurrahing sonnet was the outcome of half an hour of extreme enthusiasm as I walked home alone one day from fishing in the Elwy.' — The marked 'outriders' are: l. 1, 'ends now' 'barbarous'; l. 2, 'wind-walks'; l. 8, 'Rapturous ... greeting'; l. 9, 'azurous'; l. 10, 'Majestic ... stalwart'; l. 14, 'hurls for him ... earth for him'. (See Author's Preface, p. 10.)

16. 'THE CAGED SKYLARK. (Falling paeonic rhythm, sprung and outriding.) St. Beuno's, 1877.' In l. 13 MS. has *uncúmberèd*. Outrides: l. 4, 'drudgery'; l. 8, 'barriers'; l. 10, 'babble and'; l. 14, 'footing it'.

Line 5, *turf*, the 'turf full of clover' traditionally placed in a lark's cage; l. 11: 'But his ówn nést, wíld nést ...' (MS. 'A').

17. 'IN THE VALLEY OF THE ELWY. (Standard rhythm, sprung and counterpointed.)' 1877. — Line 1. MS. has 'I remember a house ...' G. M. H. elucidated the octave: 'The kind people of the sonnet were the Watsons of Shooter's Hill, London, nothing to do with the Elwy. ... The frame of the sonnet is a rule of three sum *wrong*, thus: As the sweet smell to those kind people so the Welsh landscape is NOT to the Welsh; and then the author and principle of all four terms is asked to bring the sum right' (*B*. pp. 76–77).

18. 'THE LOSS OF THE EURYDICE. Written in sprung rhythm, the third line has 3 beats, the rest 4. The scanning runs on without break to the end of the stanza, so that each stanza is rather one long line rhymed in passage than four lines with rhymes at the ends.' April, 1878.

Line 6, *furled*: How are hearts of oak furled? Well, in sand and sea water. ... You are to suppose a stroke or blast in a forest of "hearts of oak" . . . which at one blow both lays them low and buries them in broken earth. *Furling* (*ferrule* is a blunder for furl, I think) is proper when said of sticks and staves.' (G. M. H. in *B*, p. 52). – l. 37. 'This was that fell capsize.' (G. M. H.'s scansion); l. 47. *Cheer's death*, i.e. despair; l. 50. *Right, &c.*, i.e. 'he thought he heard Duty, stern of visage, say . . .'; l. 53. *It is even seen.* G. M. H. explains: 'I believe Hare to be a brave and conscientious man: what I say is that *even* those who seem unconscientious will act the right part at a great push.' (*B*, p. 53); l. 68, *rivelling*, (arch.) shrivelling, wrinkling (intransitive or causative); l. 89, *bygones, &c.*, i.e. consequences of the Reformation, e.g. the appropriation of Catholic cathedrals; l. 99, *riving off*, tearing away, i.e. from Catholicism; ll. 101–2 mean that the land was once so Catholic that 'Walsingham Way was a name for the Milky Way, as being supposed a fingerpost to our Lady's shrine at Walsingham [Norfolk]', (*B*, p. 53); l. 103, *And one –*, that is, Duns Scotus, champion of the Immaculate Conception (see No. 21); l. 105, *well wept:* 'It means "you do well to weep" and is framed like "well caught" or "well run" at a cricketmatch.' (*B*, p. 53); l. 112, *O Hero savest*, i.e. 'O Hero that savest' ('Omission of the relative pronoun at its worst.' – R. B.); ll. 114–15, *Have . . . heard:* see note on No. 22, l. 1.

19. 'THE MAY MAGNIFICAT. (Sprung rhythm, four stresses in each line of the first couplet, three in each of the second. Stonyhurst, May '78.)' – Stanza 6, l. 1, *bugle*, English name for the plant *ajuga reptans*, which has thick blue spikes. Cf. Keats, *Endymion*, II. 314: 'velvet leaves and bugle-blooms'.

20. 'BINSEY POPLARS, felled 1879. Oxford, March 1879.' The indentation clearly indicates the number of stresses to the line; e.g. lines 1–8: 5—5—5—4—2—2—3—6. The rhythm of l. 8 is indicated by two outrides:

'On meadow and river and wind-wandering weed-winding bank.'

Line 22, *especial*. See note to No. 22, l. 2 (p. 231).

21. 'DUNS SCOTUS'S OXFORD. Oxford, March 1879.' The rhythm is sprung and outriding. Outrides: l. 2, 'echoing . . .' swarmèd . . . charmèd'; l. 3, 'below thee'; 4, 'encounter in';

l. 8, 'keeping'; l. 10, 'lived on ... waters'; l. 11, 'all men';
l. 12, 'rarest-veinèd'; l. 13, 'insight'.

Johannes Duns Scotus (1266 or 1274–1308), Schoolman, whose
criticism of the Thomist system earned him the title of 'Subtle
Doctor'. Supposed to have worked in Oxford *c.* 1301. In
Aug. 1872 G. M. H. first read Scotus's commentaries on the
Sentences of Lombard and 'was flush with a new stroke of
enthusiasm'. See above, Journal entry for July 19, 1872 (p. 126)
and Introduction, pp. xxiii–xxv. – l. 12, *realty*, thus in MS.

22. 'HENRY PURCELL. (Alexandrine: six stresses to the line.
Oxford, April 1879.)' The rhythm is sprung and outriding.
Outrides, &c. (from 'A' and 'B' MSS.): l. 1, 'have fallen';
l. 2, 'To me'; l. 4, 'sentence ... listed'; l. 5, 'meaning'; l. 6, 'all
that'; l. 8, 'self there ... thrusts on'; l. 9, 'angels ... Lay me';
l. 10, 'sakes of him ... moonmarks'; l. 11, 'stormfowl'; l. 13,

'wuthering of his palmy snowpinions'; l. 14, 'Off him ...
motion'.

Lines 1–2:

> 'Have fáir fállen, O fáir, fáir háve fállen, so déar
>
> To me, so árch-espècial....'

G. M. H. explains: '"Have fair fallen". *Have* is the sing.
imperative (or optative if you like) of the past, a thing possible
and actual both in logic and grammar, but naturally a rare one.
As in the second person we say "Have done" or in making
appointments "Have had your dinner beforehand", so one can
say in the third person not only "Fair fall" of what is present or
future but also "Have fair fallen" of what is past. The same
thought (which plays a great part in my own mind and action)
is more clearly expressed in the last stanza but one of the
Eurydice....' (*B*, p. 174). Again: 'I *meant* "fair fall" to mean *fair*
(*fortune be-*) *fall*' (*ibid.*, p. 171). Cf. *King John*, I. i. 78: 'Fair fall
the bones that took the pains for me.' In *B*, p. 170, G. M. H.
says: 'The sonnet on Purcell means this: 1–4. I hope Purcell is
not damned for being a Protestant, because I love his genius.

5-8. And that not so much for gifts he shares, even though it shd. be in higher measure, with other musicians as for his own individuality. 9-14. So that while he is aiming only at impressing me his hearer with the meaning in hand I am looking out meanwhile for his specific, his individual markings and mottlings, "the sakes of him". It is as when a bird thinking only of soaring spreads its wings: a beholder may happen then to have his attention drawn by the act to the plumage displayed.' Line 2. For the Scotist significance of 'especial', both here and in No. 20, l. 22, see Introduction, pp. xxiii–xxv.

Line 3, *with the reversal, &c.*: 'so that the heavy condemnation under which he outwardly or nominally lay for being out of the true Church may in consequence of his good intentions have been reversed.... "listed", by the by, is "enlisted".' (*B*, p. 171.) – l. 6, *nursle* (arch.), foster; l. 10, *sakes*: 'Sake is a word I find it convenient to use: I did not know when I did so first that it is common in German, in the form *sach*[e] (*sach-* in compounds). It is the *sake* of "for the sake of", *forsake, namesake, keepsake*. I mean by it the being a thing has outside itself, as a voice by its echo, a face by its reflection, a body by its shadow, a man by his name, fame, or memory, *and also* that in the thing by virtue of which especially it has this being abroad, and that is something distinctive, marked, specifically or individually speaking, as for a voice and echo clearness; for a reflected image light, brightness; for a shadow-casting body bulk; for a man of genius, great achievements, amiability, and so on. In this case it is, as the sonnet says, distinctive quality in genius.' (*B*, p. 83.) – l. 10, *moonmarks*: 'I mean crescent shaped markings on the quill-feathers, either in the colouring of the feather or made by the overlapping of one on another.'; l. 13, *wuthering*, 'is a North-country word for the noise and rush of wind' (*B*, p. 83); l. 14, *but*, only, merely. (See p. 233.)

23. 'PEACE. Oxford, 1879.' A Curtal Sonnet in 'standard' Alexandrines. – Line 4, *own my heart*, 'is merely "my own heart", transposed for rhythm's sake and then *tamquam exquisitius*, as Hermann would say. *Reave* (l. 7) is for rob, plunder, carry off.' (*B*, p. 196); l. 9, *plumes*, grows, becomes 'fledged', &c.

24. 'THE BUGLER'S FIRST COMMUNION. (Sprung rhythm, over-

Henry Purcell.

Have fair fallen, O fair, fair have fallen, so dear
To me, so arch-especial a spirit as heaves in Henry Purcell,
An age is now since passed, since parted; with the reversal
Of the outward sentence low lays him, listed to a heresy, here.

Not mood in him nor meaning, proud fire or sacred fear,
Or love, or pity, or all that sweet notes not his might nursle:
It is the forgèd feature finds me; it is the rehearsal
Of own, of abrupt self there, so thrusts on, so throngs the ear.

Let him oh! with his air of angels then lift me, lay me, ! only I'll
Have an eye to the sakes of him, quaint moonmarks, to his pelted
                              plumage under
Wings: so some great stormfowl, whenever he has walked his while
The thunder-purple seabeach, plumèd purple of thunder,
If a wuthering of his palmy snow-pinions scatter a colossal smile
Off him, but meaning motion fans fresh our wits with wonder.

                                        Oxford. 1879

Reduced facsimile of poem No. 22, *Henry Purcell*, from MS. book 'B'.
(Actual size of draft 6½ by 6 in.) The versions in 'B', many of which (like
this one) are in the handwriting of Robert Bridges, are later and usually
more authoritative than those in 'A', the book into which R. B. pasted
G. M. H.'s poems as he received them. G. M. H. was remiss in keeping
copies of his own poems, so in 1883 R. B. copied the 'A' poems into the new
book, 'B'; and thereafter from time to time G. M. H. added other poems
to 'B' or, as here, entered his final corrections. The words 'oh!' (l. 9) and
'fresh' (l. 14), together with the date, are in the poet's own hand. The prin-
ted text follows the above draft, except that a stress-mark has been placed
on *self* (l. 8) to remind the reader of the significance of the 'outride' (*there*).

rove, an outride between the third and fourth foot of the fourth
line in each stanza.) Oxford, July 27 (?) 1879.'

St. 1, l. 4, 'Sháres their bést gifts súrely, fall hów things wíll.'

St. 3, l. 4, 'hóusel his'; *housel* (arch.) is the consecrated species of
the Eucharist, here the wafer. – St. 5, l. 2, *Squander*, scatter in
disorder; *ranks* (that) *sally*, rel. pron. omitted. – St. 12, l. 2,
brandle, (arch.) shake, make totter; l. 4, 'however and'; *like*
cf. 'belike', 'like enough', 'most likely'.

25. 'MORNING, MIDDAY, AND EVENING SACRIFICE. Oxford,
Aug. '79.' Line 6, *fuming*, cf. the smoke of incense; l. 17, *silk-
ash:* 'I meant to compare grey hairs to the flakes of silky ash
which may be seen round wood embers.' (*B*, pp. 97–8.) Line 21,
Your offering, &c., 'is said like "Your ticket", "Your reasons",
"Your money or your life" . . .: it is "Come, your offer of all
this (the matured mind), and without delay either!" (This
should now explode.)' (*B*, p. 98.)

26. 'ANDROMEDA. Oxford, Aug. 12, '79.' 'I enclose a sonnet. . . . I
endeavoured in it a more Miltonic plainness and severity than
I have anywhere else. I cannot say it has turned out severe, still
less plain, but it seems almost free from quaintness and in aiming
at one excellence I may have hit another." (B, p. 87.)
Line 1, *Time's Andromeda*, the Church? – as *Perseus* (l. 9) seems
to be Christ; *rock rude*, cf. Matt. xvi. 18: 'Thou art Peter and
upon this rock I will build my Church'; l. 14, / as in MS.

27. 'THE CANDLE INDOORS. (Common rhythm, counterpointed.)
Oxford, '79.' 'A companion to the Lantern (No. 11), not at
first meant to be though, but it fell in.' (*B*, p. 84.) Line 4, *to-fro
tender trambeams, &c.* Silk threads used for the weft of the best
silk goods are called 'trams', 'tram-silk'; also, in 1879 'tram'
could mean a continuous metal rail, as in 'tramway'. Hence
trambeams are those fine radiating lines of light which, like
antennae ('tender'), dart out *from* and back *to* the candle as the
eyelids of the beholder are slightly lowered or raised; *truckle at*,
'cower away, timidly draw back' on contact with the fully
opened eye (cf. 'wince *at* a blow', 'quail *at* the sight' – R.-V.
Schoder, S.J., in *Immortal Diamond*, pp. 206–7); l. 8, the oblique
line, /, (such as G. M. H. often used in his prose, e.g. on p. 149,
l. 21) indicates a brief pause, cf. No. 26, l. 14; ll. 9–14, cf.
Matt. vv. 13–16, and vii. 1–5.

28. 'THE HANDSOME HEART. (Common rhythm counterpointed.) Oxford, '79.' G. M. H. called this sonnet 'autobiographical. . . . Last Lent two boys of our congregation gave me much help in the sacristy in Holy Week. I offered them money for their services, which the elder refused, but being pressed consented to take it laid out in a book. The younger followed suit; then when some days after I asked him what I shd. buy answered as in the sonnet.' (B, pp. 84, 86.) Line 7, *self-instressed*, moved by its own natural impulse, i.e. towards the Good.

29. 'AT THE WEDDING MARCH. (Sprung rhythm.) Bedford, Lancashire, Oct. 21, '79.' Four stresses to the line, e.g.: 'Í to hím túrn with téars.'

30. 'FELIX RANDAL. (Sonnet: sprung and outriding rhythm; six-foot lines.) Liverpool, Apr. 28, '80.' Outrides: l. 1, 'Randal . . . farrier . . . dead then!'; l. 3, 'pining . . . rambled in it'; l. 5, broke him. . . . Impatient,'; l. 7, 'earlier'; l. 8, 'to him. . . . Ah well'; l. 11, 'heart, child, Felix,'; l. 12; 'forethought of'; l. 13, 'random'; l. 14, 'drayhorse'. – Line 7, *sweet reprieve, &c.*, Holy Communion and all it implies; l. 8, *áll road*, cf. dial. 'any road', anyway, anyhow; hence, 'in whatever manner he may ever have sinned'; l. 13, *random* (archit.) built with rough irregular stones; l. 14, *fettle*, make ready. (See p. 236.)

31. 'BROTHERS. (Sprung rhythm; three feet to the line; lines free-ended and not overrove; and reversed or counterpointed rhythm allowed in the first foot.) Hampstead, Aug. 1880.'

32. 'SPRING AND FALL. (Sprung rhythm.) Lydiate, Lancashire, Sept. 7, 1880.' Line 8, *worlds of wanwood, &c.*; 'wanwood' (noun) seems to 'inscape' or fuse together the obs. 'wan' (dark, gloomy), the obs. prefix 'wan-' (indicating deficiency, as in 'wanworth'), and the arch. 'wan' meaning 'pale, bloodless', the last sense being caught up in the adverbial *leafmeal* (cf. 'piece-meal'): one by one the leaves fall, and then rot into mealy fragments; l. 11, *the same*, i.e. all sorrows have virtually *one* source; l. 13, *ghost*, (arch.) spirit (of the living).

⑯ Felix Randal

Félix Rándal, the fárrier, O is he dead then?, my dúty all ended,
Who have watched his mould of man, big boned & hardy-handsome
Pining, pining, till time when reason rambled in it, and some
Fatal four disorders, fleshed there, all contended?
Sickness broke him. Impatient, he cursed at first, but mended
Being anointed & all ; tho' a heavenlier heart began some
Months earlier, since I had our sweet reprieve & ransom
Tendered to him. Ah well, God rest him all road ever he offended!

This often seeing the sick endears them, to us, us too it endears.
My tongue had taught thee comfort, touch had quenched thy tears,
Thy tears that touched my heart, child, Felix, poor Felix Randal;
How far from then forethought of, all thy more boisterous years,
When thou at the random, grim forge, powerful amidst peers
Didst fettle for the great grey dray horse his bright & battering sandal!

1880

Reduced facsimile of poem No. 30, from MS. book 'B'. (Actual size of
draft 5½ by 6 in.). This copy is in R. B.'s handwriting, with G. M. H.'s
corrections. Printed text is from MS. book 'A' with the corrections of 'B'.

33. 'INVERSNAID. Sept., 1881.' Line 3, *coop . . . comb*, verb-nouns, the first one meaning 'enclosed space' or 'water cooped up', the second 'water combing freely over stones, etc.' (Cf. *N*, p. 49: 'Brush and comb (how vastly absurd it is!) both apply to . . . of water ribs.' See also poet's sketch opp. p. 106 of *N*.); l. 6, *twindles*: this is conceivably a verb from the obs. 'twindle', = a twin; also a portmanteau word inscaping 'twists', 'twitches', and 'dwindles' (cf. p. 127); l. 9, *degged*, (dial.) sprinkled; l. 11, *heath-packs*, from 'heath', heather; *flitches*, ragged, russet tufts.

34. '*As kingfishers, &c.*' Line 3, *tucked*, (obs.) plucked; l. 7, *Selves*, (verb), asserts its own nature, individuality; l. 9, *justices* (verb), 'acts in a godly manner, lives fully energized by grace, justness, sanctity' (R. V. Schoder, S.J.). With the theme of this sonnet cf. *N*, p. 342: 'All things therefore are charged with love, are charged with God, and if we know how to touch them give off sparks and take fire, yield drops and flow, ring and tell of him.' (Cf. also No. 8.)

35. 'RIBBLESDALE. Stonyhurst, 1882.' One MS. adds: 'companion to No. 10' (= No. 17 in this edn.) The MSS. quote, in Latin, Romans, viii. 19 and 20: 'For the earnest expectation of the creation waiteth for the revealing of the sons of God. For the creation was subjected to vanity, not of its own will, but by reason of him who subjected it.' Line 1, *throng*, 'I mean "throng" for an adjective as we use it here in Lancashire'. (*D*, p. 109.) – l. 2, *louchèd*, 'a coinage of mine and is to mean much the same as *slouched, slouching*' (*ibid.*). As R. B. noted, the word is found in the *Eng. Dialect Dict.*; l. 7. I take *down* to be an adv. attached to *deal* in l. 6; cf. G. M. H.'s note to No. 12 (p. 226); 'paying or dealing out and down . . .'; l. 12, *reave*, see note to No. 23, l. 7.

36. 'THE LEADEN ECHO AND THE GOLDEN ECHO. Stonyhurst, Oct. 13, '82.' Written for the drama on St. Winefred; see No. 58. On one MS. G. M. H. wrote: 'I have marked the stronger stresses, but with the degree of stress so perpetually varying no marking is satisfactory. Do you think all had best be left to the reader?'
The Leaden Echo, l. 1, *keep* ⌢ . . . *lace* ⌢ (thus in MS.; see 'Author's Preface', p. 10); ll. 1–2: 'I cannot satisfy myself about the first line. You must know that words like *charm* and *enchantment* will

not do: the thought is of beauty as of something that can be physically kept and lost and by physical things only, like keys: then the things must come from the *mundus muliebris;* and thirdly they must not be markedly oldfashioned. You will see that this limits the choice of words very much indeed. . . . *Back* is not pretty, but it gives that feeling of physical constraint which I want.' (*B*, pp. 161–2.) – l. 4, *Down?*, adv., completes 'frowning' in l. 3.

The Golden Echo, l. 13, *own best being*, i.e. the body after the Resurrection; ll. 22–3, explained by G. M. H.: 'Nay more: the seed that we so carelessly and freely flung into the dull furrow, and then forgot it, will have come to ear meantime, &c.' (*B*, p. 159.) – l. 26, *fashed* (dial.); troubled, vexed; *cogged* (arch.), deceived, cheated.

37. 'MARY MOTHER OF DIVINE GRACE COMPARED TO THE AIR WE BREATHE. Stonyhurst, May '83.' (Later title from MS. 'B'.) A 'Maypiece', written to be hung up among the verse-compositions, 'in the tongues' (*D*, p. 108). Line 5, *-flixed*, from 'flix', fur; cf. *N*, p. 124: 'flix or fleece' (of a cloud).

38. 'TO WHAT SERVES MORTAL BEAUTY? (Common rhythm highly stressed: sonnet) Aug. 23, '85.' G. M. H. explains the term 'highly stressed': '. . . alexandrines: the mark ⌐───⌐ over two neighbouring syllables means that, though one has and the other has not the metrical stress, in the recitation-stress they are to be about equal, e.g. "To wha͡t serves mortal beauty – ¹ da͡ngerous; . . . (l. 3) keeps warm/Me͡n's wits . . ."' (*D*, p. 129). – Line 7, *Gregory*, i.e. Pope Gregory I, 'the Great' (*c*. 590–604), who saw the Angles in the Roman slave-market and sent Augustine to England.

39. 'SPELT FROM SIBYL'S LEAVES. (Sonnet: sprung rhythm: a rest of one stress in the first line.)' Eight feet in each line. In *B*, p. 246, G. M. H. says: 'Of this long sonnet above all remember what applies to all my verse, that it is, as living art should be, made for performance and that its performance is not reading with the eye but loud, leisurely, poetical (not rhetorical) recita-tion, with long rests, long dwells on the rhyme and other marked syllables, and so on. This sonnet shd. be almost sung:

it is most carefully timed in *tempo rubato*.' With the title and theme cf. the *Dies irae*: 'As David and the Sibyl testify . . . what terror shall affright the soul when the judge comes . . .' Cf. also the *Aeneid*, Bk. vi. – Line 3, *hornlight*, the last 'horny rays' of the setting sun (cf. Journal, p. 108); l. 6, *throughther* (Scots), syncope for 'through-other'; R. B. quotes Burns's *Halloween*: 'They roar an' cry a' throughther'; l. 7, *Disremembering* (Irish), forgetting; *round* (arch.), whisper to, counsel; l. 8, *With, &c.*, i.e. *with your warning that, &c.*; the heart is speaking. – (R. B.); l. 9, *damask* (verb), 'pattern', as in the damascene work on a sword-blade; l. 11, *part, pen, pack*, imperatives of the verbs, in the sense of sorting 'the sheep from the goats' – (R. B.); l. 14, *sheathe-*, thus in MSS.

40. (THE SOLDIER). 'Clongowes, Aug. 1885.' No title in MS. Six stresses to the line: rhythm similar to that of No. 38. Line 10, *reeve*, MS. had 'reave', an obvious mis-spelling.

41. (CARRION COMFORT). Probable date, 1885; this may be the sonnet 'written in blood' about which G. M. H. wrote to R. B. in that year. Title and the hyphen in *heaven-handling* (l. 12) added by R. B. The rhythm is sprung and outriding, six stresses to the line. Outrides in the MSS: l. 1, 'comfort'; l. 5, 'terrible'; l. 8, 'tempest, me heaped there'; l. 12, 'heaven-handling'; l. 13, 'Me . . . fought him? O which one? . . . each one?'; l. 14, 'darkness'. – Line 5, *rude*, used with adverbial force: 'in an uncouth, violent, barbarous manner'; l. 6, *rock*, (verb), 'wouldst rock' governs 'foot'. Early draft has: 'Yet why wouldst thou rock rude on me/ Thy wring-earth tread. . . .'

42. 'No worst, there is none.' 1885? Rhythm: basis 'standard', but so freely counterpointed and in parts sprung as to be virtually sprung throughout. – (Ed.) Line 6 has a 'hurried foot': wórld-sorrow; on an áge-old ánvil . . .'; l. 8, *fell*, thus in MS.; *force*, cf. Shakespeare's 'of force' and 'force perforce' (of necessity).

43. 44, 45, 46. These four sonnets (together with No. 62) were found among G. M. H.'s papers after his death. It was probably to these that he referred in a letter to R. B. of Sept. 1, 1885: 'I

shall shortly have some sonnets to send you, five or more. Four of these came like inspirations unbidden and against my will. And in the life I lead now, which is one of a continually jaded and harassed mind, if in any leisure I try to do anything I make no way – nor with my work, alas! but so it must be.'

I have decided to give these poems what is, in all probability, their correct chronological position.

43. *'To seem the stranger.'* 1885. Line 8, *wars*, i.e. the Irish struggle for political freedom; l. 9, MS. has 'now Í am at a third'; l. 14, *began*: R. B. glosses the line, 'leaves me a lonely (one who only) began'; but W. A. M. Peters says: *'Began* is a noun ... the poet calls himself a "began", not a beginner'. For a similar modified preterite cf. the turf slang, 'an also-ran'.

44. *'I wake and feel.'* 1885. Line 2, *hoūrs*, in MS. *hoūrs*; l. 12, *dull dough*, for rejected 'my selfstuff'; l. 13, *The lost*, those in Hell; according to G. M. H.'s theology, *their* plight was necessarily worse than his. The 'terrible crystal' is in the narrow margin of difference.

45. *'Patience.'* 1885. Line 2, *Patience is.* 'The initial capital is mine, and the comma after *ivy* in line 6.' – (R. B.); l. 8, *eyes*, berries; l. 10, *dearer* (arch.), more grievously; l. 14, *combs*, honeycombs.

46. *'My own heart.'* 1885. Line 6, 'I have added the comma after *comfortless*; that word has the same grammatical value as *dark* in the following line. "I cast for comfort, (which) I can no more find in my comfortless (world) than a blind man in his dark world ..."' – (R. B.); l. 9, *Jackself*, cf. the Eliz. 'Jack', a common fellow, and also 'jack-of-all-trades', 'jack-plane', etc. The plodding, workaday Hopkins! – l. 11, MS. accents *let*. – (R. B.); *size*, grow, increase; ll. 11–12: 'Be reconciled to having your pleasure whenever and however God wills it.' Line 14, *between-pie*: *'pie* apparently makes a compound with *between*, meaning "as the sky seen between dark mountains is brightly dappled", the grammar such as *intervariegates* would make. The word might have delighted William Barnes, if the verb "to pie" existed. It seems not to exist, and to be forbidden by homophonic absurdities.' – (R. B.) For G. M. H. any word 'existed' as soon as he felt the need for it: 'pie' (verb) is a back-formation

from 'pied', with support from 'magpie'. (cf. the word
'pieings' in Journal entry for June 16, 1873 – above, p. 128.)

47. 'TOM'S GARLAND. Sonnet: common rhythm, but with hur-
ried feet: two codas. Dromore, Sept. '87.' With the codas cf.
those in Milton's sonnet *On the New Forcers of Conscience.*

Examples of 'hurried feet' are: l. 3, 'By him and rips . . .'; l. 5,

'lüstily he his low lot (feel'; l. 10, 'hónour enough in áll us'.
Line 2, *fallówbootfellow*, i.e. Tom's workfellow now stamping
off duty with his similar reddish-yellow clay-caked heavy boots
(a compound built up on the analogy of some more likely
expression such as 'doss-house-bedfellow'). I retain R. B.'s long
note:

The author's own explanation of this poem may be read in a
letter written to me from Dublin, Feb. 10, '88: '. . . I laughed
outright and often, but very sardonically, to think you and the
Canon could not construe my last sonnet; that he had to write
to you for a crib. It is plain I must go no farther on this road:
if you and he cannot understand me who will? Yet, declaimed,
the strange constructions would be dramatic and effective. Must
I interpret it? It means then that, as St. Paul and Plato and
Hobbes and everybody says, the commonwealth or well ordered
human society is like one man; a body with many members
and each its function; some higher, some lower, but all honour-
able, from the honour which belongs to the whole. The head
is the sovereign, who has no superior but God and from heaven
receives his or her authority: we must then imagine this head
as bare (see St. Paul much on this) and covered, so to say, only
with the sun and stars, of which the crown is a symbol, which
is an ornament but not a covering; it has an enormous hat or
skull cap, the vault of heaven. The foot is the daylabourer,
and this is armed with hobnail boots, because it has to wear
and be worn by the ground; which again is symbolical; for it
is navvies or daylabourers who, on the great scale or in gangs
and millions, mainly trench, tunnel, blast, and in other ways
disfigure, "mammock" the earth and, on a small scale, singly, and
superficially stamp it with their footprints. And the "garlands"
of nails they wear are therefore the visible badge of the place

they fill, the lowest in the commonwealth. But this place still shares the common honour, and if it wants one advantage, glory or public fame, makes up for it by another, ease of mind, absence of care; and these things are symbolized by the gold and the iron garlands. (O, once explained, how clear it all is!) Therefore the scene of the poem is laid at evening, when they are giving over work and one after another pile their picks, with which they earn their living, and swing off home, knocking sparks out of mother earth not now by labour and of choice but by the mere footing, being strong-shod and making no hardship of hardness, taking all easy. And so to supper and bed. Here comes a violent but effective hyperbaton or suspension, in which the action of the mind mimics that of the labourer – surveys his lot, low but free from care; then by a sudden strong act throws it over the shoulder or tosses it away as a light matter. The witnessing of which lightheartedness makes me indignant with the fools of Radical Levellers. But presently I remember that this is all very well for those who are in, however low in, the Commonwealth and share in any way the common weal; but that the curse of our times is that many do not share it, that they are outcasts from it and have neither security nor splendour: that they share care with the high and obscurity with the low, but wealth or comfort with neither. And this state of things, I say, is the origin of Loafers, Tramps, Cornerboys, Roughs, Socialists and other pests of society. And I think that it is a very pregnant sonnet, and in point of execution very highly wrought, too much so, I am afraid.' (B, pp. 272–4.)

48. 'HARRY PLOUGHMAN. Dromore, Sept. 1887.' R. B. notes: G. M. H. thought well of this sonnet and wrote on Sept. 28, 1887: 'I have been touching up some old sonnets you have never seen and have within a few days done the whole of one, I hope, very good one and most of another; the one finished is a direct picture of a ploughman, without afterthought. But when you read it let me know if there is anything like it in Walt Whitman; as perhaps there may be, and I should be sorry for that.' And again on Oct. 11, 1887: 'I will enclose the sonnet on Harry Ploughman, in which burden-lines (they might be recited by a chorus) are freely used: there is in this very heavily

Harry Ploughman

Hard as hurdle arms, with a broth of goldish flue
Breathed round; the rack of ribs; the scooped flank; lank
Rope-over thigh; knee-nave; and barrelled shank —
    Head and foot, shoulder and shank —
By a grey eye's heed steered well, one crew, fall to;
Stand at stress. Each limb's barrowy-brawned thew
That onewhere curded, onewhere sucked or sank —
    Soared or sank —,
Though as a beechbole firm, finds his, as at a rollcall, rank
And features, in flesh, what deed he each must do —
    His sinew-service where do.
He leans to it, Harry bends, look. Back, elbow, and liquid waist
In him, all quail to the wallowing o' the plough. 'S cheek
Wag or crossbridle, rind and loft or in and laced —
    See his wind- lilylocks -laced —;
Churlsgrace too, child of Amansstrength, how it hangs or hurls
Them — broad in bluff hide his frowning feet lashed! raced
With, along them, cragiron under and cold furls —
    With-a-wet-sheen-shot furls.

            Dromore Sept. 1887

Reduced facsimile of G. M. H.'s autograph of poem No. 48, from MS.
book 'B'. (Actual size of draft 6 by 6 in.)

loaded sprung rhythm a call for their employment. The rhythm
of this sonnet; which is altogether for recital, and not for perusal
(as by nature verse should be), is very highly studied. From
much considering it I can no longer gather any impression of
it: perhaps it will strike you as intolerably violent and artificial.'
And again on Nov. 6, '87: 'I want Harry Ploughman to be a
vivid figure before the mind's eye; if he is not that the sonnet
fails. The difficulties are of syntax no doubt. Dividing a com-
pound word by a clause sandwiched into it was a desperate
deed, I feel, and I do not feel that it was an unquestionable
success.' (B, pp. 262-3, 265). For the elaborate metrical notation
used in this poem see the facsimile of the MS. 'A' version
opposite p. 262 in B and that of the 'B' version on p. 243 of
this book. Each of the 14 basic lines has five metrical stresses.
Especially important are the hurried feet and outrides in:

> ll. 9-10: 'Though as a beechbole firm, finds his, as at a rollcall,
> rank...'

> l. 12: 'He leans to it, Harry bends, look.' (MS. 'A'.)

> l. 13: 'In him, all quail to the wallowing o' the plough:'

> l. 16: 'Churlsgrace, too, child of Amansstrength,'

> l. 17: 'Them—broad in bluff hide...'

Line 3, *knee-nave*, i.e. -boss, -cap; l. 6, *barrowy*, from 'barrow',
a mound; l. 7, *curded*, formed into lumps, knotted; l. 10,
features is the verb. — (R. B.); l. 15, a tmesis: more boldly
inscaped than 'his lilylocks windlaced' (for another tmesis see
No. 5, st. 8, l. 6); l. 16, *churlsgrace*, from 'churl' (arch.) peasant,
labourer; l. 17, *frowning*, points to the 'frowning wrinkles' in
the broad tough insteps of Harry's boots; ll. 17-19: 'The
grammar intends: "How his churl's grace governs the move-
ment of his booted (in bluff hide) feet, as they are matched in
a race with the wet shining furrow overturned by the share."' —
(R. B.). Line 19, earlier variant rejected by R. B. and present
editor is 'With-a-wet-sheen-shot furls'.

49. 'THAT NATURE IS A HERACLITEAN FIRE AND OF THE

COMFORT OF THE RESURRECTION. (Sprung rhythm, with many outrides and hurried feet: sonnet with two [sic] codas.) July 26, 1888. Co. Dublin. The last sonnet [i.e. this one] provisional only.' There are actually *three* codas. All the longer lines have six stresses, three on each side of the caesural bar, e.g.:

'Cloud-púffball, torn túfts, tossed píllows ¹ flaunt fórth, then chévy on an aír-
built thóroughfare:...'

On Aug. 18, 1888, G. M. H. wrote to R. B.: 'I will now go to bed, the more so as I am going to preach to-morrow and put plainly to a Highland congregation of MacDonalds, Mackintoshes, Mackillops, and the rest what I am putting not at all so plainly to the rest of the world, or rather to you and Canon Dixon, in a sonnet...' See also above, Letter XXVI (p. 210).

Title: Heraclitus (c. 535–c. 475 B.C.) taught that everything is in a state of flux, since all existence, including the human body and soul, is a cyclic manifestation of the various forms taken by one basic, rational, intelligent principle – fire. Through 'strife' (πόλεμος), fire changes into water, water into earth, and then the process is reversed; but all things are ultimately resolvable into fire.

Line 1, *chevy*, race, scamper; l. 4, *shivelights*, strips of light (see note to No. 65, l. 38); l. 6, R. B. notes: '*rutpeel* may be a compound word, MS. uncertain'. But the line makes better sense as printed: the 'bright wind' (l. 5) *parches* the peel (flat cakes of mud from wheels, etc.) in pool and rut; 'wind' is also the subject of *Squandering*, *stanches* ('makes staunch', firm) and *starches* (makes stiff, then powdery); l. 8, probably = *manmarks* (that) *treadmire toil*, &c.; l. 12, MS. has no caesural mark, but

the scansion is given: 'Bóth are in an únfáthomable, áll is in an enórmous dárk'; l. 14, *disseveral*, portmanteau word from 'dissever' and 'several'; l. 18, *foundering deck*, cf. the shipwreck as symbol in No. 5; l. 23, *Jack*, a common fellow; *patch* (arch.) fool, ninny; also, a detached piece, makeshift fragment; cf. the *potsherd* with which Job scraped his sores (Job, ii. 8).

50. 'ST. ALPHONSUS RODRIGUEZ.' 1888. R. B. quotes a letter of

Oct. 3, 1888: 'I ask your opinion of a sonnet written to order on the òccasion of the first feast since his canonisation proper of St. Alphonsus Rodriguez, a laybrother of our Order, who for 40 years acted as hall-porter to the College ·of Palma in Majorca; he was, it is believed, much favoured by God with heavenly light and much persecuted by evil spirits. The sonnet (I say it snorting) aims at being intelligible.' (*B*, pp. 292–3. See also above, Letter XXVII, pp. 213–14.)

The rhythm is 'standard', with 'heavy stressing' (as in l. 2, 'gashed flesh', 'galled shield') and frequent Miltonic elision ('by of world', 'Majórca Alfónso' – ll. 13–14). For the thought, cf. the sestet of *The Windhover*, No. 13.

51. '*Justus es, &c.* Jer. xii. i (for title), March 17, '89.' In a letter to R. B. (March 20, '89) G. M. H. says: 'Observe, it must be read *adagio molto* and with great stress.' (*B*, p. 303). Line 3, 'Why do sinners'; l. 4, 'Disappointment; l. 11, *chervil*, cow-parsley.

52. '*The shepherd's brow.*' 'Various consecutive full drafts on the same sheet as No.·52, and date April 3, 1889. The text is what seems to be the latest draft; it has no corrections. It might be argued that this sonnet has the same right to be recognized as a finished poem with the sonnets 43–46, but those had several years' recognition whereas this must have been thrown off one day in a cynical mood, which he would not have wished permanently to intrude among his last serious poems.' – (R. B.). This sonnet, being the last of five careful drafts, was obviously not 'thrown off' or lightly taken. Supported by Robert Boyle S.J., who says (in his *Metaphor in Hopkins*, 1961): 'This poem is not cynical ... Hopkins is facing realities', I have decided to give this sonnet its proper place in the canon. – Line 8, *viol*, cf. Isaiah, xiv. 11: 'Thy pomp is brought down to the grave, ·and the noise of thy viols.'

53. '*TO* R. B. April 22, '89.' Line 6, *combs:* possible meanings are: (1) 'straightens, sets in order', and (2) 'stores and matures, as in a honeycomb'.

UNFINISHED POEMS AND FRAGMENTS (1876–1889)

54. 'MOONRISE. June 19, 1876.' Line 5, *fanged*, (dial.) seized, held.

55. 'THE WOODLARK.' G. M. H. left only disordered fragments,
dated July, 1876. An admirable recension, by the late Rev.
Geoffrey Bliss, S.J., of the 1st edn. text produced the version
given here. The lines in square brackets are his, and the present
editor identifies himself with Fr. Bliss's note: 'The excuse for
this impiety is a pious one: I would have the effect of a lovely
piece of verse to be, at least for a moment, not interrupted by
gaps in the strain.' The four-stress lines illustrate the great
flexibility of Sprung Rhythm, from 'Fláme-rásh rúdréd' (l. 23)
to

'Tátter-tassel-tángled and dingle-a-dánglèd' (l. 25).
Line 23, *rudred*, (obs.) rosy-cheeked.

56. 'CHEERY BEGGAR.' Probable date is 1879, when G. M. H.
was preacher at St. Aloysius's Church, Oxford.

57. '*The furl of fresh-leaved dogrose down.*' 1879. R. B.'s interpretation
of some unfinished disordered verses. Line 1, *down*, see note on
fleecèd bloom in No. 58, p. 75, l. 24.

58. 'ST. WINEFRED'S WELL.' Fragments (written between 1879 and
1885), for which No. 36 is a chorus. Of the rhythm G. M. H.
says: 'It is in an alexandrine verse, which I sometimes expand
to 7 or 8 feet, very hard to manage but very effective when well
used.' (*D*, p. 143.) Again: '... as the feeling rises the rhythm
becomes freer and more sprung.' (*B*, p. 212.)

According to Butler (*Lives of the Saints*), Winefred, daughter
of Teryth, was instructed in Christian piety by her uncle,
St. Beuno. The chieftain Carádoc, thwarted in an attack on her
chastity, severed her head from her body. St. Beuno restored her
to life and she died an abbess fifteen years later. The famous
spring, still visited by pilgrims, is supposed to have gushed forth
from the spot where Winefred's head fell. In G. M. H.'s play,
Carádoc was to 'die impenitent, struck by the finger of God'.
(*B*, p. 212.) – Page 75, l. 51, *fleecèd bloom*, 'I mean the velvetiness
of roseleaves, flesh, and other things, *duvet*'. (*B*, p. 215.)

59. (MARGARET CLITHEROE). Undated and without title. Sen-
tenced by Judge Clinch, Margaret Clitheroe was pressed to
death at York in 1586 for contravening the laws against Roman
Catholics.

61. 'ON A PIECE OF MUSIC.' Undated. The text printed here is
my own interpretation of stanzas written, without final

arrangement, on two separate sheets – Stanza 7, l. 4, *one*: there can be no doubt that this means 'Christ' (cf. No. 64, l. 20). St. 10 suggests that moral beauty ('right') is a higher perfection than the 'fault-not-found-with good' of art. See also Letter XXI, p. 198.

62. (ASH-BOUGHS). 1885 (R. B.s' title). A Curtal Sonnet, with expanded variation from the seventh line. I omit R. B.'s 'brackets to show what I think would make the best version of the poem'.

63. '*Thee, God, I come from.*' 1885. R. B. notes: 'After the verses printed in text there is some versified *credo* intended to form part of the complete poem; thus:

> "Jesus Christ sacrificed
> On the Cross. . . .
> Moulded, he, in maiden's womb,
> Lived and died and from the tomb
> Rose in power and is our
> Judge that comes to deal our doom."'

64. 'ON THE PORTRAIT, &C. Monastereven, Co. Kildare, Christmas, 1886.'

Stanza 2, l. 4, *heft*, (obs. and dial.) from 'heave'. Cf. *The Winter's Tale*, II. i. 45: 'he cracks his gorge, his sides/With violent hefts.' G. M. H.'s use of 'heft' suggests (1) the strain of rearing, bringing up, nurturing (cf. *King Lear*, II. iv. 167: 'thy tender-hefted nature'); or (2) effort to rise, aspiration, ambition.

St. 3, l. 4, *burling*, cf. dial. 'burl', to pour; also bubbling, swirling, purling.

St. 7, l. 1, *list*, cf. obs. 'pleasure', 'desire', with mod. 'leaning'.

St. 8, l. 1. The ellipsis obviously intends: 'Physical graces you have in abundance, such as . . .'; l. 3: 'The worst (vices, men) will always prey upon, vitiate, the best (qualities, people).'

65. 'EPITHALAMION.' I give R. B.'s original note: 'Four sides of pencilled rough sketches, and five sides of quarto first draft, on "Royal University of Ireland" candidates' paper, as if G. M. H. had written it while supervising an examination. Fragments in disorder with erasures and corrections; undated. . . . The text, which omits only two disconnected lines, is my arrangement of

the fragments, and embodies the latest corrections. It was to have been an Ode on the occasion of his brother's marriage, which fixes the date as 1888.'

Line 4, *dene*, dell, valley; *clough*, ravine (rhymes with 'rough'); *cleave*, like 'clough', from O. E. *cleofa*, a cleft (see extract from Journal, Sept. 6, 1874 – above p. 132); l. 9, *cover* = 'covert' – (R. B.); l. 11, *of* may be *at*, MS. uncertain. – (R. B.); l. 36, *coffer*, box-like basin, cf. (engin.) 'coffer-dam'; l. 37, *selfquainèd:* cf. Journal passage beginning, 'I was arguing about the planing of rocks . . .' (above, p. 115). For G. M. H.'s use of the unusual 'quain' (noun) see Journal, March–April 1871 (above, p. 122). It is dialectal for 'quoin' (= coign), external angle of a wall, wedge-shaped block. Cf. 'And if you look well at big pack-clouds overhead you will soon find a strong large quaining and squaring in them which makes each pack impressive and whole.' *N*, p. 141.) But 'quain' also suggests a back-formation from 'quaint' (singular, fanciful). Cf. the 'peaked quains' of the ash-spray (p. 122), and see Note B, below Line 38, *shivès*: obs. 'shive' = splinter, slice, sliver (cf. *shivelights* in No. 49); *shoots* is the noun.

(b) ADDITIONAL NOTES ON THE PROSE

Note A, p. 188. In a letter to R. B. on *The Deutschland* and Sprung Rhythm, G. M. H. says:

'Why do I employ sprung rhythm at all? Because it is the nearest to the rhythm of prose, that is the native and natural rhythm of speech, the least forced, the most rhetorical and emphatic of all possible rhythms, combining, as it seems to me, opposite and, one wd. have thought, incompatible excellences, markedness of rhythm – that is rhythm's self – and naturalness of expression – for why, if it is forcible in prose to say "láshed ród" [Poem No. 5, st. 2. l. 2.], am I obliged to weaken this in verse, which ought to be stronger, not weaker, into "láshed birch-ród" or something?

'My verse is less to be read than heard, as I have told you before; it is oratorical, that is the rhythm is so.' (*B*, pp. 44–47.)

Note B, p. 122. Frequently 'quain' means something like the angular excrescences of the conventional star-shape, or any similar pinked, 'fretted', or 'lacy' *scaping*. Cf. the following note on clouds (N, p. 140): 'The bright woolpacks that pelt before a gale in a clear sky are in the tuft and you can see the wind unravelling and rending them finer and finer than any sponge till within one easy reach overhead they are morselled to nothing and consumed – it depends of course on their size. Possibly each tuft in forepitch or origin is quained and a crystal.'

Most revealing is a passage from an early essay called *Poetry and Verse*. Speaking of the running *inscape*, or repeated figure, of verse as opposed to prose, G. M. H. says: 'The figure may be repeated runningly, continuously, as in rhythm (ABABAB), or intermittently, as in alliteration and rhyme (ABCDABEFABGH). The former gives more tone, *candorem*, style, chasteness; the latter more brilliancy, starriness, quain, margaretting' (N, p. 251).

Note C, p. 133. I began to learn Welsh. In a letter to Baillie (Jan. 6, 1877), G. M. H. said: 'I have learnt Welsh, as you say: I can read easy prose and speak stumblingly, but at present I find the greatest difficulty, amounting almost to total failure, in understanding it when spoken, and the poetry, which is quite as hard as the choruses in a Gk. play – and consider what those would be with none but a small and bad dictionary at command – I can make very little way with.' (F, pp. 94-5.) Yet he learnt enough to write a passable Welsh poem himself (3rd edn., Nos. 134, 135) and to master, and partly adopt into his own English verse, the strict and elaborate system of alliteration and internal rhyme called *cynghanedd*. Almost entirely due to the 'starriness', 'quain', rich texture of classical Welsh poetry are such lines as the following:

'Warm-laid grave of a womb-life grey' (No. 5, vii. 3).
  a   *b*   *c*   *a*   *b*   *c*

'Left *hand* off *land* I hear the lark ascend' (No. 12).
'... bow or brooch or braid or brace, lace, latch or catch or key to keep
Back beauty....' (No. 36, l. 1.)

'... your land*mark*, sea*mark*, or soul's star?' (No. 64, v.)

For a full account of the Welsh influence see Gweneth Lilly in *The Modern Language Review*, July 1943, or the present editor's *Gerard Manley Hopkins*, Vol. II (1949; 2nd edn., 1962), pp. 143-57.

Note D, p. 145. St. Ignatius Loyola (1491–1556), the Spanish founder of the Society of Jesus, a Catholic order dedicated, in the first place, to the service of the Counter-Reformation. *The Spiritual Exercises* still provide the practical basis for every Jesuit's spiritual training. As such the work exerted a profound influence upon the life, character and poetry of G. M. H.

Note E, p. 152. Marcus Andrew Hislop Clarke (1845–1881) went to Australia, where he became a journalist and wrote several novels, the best known being *For the Term of His Natural Life*. That G. M. H. had made a deep impression on Clarke is proved by direct references to 'Hopkins' and 'Gerrard' in two of his stories. (See *N*, p. 355, and the *Life of G. M. H.* by E. Ruggles, pp. 223–4.)

Note F, p. 153. Alexander William Mowbray Baillie (1843–1921) was educated at Edinburgh Academy and Balliol College, Oxford. Took a First Class in Classical Mods. and Greats, was called to the Bar, went to N. Africa to throw off consumption, and lived most of his life as a retired scholar. Though a rationalist, Baillie regretted his lack of belief in a second life because he wanted so badly 'somewhere, somehow, to meet Gerard Hopkins again'. (*F*, p. 449.) The correspondence with B. lasted from 1863 to 1888 and covered poetry, politics, etymology, Egyptology, Homeric studies, etc.

Note G, p. 162. Like G. M. H. and Baillie, Addis took a First Class in Classical Mods. and Greats. After his ordination as a Catholic priest in 1872 he was parish priest at Sydenham from 1878 to 1888. In the latter year he left the Church of Rome and in 1901 returned to the Church of England. After being Professor of Old Testament Criticism at Manchester College, Oxford, he became eventually vicar of All Saints, Knightsbridge (1910–1917). He published works on Church history. The correspondence between him and G. M. H. seems to have been destroyed.

Note H, p. 172. Robert Seymour Bridges (1844–1930) was educated at Eton and Corpus Christi College, Oxford. After taking Classical Schools he qualified as a medical doctor and practised until 1882, after which year he gave all his time to writing. In 1913 he was appointed Poet Laureate. Works by R. B. mentioned in the selected letters are: *Poems*, 1873 (Letter XV), *The Growth of Love*, 1876 (*ibid.*), *Prometheus the Firegiver*, 1883 (Letters XXI, XXIII), *The Return of Ulysses* (Letter XXIII), *Nero*, Part I, 1884 (Letter XXIII), *Eros and Psyche*, 1885 (Letter XXII). The correspondence with G. M. H. extended from 1865 to 1889. R. B. destroyed his own letters but earned our gratitude by preserving all G. M. H.'s mature poems and editing the first complete edition in 1918.

Note I, p. 180. Richard Watson Dixon (1833–1900) was educated at King Edward VI School, Birmingham, and Pembroke College, Oxford, where he became a member of the Pre-Raphaelite Brotherhood and enjoyed the friendship of Burne-Jones, Wm. Morris, and (through them) of Rossetti. After his ordination he was for a short time assistant master at Highgate School (1861), where he met G. M. H. In the same year he began to publish the poetry which was praised by both Rossetti and Swinburne. In later years he was successively vicar of Hayton, Cumberland, and of Warkworth, Northumberland. His poetical works still in print are: *Christ's Company* (1861); *Historical Odes* (1863); *Mano: a Poetical History* (1883); *Odes and Eclogues* (1884); and *Lyrical Poems* (1887). A selection of his best poems was edited, with a memoir, by R. B. in 1909. Dixon's chief prose work is *The History of the Church of England from the Abolition of the Roman Jurisdiction*, in six vols. (1878–1902). Dixon was the first person to recognize and tersely define the special poetic quality of G. M. H. (See Introduction.)

Note J, p. 203. '... But the Greek gods are rakes, and unnatural rakes ... Indeed they are not brave, not self controlled, they have no manners, they are not gentlemen and ladies. They clout one another's ears and blubber and bellow. You will say this is Homer's fun, like the miracle-plays of Christendom. Then where is his earnest about them? At their best they remind me of some company of beaux and fashionable world at Bath in its palmy days or Tunbridge Wells or what not. Zeus is like the Major in *Pendennis* handsomer and better preserved sitting on Olympus as behind a club-window and watching Danae and other pretty seamstresses cross the street – not to go farther. You will think this is very Philistine and vulgar and be pained.

But I am pained: this is the light in which the matter strikes me, the only one in which it will; and I do think it is the true light.

'But I grant that the Greek mythology is very susceptible of fine treatment, allegorical treatment for instance, and so treated gives rise to the most beautiful results. No wonder: the moral evil is got rid of and the pure art, morally neutral and artistically so rich, remains and can be even turned to moral uses.' (*D*, pp. 146-7.) Cf. the symbolism in *Andromeda*, No. 26.

Note K, p. 206. Coventry Kersey Dighton Patmore (1823-96), son of P. G. Patmore – author, dandy, and friend of Hazlitt – was educated in France. His first volume, *Poems* (1844), won him the friendship of Tennyson, Carlyle, and Ruskin. Marital love and his own first marriage were idealized in *The Angel in the House* (1854-1856), a domestic epic which had a great popular success. In 1864 his second marriage brought him a fortune. He became a Roman Catholic and lived the life of a country squire, first at Heron's Ghyll near Uckfield, then at Hastings, where G. M. H. visited him in 1885. After a sequel to *The Angel – The Victories of Love* (1862) – Patmore produced his finest poetry in *The Unknown Eros* (1877). His collections of essays and meditations include *Principle in Art* (1899), *Religio Poetae* (1899) and *The Rod, the Root and the Flower* (1895). Patmore alleged that a word of moral disapproval from G. M. H. had caused him to burn the MS. of a whole prose work – the *Sponsa Dei;* yet he could not get past the 'obscuring novelty of mode' in G. M. H.'s poetry, which for him had the effect of 'veins of pure gold imbedded in masses of impracticable quartz.'

Note L, p. 211. Manley Hopkins (1818-1897) was head of a firm of Average Adjusters. His published works include: *A Philosopher's Stone* (verse, dedicated to Thomas Hood: 1843); *A Handbook of Average* (1857); *Hawaii: An Historical Account of the Sandwich Islands* (1862, 1866); *A Manual of Marine Insurance* (1867); *The Port of Refuge, or advice and instructions to the Master-Mariner in situations of doubt, difficulty, and danger* (1873; 3rd edn. 1888); *Spicilegium Poeticum* (verse privately printed: *c.* 1890).

Note M, p. 212. *Gifted Hopkins.* The allusion is not clear. A footnote in Vol. III of Dixon's *History of the English Church* (1885) had acknowledged help received from 'my gifted friend the Rev.

Gerard Hopkins, S. J.' G. M. H.'s comment to R. B. was: 'Alas! has "the gifted Hopkins" appeared in C. D.'s "abrupt note"? – too plainly the son and literary executor of [Andrew] Lang's Gifted Hopkins. . . .' This is a reference to G. M. H.'s letter (to R. B.) of Oct. 16, 1882: 'Look at this: *Saturday Review* Oct. 14, 1882: *The Sorrows of Prince Bismarck:* "On some luckless day the bookseller sends out his catalogue, with such items as '*Love Lies Bleeding*. By G. Hopkins. Pages unopened [this is wrong: it should be *uncut*]. Autograph poem and inscription by the author. Published at Five Shillings. Fourpence.' Then these catalogues fall into the hands of Hopkins and his friends, and there is wailing and shrieking on Parnassus." It seems to be meant for me. Andrew Lang perhaps or somebody who knows of me through you. . . . Be careful not to betray me to suspects and dangerous people.'

Note N, p. 126. Johannes Duns Scotus (1265?–1308), born in the north of Britain or in Ireland, became a Franciscan and lectured at Oxford about 1301 (see poem No. 21), whence he moved to Paris and Cologne. Entitled 'Dr Subtilis', he was an acute critic of Thomas Aquinas. In philosophy he revived nominalism, and in theology he strongly upheld the doctrine of the Immaculate Conception (see poem No. 21, l. 14). His chief work is the *Opus Oxoniense*, a massive commentary on the Bible, Aristotle, and the *Sentences* of Peter Lombard.

SHORT BIBLIOGRAPHY

[For the published works of Gerard Manley Hopkins
see p. 221]

G. F. LAHEY, S.J.: *Gerard Manley Hopkins: A Life* (O.U.P., 1930).

F. R. LEAVIS: essay on G. M. H. in *New Bearings in English Poetry* (Chatto and Windus, 1932; Penguin Books, 1962).

E. E. PHARE: *The Poetry of Gerard Manley Hopkins* (C.U.P., 1933).

JOHN PICK: *Gerard Manley Hopkins, Priest and Poet* (O.U.P., 1942). *A Hopkins Reader* (O.U.P., 1953).

ELEANOR RUGGLES: *Gerard Manley Hopkins: A Life* (Bodley Head, 1944).

KENYON CRITICS: *Gerard Manley Hopkins* (New Directions, 1945).

W. A. M. PETERS, S.J.: *Gerard Manley Hopkins: A Critical Essay towards the Understanding of his Poetry* (O.U.P., 1948).

NORMAN WEYAND, S.J. (Editor): *Immortal Diamond: Studies in Gerard Manley Hopkins* (Sheed and Ward, 1949).

W. H. GARDNER: *Gerard Manley Hopkins: A Study of Poetic Idiosyncrasy in Relation to Poetic Tradition.* Vol. I (Secker & Warburg, 1944), 2nd edn. (Secker & Warburg and Yale University Press, 1948); Vol. II (Secker & Warburg and Yale University Press, 1949). Vols. I and II (O.U.P., 1958; 2nd edn. 1962).

ALAN HEUSER: *The Shaping Vision of Gerard Manley Hopkins* (O.U.P., 1958).

DAVID A. DOWNES: *Gerard Manley Hopkins: A Study of his Ignatian Spirit* (Bookman Associates, N.Y., 1959).

JEAN-GEORGES RITZ: *Robert Bridges and Gerard Manley Hopkins: A Literary Friendship* (O.U.P., 1960).

R. BOYLE: *Metaphor in Hopkins* (University of North Carolina Press, 1960).

INDEX OF FIRST LINES

INDEX TO THE PROSE

MORE ABOUT PENGUINS, PELICANS AND PUFFINS

For further information about books available from Penguins please write to Dept EP, Penguin Books Ltd, Harmondsworth, Middlesex UB7 ODA.

In the U.S.A.: For a complete list of books available from Penguins in the United States write to Dept DG, Penguin Books, 299 Murray Hill Parkway, East Rutherford, New Jersey 07073.

In Canada: For a complete list of books available from Penguins in Canada write to Penguin Books Canada Ltd, 2801 John Street, Markham, Ontario L3R 1B4.

In Australia: For a complete list of books available from Penguins in Australia write to the Marketing Department, Penguin Books Australia Ltd, P.O. Box 257, Ringwood, Victoria 3134.

In New Zealand: For a complete list of books available from Penguins in New Zealand write to the Marketing Department, Penguin Books (N.Z.) Ltd, P.O. Box 4019, Auckland 10.

In India: For a complete list of books available from Penguins in India write to Penguin Overseas Ltd, 706 Eros Apartments, 56 Nehru Place, New Delhi 110019.

BLAKE

A selection by Jacob Bronowski

No English poetry is more rewarding or difficult to plumb, more surprising or inspiring to read than that of William Blake. In his own lifetime (1757–1827) his art – the poetry, engraving and painting that he believed to be the expression of a single genius – went virtually unrecognized, although Wordsworth declared that 'there is something in the madness of this man which interests me more than the sanity of Lord Byron and Walter Scott'; and later T.S. Eliot described how 'because he was not distracted, or frightened, or occupied in anything but exact statements, he understood. He was naked, and saw man naked, and from the centre of his own crystal ... There was nothing of the superior person about him. This makes him terrifying.'

This edition contains selections from Blake's early lyrics, including *Songs of Innocence* and *Songs of Experience*, passages from the prophetic books, and some of Blake's annotations and letters that give a flavour of the man and of the circumstances in which he worked. Jacob Brownowski's succinct and illuminating introduction provides the essential background to Blake's rebellious philosophy and life.

COLERIDGE

A selection by Kathleen Raine

'His genius . . .' wrote William Hazlitt, 'had angelic wings and fed on manna. He talked on for ever; and you wished him to talk on for ever . . .'

Like no other poet Coleridge was, in five short years, 'visited by the Muse'. The great flowering of his poetry happened in the single year from the summer of 1797 when he first became friends with Dorothy and William Wordsworth. That was the year in which he wrote *The Ancient Mariner*, the first part of *Christabel*, *Kubla Khan* and other poems that were, as Kathleen Raine writes, 'the works not of his talent but of his genius'.

As well as Coleridge's finest poems, this Penguin edition contains selections from his letters and his main critical writings, including extracts from *Biographia Literaria* and several of his revolutionary essays on Shakespeare.

KEATS

A selection by J. E. Morpurgo

'I would sooner fail than not be among the greatest.'

Thus wrote Keats in 1818. His first volume, *Poems*, was published in 1817; four years later he died of consumption at the tragically early age of twenty-five. Yet, despite his short creative life, he has, in the words of one eminent critic, 'become a symbolic figure, the type of poetic genius, a hero and martyr of poetry'. This volume contains almost everything of his mature achievement, together with much of his early work and extensive selections from his longer poems.

During his lifetime Keats met with much criticism and with 'some good success among literary people'. Through his worship of beauty he is often thought of as the supreme practitioner of 'art for art's sake'. But the richness, warmth and sensuous vitality of his verse reveal his joy in art and his irresistible delight in life itself.

Poetry in Penguins

THE PENGUIN BOOK OF
VICTORIAN VERSE

Edited with an introduction by George MacBeth

'Victorian poetry has for a long time been the subject of neglect, misunderstanding and abuse.'

Setting Tennyson, Browning, Swinburne, Kipling, Christina Rossetti and Gerard Manley Hopkins alongside a wealth of lesser-known poets, George MacBeth brilliantly defines a fresh approach to Victorian poetry. His selection and his elegant and thought-provoking introduction combine to emphasize the sheer inventiveness of the Victorians: how many of the best poets explored forbidden subjects – violence, religious doubt, eroticism, crime or passion – behind the mask of the dramatic monologue and in the extraordinary narrative poems which are at the heart of this 'great age of fiction in English poetry'.

'It is the great and crucial merit of *The Penguin Book of Victorian Verse* that it changes one's attitude to contemporary poetry, as well as to that of the period it sets out to cover' – Edward Lucie-Smith.